12272648

WITHDRAWN

Projects and Procedures for
SERIALS ADMINISTRATION

CURRENT ISSUES IN SERIALS MANAGEMENT

Projects and
Procedures for
SERIALS
ADMINISTRATION

Compiled and edited by
Diane Stine

THE PIERIAN PRESS
1985

Library of Congress Catalog Card Number 85-60593
ISBN 0-87650-190-0

THE PIERIAN PRESS
P.O. Box 1808
Ann Arbor, MI. 48106

Contents

Introduction

Why a book on processing serials? Ask any serials librarian. We all encounter the same problems even if our environments are not identical. Bob Migneault discusses these problems in the first essay. To provide access to serials for our patrons, we are constantly searching for better procedures. We can always learn from someone else's experience and, one hopes, keep from making as many mistakes. Reading about another librarian's project can help one to plan one's own. The facts and figures may vary but the basic guidelines remain the same.

Some of the essays deal with all--encompassing projects such as the "Serials Reconciliation Project at the University of New Mexico General Library" by Marilyn Fletcher. This project encom--passed the fiscal and bibliographic reconciliation of serials records as well as collection development aspects of the serial titles. After reading Marilyn's article one is more confident that such a mam--moth undertaking can actually be accomplished. Other projects which may have been done for a specific reason at one institution may be applicable to another library's needs. Barbara Pinzelik's article on serials deacquisitions states that the library was forced to weed because of space constraints. Most libraries have this same problem. She provides a process for handling a large number of titles quickly by assigning categories and making broad--based assumptions. Marilyn's article, on the other hand, provides a long--term title by title analysis. Depending on the particular needs of the institution, librarians can choose one method or the other or a combination.

I have included several essays on handling monographic series and analyzed serials because this is an area which is especially problematic. Wellesley's experience, described by Betty Landsman, provides a good model for a smaller academic library which can update all titles in a series to AACR 2 form of entry as a new title arrives. Susan Matson's description of Southern Illinois University Library's procedures is applicable to any large operation. A library in this situation cannot afford to recatalog titles in series so that the entire catalog will be in AACR 2 form. Rather, Sue describes procedures for linking older and new forms of heading. The operation at SIU is an example of intensive series authority control handled by serials experts. Not only does she describe the procedures used but also the level of staffing needed for each step in the process of establishing series. Although the series work done is quite time–consuming it saves time in the long run by allowing monographic catalogers to process more items because they are not bogged down in the difficult task of establishing series.

I have made an effort to include articles by librarians using various manual and automated systems so that librarians can use this information to help decide between systems. Libraries which have already been committed to a system can follow the applicable procedures for implementation. I hope that serials librarians will be able to use the procedures outlined here to make their jobs a little easier and their operations run more smoothly.

Serials: An Introductory Perspective

Robert L. Migneault
Assistant Dean for Technical Services
University of New Mexico Library

Whenever an informed serialist presents his or her views on serials, it is bound to raise, sooner or later, at least two questions. What, after all, is a "serial?" And, do "serials" necessarily require special handling? Now, these questions may appear to be simple, leading to simple answers. Experience, however, reveals otherwise. For serialists, the process of defining the term "serial" and reaching a generally agreed upon practice on how best to handle serials invariably involves more than a simple referral to a dictionary or accepting without reservation a given serials operation (a model) as the only way to go. The process involves a number of practical as well as theoretical considerations, not the least of which is consideration of the cause and effect relationships between definition and practice. These relationships, whatever they may be, have been topics of discussion, not infrequently of debates, on whether or not practice is a function of definition, or whether or not practice has primacy over form.

The serialist Andrew Osborn, for example, has devoted considerable attention in *Serial Publications* to the relationships between definition and practice. Incidentally, he also has been quick to point out that definitions aimed at explaining the intricacies of the "serial," including efforts to reach its precise definition, have been ongoing efforts for sometime. As Osborn explains: "A sound definition of a serial . . . has long been sought, especially in booktrade, legal, and library circles, as well as by bibliographers and literary historians."[1] Mind you, the professional literature is replete with attempts to settle matters with respect to defining the term "serials" and the corollary of how best to handle them. As one considers the numerous attempts by countless numbers of people to capture, once and for all, the true definition of a serial, one can easily agree with Osborn that the "futility of the quest" is historically evident.

In considering the matter of definition, no better point of departure is Osborn himself. He explains that the term "serial"

1

is an inclusive term referring to publications, or works, that normally have "(1) a name and (2) either periodical or serial numbering of the successive parts of a work which appear under the original name or a later name."[2] Serial being a generic term, a given serial may be a periodical (i.e., a magazine or a journal), a continuation (e.g., a numbered set of monographs), or what Osborn refers to as a provisional serial (a main work having cumulative supplements), or to a pseudoserial. "A pseudoserial is a frequently reissued and revised publication which quite properly may be, and on first publication generally is, considered to be a monograph."[3]

Clara Brown, a serialist who has worked with serials for over thirty years, offered these remarks: "Magazines, periodicals, serials and continuations have been defined and discussed in all the earlier books (pre-1975) on serials. The terms vary so much and so many exceptions to the terms are permitted that an intelligent discussion often is not possible. They [serials] contain two ingredients: they are numbered; they intend to continue for an indefinite period, as opposed to sets which start out with a definite decision on how many volumes will be published. 'Magazines' seem generally to mean popular titles read by the general public. 'Periodicals' on the other hand might be considered somewhat more scholarly but still have a distinctive title. 'Continuations' are publications by corporate bodies and are designed as 'bulletins', 'proceedings', 'transactions', etc. 'Serials' are most generally considered to include all the above categories, although in England and Europe the word is somewhat frowned upon and in Germany the definition was at one time broken into intricate small parts. This is still the case in the definition of legal publications."[4]

At the American Library Association annual Conference in Dallas in 1971 the Serials Section of the Resources and Technical Services Division established the *Ad Hoc* Committee to Study Manually Maintained Serial Records. Herbert Linville, UC Santa Barbara, was appointed chairman. Assisting him on the committee were Judith Kharbas, University of Rochester Library, and Le Roy Ortopan, General Library, UC Berkeley. As time passed, Ortopan succeeded Linville as chairman and, in time, Mary Sauer, Serials Record Division, Library of Congress, was appointed to fill a vacancy on the committee. The committee's primary task was to produce a state of the art report on the maintenance of serial records by manual methods in libraries of all types. The committee sent questionnaires to some 150 libraries. Interestingly enough, the committee found that most of the libraries that responded were at variance in defining serials, the result of which indicated that the same libraries also handled their serials quite differently. For its purposes, the committee utilized the definition which can be found in the *Anglo--American Cataloging Rules* (North American Text, 1967): a serial is "A publication issued in successive parts bearing numerical or chronological designations and intended to be con--tinued indefinitely. Serials include periodicals, newspapers, annuals (reports, yearbooks, etc.), the journals, memoirs, proceedings, trans--actions, etc., of societies and numbered monographic series."[5]

The *Ad Hoc* Committee to Study Manually Maintained Serials Records confirmed what practicing serials librarians already knew: serialists cannot agree on a definition of the term "serial." Most authorities on serials have agreed that the reason generates from two problems: serials are objects of constant change, and they are lacking when it comes to standards and standardization. In explaining this phenomenon, serialists frequently compare the serial to "the book." Consider the following comments as an example: "Almost all books are published by sophisticated, experi--enced, well financed professionals who understand their self--interest in as well as their customers' need for bibliographic consistency. Problems abound, but the standard is well--defined and usually ad--hered to. On the other hand any knucklehead with a typewriter and access to an offset press can publish a serial."[6]

How often has a serialist heard this question? What the dif--ferences between a "serial," a "series," and a "set?" To try to explain the differences so that the uninitiated can gain a clear under--standing is like trying . . . to well, let us say that at best it is an effort. When faced with the question, one might be wise to avoid what is guaranteed to be a frustrating exercise by adopting the strategic posture: "If you must ask the question I'm afraid you'll not understand the answer!"

At the expense of suffering a kaleidoscopic spin one might pause to reflect on shifting comparisons. A "serial" is a work issued in successive parts. A "series" is a separate work issued in succession. A "set" is a work issued in parts in succession to form a multi--volume entity. One may say a "serial" continues indefinitely, a "series" may be short--lived, or ongoing endlessly, and a "set" has a planned duration. A "serial" has stated intervals of publication and each successive part is designated chronologically, perhaps numerically, perhaps not. A "series" may be numbered, or it may not. However, the individual volumes in the "series" are related to one another through a collective title. A "set" may be something that is published all at once, or parts may be published in succession, and the intervals between publication may be daily, weekly, month--ly, quarterly, annually, bi--annually, every five years, each decade, or whatever. In the case of "set" the distingushing factor is that the publisher knows in advance when the publication(s) will end. It is interesting to note that Doris Carson, in "What Is a Serial

Publication," postulated that "the traditional scope of serial pub-lications, which included serials, series, and sets, is untenable and that serials alone are serial publications."[7] To Carson, series and sets should be excluded from the definition of the term "serials."

When the new and controversial *Anglo–American Cataloguing Rules* (second edition) was released in 1978, the work as a new set of rules was received with mixed emotions by practicing librarians. Even so, *AACR 2* offered what may be recognized as the single most utilitarian and commonly acceptable authoritative definition of "serial" currently in use. Although it continues to be generally recognized that "[n]o standard definition of *serial* exists, . . . the second edition of the *Anglo–American Cataloguing Rules (AACR 2)* defines the term well . . . [and] is close to a standard definition for English–speaking librarians."[8] Referring to *AACR 2,* "serial" is defined as "A publication in any medium issued in successive parts bearing numerical or chronological designations and intended to be continued indefinitely. Serials include periodicals; news--papers; annuals (reports, yearbooks, etc.); the journals, memoirs, proceedings, transactions, etc., of societies; and numbered mono--graphic series."[9]

Two years after *AACR 2*'s debut, Michael Gorman, a principal editor of the *Rules,* offered in *American Libraries* his personal opinions on the definition of the term "serials" and on related matters. In effect, Gorman acknowledged that serials have their peculiarities, that they require special handling, and that in the best of times the handling of serials can wear down the most brave of the brave. With practicing librarians in mind, Gorman opined that "the most harried members of the library profession are serials librarians. The vagaries of serials wear down the stoutest of hearts. Who can spend a lifetime coping with changes of title, or format, of content, of price, of anything that can be changed? For many years librarians have been wrestling with the definition of a serial. My offering is that a serial is any library material that can and does change."[10]

David C. Taylor offers an interesting definition: "A serial is a publication reproduced in more than one copy and more than one issue. It has a common name identifying the issues, and dating or numbering to show the distinction and connection between one issue and another. It has no intended point of completion. The essential elements to this definition are:

1. Publication

2. Reproduction in more than one copy

4

3. Appearance more than once

4. A name or title shared by the multiple copies and issues

5. A numbering or dating system

6. Indefinite appearance".[11]

The practicing serials librarian is not likely to find theoretical definitions in and of themselves of much practical use. It is fair to say that on the one hand abstraction has its place; yet, on the other so does the so--called "real" working definition. Thus we come to the point where form and function meet, the culmination known as serials librarianship.

Practicing serials librarians recognize that serials are different from other library materials, that serials are subject to consequential changes, and that serials lack standardization and standards. Conse--quently, as someone unabashedly stated, "Librarians cannot agree on a definition of the *serial.*"[12] Because of these realities, practicing serials librarians must recognize the need to apply flexible interpre--tations to the definition(s) of a serial. To be meaningful in practice the term "serials" must always be accompanied by the appropriate qualifier(s). Osborn, for example, lists eleven qualifications that need to be added to even the best of the library definitions of a serial, viz., the one found in *AACR 2* mentioned earlier. Assuming a decision can be (and is) made to the effect that serials, however defined, are to be treated in a certain manner, any library material that lends itself to be treated in that manner may in practice be or become a "serial." In practice, a serials librarian may treat a given publication as a serial because the publication was first defined as a serial; or, a publication not originally defined as a serial may be treated as one if the publication lends itself to be treated as a serial. The author appreciates fully Anne Marie Allison's observa--tion: "Perhaps a serial is any item any serial librarian chooses to call a serial."[13] One cannot help remembering the logic applied by Humpty Dumpty:

"When I use a word," Humpty Dumpty said, in rather a scornful tone, "it means just what I choose it to mean -- neither more or less."

"The question is," said Humpty Dumpty, "Which is to be mas--ter -- that's all."

Alice was too much puzzled to say anything; so after a minute

Humpty Dumpty began again.

"They've a temper, some of them – particularly verbs: they're the proudest – adjectives you can do anything with, but not verbs -- however, I can manage the whole lot of them! Impene-- trability! That's what I say!"

"Would you tell me, please," said Alice, "what that mean?"

"Now you talk like a reasonable child," said Humpty Dumpty, looking very much pleased. "I mean by 'impenetrability' that we've had enough of that subject, and it would be just as well if you'd mention what you mean to do next, as I suppose you don't mean to stop here all the rest of your life."

"That's a great deal to make one word mean," Alice said in a thoughtful tone.

"When I Make a word do a lot of work like that," said Humpty Dumpty, "I always pay it extra."[14]

Journal des Scavans is generally considered to be the first true scholarly journal. As well, it may be considered to have been the first independent serial to be mercilessly unleashed on unsuspecting souls! *Journal des Scavans* was first published in Paris on January 5, 1665. With the birth of modern serials in the latter part of the 17th century, the effect of serials on libraries was and continues to be profound. "Ever since then, libraries have been trying, with varying degrees of success, to cope with the many problems associ-- ated with the development of collections of these indispensable publications."[15]

The problems related to the care and handling of serial publica-- tions were a matter for discussion at the first meeting of the then newly formed American Library Association in 1876.[16] Subse-- quently, authors having articles published in library literature began openly to acknowledge that the problems of serial publications in libraries were becoming significant. To the author's knowledge the first separately published work on serials was produced by Pearl Holland Clark in 1930. This work was published by the Uni-- versity of Chicago and is entitled *The Problem Presented by Periodi-- cals in College and University Libraries.*

Clark claimed that her study "originated in an attempt to devise a more efficient procedure for keeping complete the files of incom-- ing numbers of periodicals in college and university libraries."[17] At the time of her study, Clark thought best to deal only with those factors entering into the treatment of periodicals from the time they are ordered until they are bound. Concerning the existing practices at the time, Clark reported that there were "a striking variety of methods," which she attributed "to local conditions."[18]

According to Cabeen and Cook, sometime between 1932 and the early 1940s libraries began a trend towards the consolidation of records for serials.[19] During these years, if one turned to the professional literature for guidance, most likely one would have been left with the impression that most authors writing about serials favored centralizing *all* serials functions, not just records for serials.

In 1937, J. Harris Gable produced a professionally recognized work on serials, now of historical importance. It contained information about the nature of serial publications and how they were being handled in libraries. "Although serials routines were different from one institution to another one can discern some effort to centralize functions and to standardize routines."[20] Gable's work was followed in 1940 by an equally important work, authored by Rothman and Ditzion.

Rothman and Ditzion criticized Gable by saying they believed Gable erred in minimizing the progress that had been made by libraries in centralizing serial activities. They (Rothman and Ditzion) also had a different opinion about priorities: "Gable made service to the public his sixth and last point in planning for a reorganization of serials procedures; it is our feeling that first place be given to the improvement of service to the public, and that economy and ease of operations are secondary to this end."[21]

In their "Prevailing Practices in Handling Serials," Rothman and Ditzion offered these comments:

Scientists insist that the first step in the solution of any problem is the recognition and formulation of the problem. At the first meeting of the American Library Association, the problem of care and handling of serial publications was poised . . .

This report ["Prevailing Practices in Handling Serials"] ostensibly is on prevailing practices in the handling and care of serials. To give the picture as asked for (i.e., a survey of prevailing library practices -- a report on serials) would be like asking a blind man in a dark room to find a black cat that is not there. As a result of the survey, we do feel that there is a decided trend toward centralization. This trend has taken so many forms that it can hardly be called a prevailing practice . . .

. . . there has come into being an obvious consciousness of the fact that serial publications are different from books . . .

If there is any reason at all for distinguishing periodicals from books insofar as treatment and handling are concerned, there is some reason for making the distinction for all serials publica-- tions in their entirety . . .

If distinctions are made among periodicals, serials, continuations, and government documents, the distinction in and of itself breeds a difficulty inherent in the fact that, regardless of the care with which definitions are prepared, borderline cases must be numerous . . .

As a result of the survey that has been made of methods used in the care and handling of serials in one hundred and twenty--six college, university, and public libraries, we find that *complete centralization of functions relating to serials offers the best solution of vexing problems.*[22]

What is complete centralization of functions relating to serials? For guidance, one may wish to consider the list of processes which was prepared by Augustus F. Kuhlman. Historically, "Kuhlman's nine" has been cited as being equivalent to the essential functions which constitute a totally centralized serials unit. These may be outlined:

"(1) the discovery of what is available.

(2) selection.

(3) setting up appropriate machinery.

(4) organization for use.

(5) reference service.

(6) cataloging and classification.

(7) serials checkin.

(8) binding.

(9) filling gaps."[23]

Following World War II, articles about the administration of serial processes revealed, among other things, that the Library of Congress centralized its serials operation, as did Ohio State Uni--

versity Library, the Washington Square Library of New York University, and others. Advocates of centralization felt that centralization was talked about more than practiced. Someone at the time observed that, "[w]hile there has been a tendency to speak of the centralization of serials in libraries, there has been a marked lack of converted action."[24]

The premier work on serials, of course, is Andrew D. Osborn's *Serial Publications: Their Place and Treatment in Libraries*. The first edition was published in 1955; the second in 1973; and the third in 1980. *Serial Publications* is a must reading for anyone seriously interested in serials, especially if one is interested in their treatment in libraries. One should notice that Osborn, an internationally recognized expert on serials, expresses the view that centralization is not the only answer for efficient handling of serials:

> There are three main areas of serial activity in libraries which are large enough to require specialization of functions. Each of them may have one or more staff members who work exclusively with serials. The areas are the acquisition department, which procures serials and commonly has the current checking records under its supervision; the catalog department where there is usually a serial cataloging section or division; and the current--periodical room, which is sometimes supplemented by a document or a newspaper room. Naturally other parts of a library have much to do with serials, notably the circulation and reference desks, but their concern is as a rule incidental to their general duties, as can be seen from the fact that only rarely is one of their assistants a serial specialist . . .

> It is possible for any one of the three departments -- acquisitions, cataloging, or the periodical room -- to assume the major responsibility for serials and to be called the "serial section", "serial division", etc. In point of theory, it is difficult to lay down hard and fast rules for the location of the primary serial functions, a good case can be made for each department . . .

> The orthodox arrangement is to divide the work among the three . . .

> Complete centralization is, of course, out of the question . . .

> If outright centralization is not the answer, and generally it is not, much can and should be done in many a library to coordinate serial functions better, eliminate areas of overlap, provide more adequate staff and quarters for all phases of serial work,

and conserve for the future all files of serials which should be available to the historian and the bibliographer, as well as the research worker.[25]

Between the time of Osborn's first and second edition there were at least two articles of note which described the organization of "serials" in U.S. libraries. In "Serial Practices in Selected College and University Libraries," Gloria Whetson in 1961 claimed she found a marked trend towards centralization.[26] Two years later, Robert Orr compiled data and showed that there was a high degree of centralization in regards to serial operations in medium and large libraries. Orr explained that although centralization was an acceptable option, organizational configurations were of such varieties "as to defy the identification of any discernible major present practice or of trends for the future."[27]

The Executive Board of ALA's Resources and Technical Services Division in 1964 decided that it was time to institute a study to examine library developments in the light of increased service pressures, rising costs, and automation in library technical services operation. The study was conducted by a committee composed of Richard Dougherty, Robert Wadsworth, and Donald Axman. The excerpts that follow represent highlights of the study:

. . . despite the abundance of data available to the profession, very little, unfortunately, is comparable.

The Committee believes that the fundamental weakness of this survey, as well as similar undertakings, is the inability to evaluate the effectiveness of the procedures and methods described by respondents. It does not necessarily follow that because a policy, an organizational pattern, or a new procedure is used by thirty or forty libraries it is more effective than, or even as effective as, an alternative method reported by a few libraries.

In the traditional organization, the functions normally associated with serial work are split between acquisitions and cataloging:

(a)

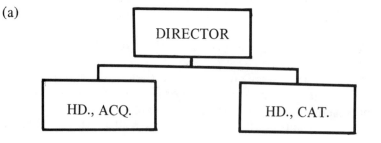

(b)

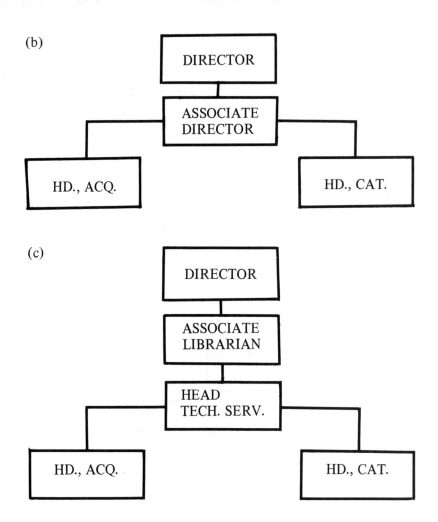

(c)

Some libraries have altered the pattern by establishing independent serials departments:

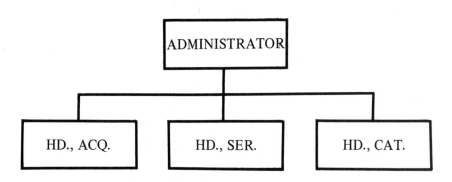

This is the pattern the Committee defined as being truly a "technical services" organization:

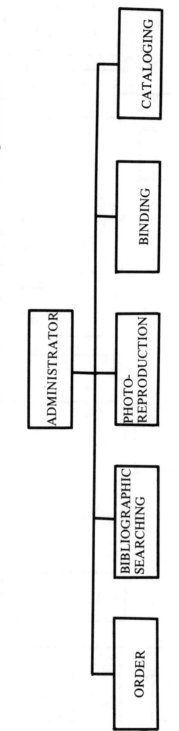

The surveyors [of a previous study] in 1955 often found it difficult to determine from the responses whether or not a library could be classified as a technical services or a non-technical services organized library. As one committee member at the time observed: "The more I look at the charts and the details of the questionnaire, the more I become convinced that libraries don't know whether they have a technical services library or not."[28] This observation still appears to be pertinent ten years later.

Analysis of the data on the organization of functions related to serials work proved to be singularly difficult and not very rewarding . . . . Again the lack of standard terms proved a bugaboo . . . . Consequently a variety of interpretations resulted . . . . [T]his lack of conformity in terminology makes any but the broadest type of generalization meaningless.

. . . if "acquisitions" is interpreted to mean selection, it would mean that technical service operating units are primarily responsible for the selection of serial--type materials.

It would appear that technical services are responsible for maintaining the official checking--in records.

Serials cataloging seems to have been most immune to reorganization. Most libraries still assign the work of serials cataloging to the cataloging department.

The Committee was trying to learn who or what unit was responsible for deciding the manner in which a serial is to be bound . . . . (Virtually all of this work has been assigned to technical services.)

Administrative Organization of Serials Unit. From responses to the question of who administers serial work, four administrative patterns emerged.

Title of Responsible Person	*Number of Libraries Reporting*
Centralized Administration:	
Serials	11
Decentralized Administration:	

13

Acquisitions and Cataloging	27
Acquisitions, Cataloging, and Binding	7
Acquisitions, Cataloging, and Technical Service Chief	2
Acquisitions, Cataloging, and Library Director	1
Acquisitions, Cataloging, and Circulation	2
Acquisitions, Cataloging, and Accounting	2
Director of Processing, Associate Director, and Reference	1
Acquisitions, Cataloging, Business Manager, and Binding	3
Not clear	7

First, serials functions are grouped within acquisitions with the exception of cataloging, which remains the responsibility of the cataloging department. Second, a serials unit independent of acquisitions is organized, but cataloging remains within the province of the cataloging department. Third, all functions related to serials work are centralized within one operating unit. Fourth, are libraries that have decentralized serials work and its administration among more than one unit.[29]

As any serialist should realize there is no universally recognized single ideal scheme for organizing any of the major organizational components of a technical services division, including Serials. Hepfer, for one, concluded that "there is not a single scheme for organizing technical services which is ideal for all libraries. The complexity of the collection is the most determinant as to whether serials specialization is really as sacrosanct as Gable, Brown and the others have contended."[30] A survey of the professional litera-- ture indicates that there are many different organizational schemes possible. However, they are for the most part based on or variations of the schemes identified by the Dougherty, Wadsworth, and Axman study mentioned earlier.

In 1969, there was a four day conference sponsored by the Graduate School of Library Science at the University of Illinois to discuss step by step the many phases of dealing with serials.[31] One of several excellent papers was delivered by Samuel Lazerow, Chief of the Serial Record Division, Library of Congress. Lazerow talked about the organization of serials activities. One could have

14

predicted in advance that Lazerow would inform the audience that there were divergent opinions about the organization of serials activities in libraries. As one possibility, he explained, in large libraries serial functions may be grouped together in one department. "It has been argued that this type of organization eliminates dupli- cation of recording, simplifies routines, reduces possibility for error, accelerates production, reduces communication problems and eliminates departmental bias. On the negative side there are the factors of expense, space requirements, and the overlapping of purely serials functions with non--serial library activities."[32]

If national libraries are appropriate models, Lazerow's remarks may be of use. "In the national libraries centralization has been the choice. The National Agricultural Library (NAL) has placed the serial recording function with the catalog and records activity; the National Library of Medicine (NLM) placed serial controls in the acquisitions area of its technical services division. The Library of Congress adopted a comprehensive approach in the early 1940s when it established its central serial record as a section of the then accessions division . . . . Since that time the Library has shifted its serial record from divisional to sectional and back to divisional status. Similarly, NAL and NLM today operate their records as independent units. We have all found that staffing and personnel requirements are more easily met in a centralized activity."[33]

With the publication of *Serials Librarian,* special attention was and continues to be given to serials. For example, the Winter 1979 issue carried an article devoted to serials administration. In the article, Hans Weber makes a strong pitch for centralization. Weber tells us that

> a major function of a serials unit is to coordinate the processing of materials relating to one *form* and to maintain accuracy of records and currency of processing . . . . The processing of like materials such as serials has been found to be a very success-- ful way to ease the flow of this particularly difficult form . . . . There is unfortunately a tendency for those who work only with monographs to shunt serials aside, perhaps in the hopes they will go away if ignored, since they can frequently be imbued with more problems and changes than one might reasonably expect . . . . For reasons such as this, it has become a trend among those administrators who truly understand this form and its trials and tribulations to assemble the various aspects of the serials function together. The greater understanding engen-- dered for serials by people who work with the whole gamut of this form cannot be overemphasized . . . . There are many ways to process serials administratively, but there comes a

point when I believe the *size* of an institution . . . make[s] it really necessary to consolidate certain functions by form for optimum efficiency.[34]

Someone once said that controlling serials is like nailing Jello to the wall. This brings to mind what may be the crux of the matter, which is the entire spectrum of the relationships between bibliog-raphic control of serials at the national level and local collections. Several observers have remarked that many of the local problems with respect to the bibliographic control of the serials collection are due to lack of direction at the national level. This, then, neces-sitates local decisions, the result of which is an increase to the overall numbers of variances and vagaries. As a matter of course, "many of the problem areas in dealing with serials on a local level are inherent in the nature of serials and will exist no matter what rules [cataloging rules for bibliographic control] are current or have been in effect over the life span of a collection."[35]

Understandably, many decisions have to made at the local level. These decisions represent an ongoing process based on a number of factors, including historical precedent, national, regional, and local practices as deemed appropriate, and human resources and talent. Frequently, the success or failure of a given serials operation depends on the decisions of the serialist(s) involved. Normally, serialists are faced with demanding responsibilities in the face of constant change and ambiguities. With this in mind, one may ask whether or not serialists, if they are to succeed in their tasks, should have, or develop, a special make--up.

Over the years the author has encountered several opinions on what constitutes an ideal serialist, verbally expressed as well as in writing. The opinions had one thing in common; nothing less than being bionic could possibly do! Weber summed it up nicely. "The type of material encountered does seem to call for an indi-vidual who, to be successful in this area, must be able to take in stride the constant change inherent in serials work . . . . [T]here appear to be some salient requisites that can be enumerated as being desirable characteristics for those who work with ser-ials . . . ."[36] Weber prepared a list of qualities which he believed would contribute much to the success of practicing serialists. In the order of importance they are:

-- Knowledge -- an all--important quality that really determines the attitude of staff and colleagues to one's work and aids greatly in engendering respect and confidence. So often knowl-edge of serials work comes about primarily by actual experience.

-- Flexibility -- absolutely essential in order to be able to cope with constant change and continuous problems.

-- Questioning attitude -- the intuitive feeling that a record, serial in hand, procedure, or policy needs correcting and/or attention is a crucial trait to keeping up an efficient flow of materials.

-- Problem solving ability -- another essential aspect of this type of work is to be able to resolve the many problems that arise with an attitude that looks upon such matters as somewhat routine.

-- Decisiveness -- a quality that is quite necessary to staff and professional supervisors if work is to proceed unencumbered with unsolved problems, bottlenecks, etc.

-- Communicativeness -- keeping open the lines of communication with staff, colleagues, and other library units is vital in order to facilitate the handling of departmental and interdepartmental matters of concern.

-- Sense of humor -- a factor most often ignored but a quality whose importance is not sufficiently realized in its ability to ameliorate tension in an environment of constant stress.

-- Leadership -- the capacity to lead, motivate, engender positive staff morale and *espirit de corps,* and develop a deep sense of cooperative effort and mutual reinforcement among serials staff are all crucial to success in serials administration.

-- Supportive attitude -- a necessary factor in maintaining positive staff morale. The staff must be acutely aware that their needs and concerns are understood and supported in relations to departmental, interdepartmental, and general library matters.

-- Service--mindedness -- this is a factor that is more difficult to place in its proper perspective in this list since it refers to the mission rather than the successful operation of a serials unit. But its importance is such that it should not be an after--thought but an integral part of daily attitudes.

-- Analytical ability -- the detail inherent in serials work makes it necessary that the people involved be comfortable in working with detail. There is perhaps no other area of the library that has so many functions that depend on correct assimilation and understanding of the importance of the amount of detail associated with serials work.

-- Planning ability -- the ability to see ahead, to determine priorities in work assignments, to look at these things in the abstract (what if?), to use one's time effectively, and to be able to be patient as the situation requires all provide a basis for confidence and proper perspective among the staff.

-- Human understanding -- the capacity for this trait is not to be minimized. Understanding why people act and react to colleagues, situations, supervisors, pressures, and a myriad of other factors that bear on one's work and life are vital to the well-being of an area that especially requires a close and cooperative interaction of people.

-- Enthusiasm -- often overlooked but an integral aspect of engendering a positive attitude towards serials, and its vagarities. If one likes the genre one looks at one's work and the world in a different light.

-- Energy -- without which the serials world cannot effectively turn.[37]

The presentation offered herein has focused primarily on two aspects of serials librarianship: defining the term "serial" and, in a general way, operations. The perspective offered herein has been based on library historical developments and conventional concepts, exemplified by the assumption that ownership of collections, as compared to access of information, continues to be the preferred library *modus operandi*. Although access to information as library practice is not likely to replace entirely the desire to own, or actual ownership of, collections it is inevitable that the idea of access, rather than outright ownership, will in an ever increasing way modify traditional library concepts and procedures. There can be little doubt that as access to information (and all of what that implies) takes on greater significance there will be corresponding changes that will affect the library profession as a whole, including such specific activities as the practice of serials librarianship.

Practicing serialists are faced with the exigencies of the here and now. In the words of Benita Weber, "While we look forward to and prepare for the changes that will affect our [library] profession, we must, nevertheless, manage the ongoing activities related to serials and organize ourselves [i.e., serials activities, procedures] in the manner that most efficiently and effectively leads to provision

18

of services and material to our [library] users."[38] To twist a phrase: what's in a name? That which we call a serial, by any other name would be the same. A serial is a serial is a serial is a serial. Serials are unique. They are different from all other library materials and they require special handling, whether or not the structure for pro-cessing serials is centralized or decentralized. Simply stated, there is no way out of it.

Ideas on how to best organize serials activties and how best to proceed in handling serials may be gained by considering the pro-cedures described in the chapters that follow. In closing, it seems fitting to reflect on the words of Cervantes: "Never look for birds of this year in the nests of the last."

NOTES

1. Andrew D. Osborn, *Serial Publications: Their Place and Treat-ment in Libraries,* 3rd edition (Chicago: American Library Association, 1980), p. 7.

2. Osborn, p. 3.

3. Osborn, p. 18.

4. Clara D. Brown, *Serials: Acquisitions & Maintenance* (Birming-ham: EBSCO Industries, Inc., n.d.), p. 5.

5. *Anglo-American Cataloging Rules,* North American Text, pre-pared by the American Library Association, The Library of Congress, The Library Association and The Canadian Library Association (Chicago: American Library Association, 1967), p. 346.

6. *Title Varies,* 1 (1974): 29.

7. Doris M. Carson, "What is a Serial Publication?" *Journal of Academic Librarianship,* 3 (September 1977): 206.

8. Marcia Tuttle, *Introduction to Serials Management,* Foundations in Library Information Science (Greenwich, Connecticut: JAI Press, Inc., 1983), p. 6.

9. *Anglo-American Cataloguing Rules,* 2nd ed., prepared by The American Library Association, The British Library, The Canadian Committee on Cataloguing, The Library Association, The Library of Congress, edited by Michael Gorman and Paul W. Winkler

(Chicago; Ottawa: American Library Association; Canadian Library Association, 1978), p. 570.

10. Michael Gorman. "Crunching the Serial," *American Libraries,* 11, (July/August 1980): 416.

11. David C. Taylor, *Managing the Serials Explosion: The Issues for Publishers and Libraries* (White Plains, New York: Knowledge Industry Publications, Inc., 1982), p. 5.

12. Tuttle, p. 1.

13. Anne Marie Allison, "Automated Serials Control: A Bibliographic Survey," in *The Management of Serials Automation: Current Technology & Strategies for Future Planning,* edited with an introduction by Peter Gellatly (New York: Haworth Press, 1982), p. 8.

14. Charles Lutwidge Dodgson, *Alice's Adventures in Wonderland & Through the Looking–Glass,* by Lewis Carroll, with illustrations by John Teniel, afterword by Clifton Fadiman (New York: Macmillan, 1963), pp. 79–80.

15. Robert W. Orr, "A Few Aspects of Acquiring Serials," *Library Trends,* vol. 3, no. 4 (April 1955), p. 393.

16. G.N. Hartje. *Centralized Serial Records in University Libraries,* University of Illinois Library School Occasional Papers, no. 24 (Urbana, Illinois: The Library School, 1951), p. 1.

17. Pearl Holland Clark, *The Problem Presented by Periodicals in College and University Libraries* (Chicago: University of Chicago, 1930), p. iii.

18. Clark, p. 3.

19. Violet Abbott Cabeen and C. Donald Cook. "Organization of Serials and Documents," *Library Trends,* 2, (October 1953): 199.

20. J. Harris Gable, "The New Serials Department," *Library Journal,* 60 (November 15, 1937): 868.

21. Fred B. Rothman and Sidney Ditzion, "Prevailing Practices in Handling Serials," *College and Research Libraries,* 1, (March

1940): 166.

22. Rothman and Ditzion, pp. 165–166.

23. Augustus F. Kuhlman, "Administration of Serial and Document Acquisition and Preparation," *The Acquisition and Cataloging of Books,* edited by William M. Randall (Chicago: The University of Chicago Press, 1940), p. 95 ff.

24. Hartje, p. 1.

25. Osborn, pp. 57–72.

26. Gloria Whetstone, "Serial Practices in Selected College and University Libraries," *Library Resources and Technical Services,* 5, (Fall 1961): 284.

27. Robert W. Orr, "The Selection, Ordering, and Handling of Serials" in *Selection and Acquisition Procedures in Medium–Sized and Large Libraries,* edited by Herbert Goldhor (Urbana, Illinois: University of Illinois, 1963), p. 72.

28. Richard M. Dougherty, Robert W. Wadsworth, and Donald H. Axman, *Policies and Programs Designed to Improve Cooperation and Coordination Among Technical Service Operating Units,* University of Illinois Graduate School of Library Science Occasional Papers, no. 86 (Urbana, Illinois: University of Illinois, August 1967), p. 8 ff.

29. Dougherty, Wadsworth, Axman, pp. 16–17.

30. William Hepfer. "Serials Organization in Academic Libraries: Is There a Better Way?" in *The Serials Collection: Organization and Administration,* edited by Nancy Jean Melin (Ann Arbor: Pierian Press, 1982), pp. 6–7.

31. Walter C. Allen, ed. *Serial Publications in Large Libraries,* (Urbana, Illinois: University of Illinois, 1970), p. v.

32. Allen, p. 109.

33. Allen, p. 110.

34. Hans H. Weber. "Serials Administration," *Serials Librarian,* 4 (Winter 1979): 148.

35. Ruth S. Carter. "Playing by the Rules -- *AACR 2* and Serials" in *Serials Management in an Automated Age: Proceedings of the First Annual Serials Conference, October 30--31, 1981, Arlington, Va.,* edited by Nancy Jean Melin (Westport: Meckler Publishing, 1982), p. 28.

36. Hans H. Weber, p. 150.

37. Hans H. Weber, pp. 150--151.

38. Benita M. Weber. "The Year's Work in Serials: 1982," *Library Resources & Technical Services,* 27, (July/September 1983): 255.

Serials Reconciliation at the
University of New Mexico General Library

Marilyn P. Fletcher
Serials Acquisitions Librarian
University of New Mexico Library

Introduction

In late 1977, a team of consultants consisting of Susan Brynte--son and Mary E. Sauer visited the UNM General Library for the purpose of studying, reviewing, and recommending changes in the organization and procedures of the Serials Department. Their report, issued in February of 1978, was quite comprehensive, covering all aspects of the functions of the Serials Department. A specific recommendation pertained to the serials record check--in system which the consultants deemed to be "seriously deficient." The report stated:

> The condition of the serial records in the University of New Mexico Library is seriously deficient; traditional bibliographic access is virtually nonexistent. The public catalog holds des--criptive bibliographic records for a percentage of serial titles but none have been added for several years. There is no one central place where University of New Mexico serial holdings may be ascertained and in order to ascertain such holdings several files must be consulted.[1]

The consultants' conclusions were indeed correct. Current receipts and location information were available on the Kardex file; bound holdings were available only on the shelf list (on a different floor of the library building); fiscal information was in yet another file; and public access to serials was largely through a serials title list on microfiche which gave title/entry, location, call number, and summary holdings.

In order to correct these deficiencies, the consultants recom--mended the establishment of a central serial record which accu--rately reflected all aspects of any given serial and which was in bibliographic agreement with forms of entry used in the public catalog and which conformed to the latest rules of cataloging.

23

Although the consultants' report advised that the central serial record (CSR) contain current titles only, it was decided internally that the CSR would contain records for all serial titles, active and inactive. This had been the tradition at the UNM General Library. The new Central Serial Record would also include bound holdings for all titles, fiscal information, and the source of the serial, whether it be a vendor, order direct, gift, exchange, deposit -- whatever.

The consultants' report recommended that the project be called "Central Serial Record Team or Serial Reconciliation Pro-- ject" and "that its mission is of profound significance to the Library and that it is an honor to be assigned to it [the project]."[2] The name chosen for the project was "Serials Reconciliation" and was naturally shortened to Serials recon.

Formulating the Plan

Late in 1978, the Head of the Serials Department, Benita M. Weber (who has remained the department head throughout the duration of the project) presented a plan to the library admini-- stration for the implementation of the serials reconciliation project. She stated that the project "would be aimed at 1) an immediate improvement of patron access to correct information both on the existing serials title fiche and CSR or checklist and thus, to the collection; 2) an inventory of all serials holdings; 3) preparation of information (other than bibliographic) to be used for creation of a true CSR at a later point."[3]

Ms. Weber proposed that a special serials reconciliation team be appointed to work on the project and the concept and the necessary funds were approved. The team members were to be appointed to temporary positions preferably with one year "ap-- pointments." The proposal originally called for two Library Technical Assistants (paraprofessional level) and one Clerical Specialist who would be supervised by a librarian (permanent staff member). Of course, the work of the serials reconciliation project touched and affected literally every member of the Serials Department throughout its existence, which is still continuing in a limited way at the present time.

As anyone who has ever worked with serials is aware, the prospect of initiating and completing such a project is mind-- boggling. At the time of its inception, the serials check--in record had approximately 25,000 titles. At UNM, the decision to place a title or series on the checklist had been determined primarily by whether or not the title could be treated as a serial. Although the placement of monographic series and sets had vacillated from

24

acquisitions to serials throughout the years, it was decided at this point to transfer all standing orders for such series and sets to the serials record as a part of the project. The only "standing orders" which were to remain in acquisitions were orders for all UNM Press publications and other blanket types of orders which could not be accounted for on a serial check–in record.

After searching much of the literature, I can find no other indications that such a mammoth project has been reported by any other academic library of our size. There are, to be sure, many articles concerning the collection development aspects of serials, i.e., coping with decreasing budgets, formulas for cancellation of serials, weeding collections. What was originally conceived at UNM as an inventory of the serials collection (including reconciliation of fiscal and bibliographic information into a central serial record) evolved into a project of much greater magnitude. This occurred because of the inclusion of collection development personnel in the process. The project then became unique because it became an intensive, comprehensive review and evaluation of the total serials collection in the University of New Mexico General Library system.

Each and every title was listed, inventoried, checked for holdings, binding condition, and so forth. The title was then verified for source and fiscal information. Then, each title was reviewed and evaluated by a subject selector for possible cancellation, continuation, location, and retention. Cancellation of titles was carefully considered due to the library's tightening budgetary situation. Although the actual amount expended for serials did not decrease during the project, it became *quid pro quo* that in order to place a new subscription, another must be cancelled. The cancellation rate has been calculated at 10–11% over the life of the project.

A few words about the collection development process at the University of New Mexico General Library may be helpful at this point. The UNM General Library has an Assistant Dean for Collection Development. Rather than having bibliographers with no other function than collection building, librarians from throughout the library participate in the collection development functions as part of their duties. For example, the science and engineering selectors are also reference librarians, the selectors in Russian, German, and French literatures are all catalogers. The selection duties in Latin– and Ibero–American studies are shared by librarians in reference, cataloging, and acquisitions. These librarians have been assigned to these duties because they have some sort of specialization or academic degree in the subject or language area. It seems to work rather well as collection building is carried on continuously by a multiplicity of library staff. Their collection development duties are overseen by a group of coordinators (Humanities, Science and Engineering, Social Science, and Education). The Latin- and Ibero-American selectors have formed a council among themselves to coordinate their collection development activities. All selectors meet monthly with the Assistant Dean for Collection Development to hear announcements and proposals concerning the library budget and to discuss common areas of concern. Selectors are an integral part of the budgetary process and each knows how much money can be encumbered and expended throughout the year. Most selectors have liaisons on the teaching faculty with whom they confer on possible acquisitions and cancellations. From the above background, it can be seen that the work of the serials reconciliation project was spread amongst many individuals throughout the entire library. The majority of those involved realized the importance of the project and were very responsive to doing the work necessary to accomplish its purpose.

Forms and Procedures

If the project were to be successful, forms and statistics had to be designed and maintained in such a manner as to show the progress of the project on a regular basis. The Head of the Serials Department, Ms. Weber, after consulting with a variety of people, designed the form which has been used from the beginning of the project to the present. The form was very well thought out and designed and includes almost every conceivable bit of information which might be necessary to reconcile a particular title. (See Figure 1).

The example of the form shows to what depth each serial was investigated. There are basically two parts for each title. The left hand side of the form was for internal serials use, and information was taken from the check--in record, the shelf--holdings, and payment information. The right hand side of the form was for the subject selectors to fill out. The internal information was generated by a member of the serials recon team and the beginning point for information gathering was the checklist. A different form was used for duplicate titles in separate locations because each needed its own fiscal and bibliographic record. A shelf check was done for all titles in the main library. Branch libraries were responsible for doing their own shelf check.

Call number, location, and frequency are fairly self--explanatory. The current disposition notes area was used to record such information as "Latest in Reference," "Library retains latest edition only," "Superseded issues discarded," and the other myriad

26

notes which are necessary in a serials check–in record. Linking notes refer to earlier and later forms of the title. At the time, the library had decided to use successive entry title for cataloging, and team members were responsible for reconciling all linking titles at the same time so that the selectors could view the title and its variants as a whole entity rather than bits and pieces. Latest issue received and date of receipt of last issue were important information. Often such information led us to the conclusion that we were dealing with a complimentary subscription or possibly an old exchange title.

Brief holdings were included as a summary statement of what the checklist record showed. If the holdings were complete, such was indicated. For gaps and missing issues, the notations "miss–ing––––" or "missing some issues," or "missing many issues" were made. In addition to filling out separate forms for linking titles, separate forms were also completed for microfilm, micro–fiche, or other formats. Even titles which were parts of microform sets such as *Early English Books* and *Early American Newspapers* had forms filled out so that a decision could be made about reten–tion.

Team members then checked the shelves for the actual pieces. Notations were made as to type of binding. The condition of the binding or lack thereof was rated from poor to excellent based upon the judgment of the recon team member. The miscellaneous notes space was used for many sorts of information. The "searched" notations were used for bibliographic reconciliation by the serials cataloging unit.

The bibliographic reconciliation (cataloging) aspects of the project proved to be the most involved and time–consuming. After a decision was made to continue and/or retain a serial, each title had to be brought up–to–date using AACR–2 rules and form of entry and entered into OCLC. The UNM General Library is currently in the process of retrospective conversion of the entire collection to machine–readable form on OCLC. Although this process actually began for serials with the beginning of the recon–ciliation project, it is now in effect for monographs as well, and the two functions have become enmeshed as far as bibliographic reconciliation is concerned. Although the fiscal reconciliation process has been mostly completed, the only sizable backlog that remains is that of bibliographic reconciliation. Over 7,000 titles have been bibliographically reconciled, and the remainder will be done as time and staff permit.

For over ten years, the library has utilized computer output microfiche for public access to serials information. At its inception, the serials list was produced in paper format, but evolved in time

Figure 1
Serial Reconciliation Form

Call No.   Entry: _____
               _____
               _____
               _____
               _____

               Date: _____ Team Member: _____
Location: _____ Multiple locations on one checklist card: __

Frequency: _____

Current disposition notes: _____
_____
_____

Linking notes: _____
_____
_____

Latest issue recd: _____ Date recd: _____

Brief holdings: _____
_____
_____

Type of binding: _____ Condition: _____

Notes: Searched: _____ SL
                                      _____ Checklist
                                      _____ PC
                                      _____ Shelf
                                      _____ Circulation
                                      _____ SAF
                                      _____ CSO
                                      _____ Withdrawn

FISCAL INFORMATION

Vendor # _____ Source if not SUB/STO _____

Agency: _____ Fund: _____ Price: $ _____

Date of last payment/period covered: _____

Indexed: _____

28

Coordinator _____ Selector _____ Date _____

I. <u>Location</u>
    Current location is O.K. _____
    Change to _____ (justification needed, use verso)
    Put on current display (PER) _____
    Remove from current display (PER) _____

II. <u>Currently Received SUB or STO</u>
    Continue SUB or STO _____ (If yes, complete Sections II & III)
    Cancel SUB or STO; yes ___ no ___ (If yes, must complete Section IV)
    Claim missing issues (previous one year only) _____
    Fill in gaps - attach order form _____
    If subscription is duplicate, justify: _____
    _____
    Has correct fund been charged? yes ___ no, should be _____
    Withdraw hard copy back run _____

III. <u>Retention</u>
    Discard hard copy (H.C.) and keep subscription backfile in M.F. (attach
       order if necessary) _____
    Current disposition notes O.K. (noted on workform) _____
    If "latest in", review disposition of superseded issues or give
       disposition if not noted: _____
    _____
    Changes/additions to disposition instructions _____
    _____
    1) Send duplicates to action review _____, or 2) Add duplicates up to
    3) Send duplicates to gifts _____   _____ copies, or
    <u>Binding:</u> Change to Class _____
       Do not bind; retain only current ___ years
       Not presently bound; bind Class _____

IV. <u>Cancelled or Inactive Title Decisions</u>
    If cancelled SUB or STO, retain holdings _____
    If cancelled SUB or STO, withdraw holdings _____
    <u>Approval or Purchase Titles:</u> (Recent volume(s) acquired via purchase,
                            approval or blanket plan)
       Place STO - submit order form and evaluation to coordinator
       Recent volume acquired via purchase, approval or blanket order.
          No STO wanted _____
       Retain piece(s) _____
       Withdraw piece(s) _____
    <u>Widely Scattered Holdings</u>
       Withdraw _____
       Retain _____ (If yes, use verso for justification)
       Place current subscription or STO: yes ___ no ___ (If yes, submit
          order and evaluation to coordinator)
       Fill in gaps, order backfile in hard copy _____
       Order backfile in M.F. _____
          Withdraw hard copy when film arrives _____
          Withdraw hard copy now _____
          Retain hard copy _____ (If yes, use verso for justification)
    <u>Fairly Complete Run</u>
       Withdraw _____
       Retain _____
          Fill in gaps, order backfile in hard copy _____
          Place current subscription to hard copy _____
       Acquire M.F. run in addition to hard copy: yes ___ no ___ (If yes,
          use verso for justification)
       Replace with M.F. _____
       Order backfile in M.F. _____
       Place current subscription for M.F. _____
       Disposition of hard copy:
          Retain: yes ___ no ___ (If yes, use verso for justification)
          Withdraw hard copy when film arrives _____

Selector: _____ Date: _____

© University of New Mexico General Library

29

to a COM format which is issued monthly. This has been especially helpful because all periodicals and periodical indexes are shelved on one floor of the library, separate from the monographic collection and the card catalog. Patrons often utilize the microfiche list as they can go directly from the periodical indexes to the fiche list without having to consult the public catalog. Copies of the COM list are located throughout the library. The public fiche entries for each serial include: location, call number, entry (corporate author/title or title), and summary holdings and linking title notes. The internal use fiche also contains ISSN numbers, control number, and OCLC number.

For a period of several years, the UNM General Library decided not to put cards in the public catalog for periodicals, but rather to file a card in the shelf list only and rely on the COM list for access to journals. With the onset of OCLC, this decision was reversed and all periodicals cataloged during that period have now been entered on OCLC and complete card sets produced and filed. Part of the bibliographic reconciliation process included verifying the accuracy of the COM list and correcting it if necessary.

Fiscal information was and is a vital part of the reconciliation process. The UNM General Library has bee using the BATAB acquisitions system for monographs and serials for ten years. Although the system was designed for the acquisition of monographs, at UNM drastic changes were made to make the system function for serials. It was necessary to maintain the records in the BATAB system in order to properly encumber and expend to the correct fund. However, it was also thought that this accounting information must be included as part of the Central Serial Record so that all data concerning a serial title would be in one place. Thus, the idea of the fiscal record card (or "green card," as we have come to call it affectionately) came into being. The green color was selected because it would distinguish the card as a fiscal record as distinctive from a checkin record and also because a pale green color is the one most used for accounting systems. (See Figure 2)

The fiscal information recorded on the recon form was taken from the data in the BATAB system. Recon team members searched for the entries in BATAB in order to establish vendor number, source, and so forth. "Agency" and "Fund" refer to the hierarchy of funds in the BATAB system, i.e., SUB is the agency used for all subscriptions, STO is the agency used for all standing orders, and funds are ordinarily subject related (HIST–history, ARCH–Architecture, ELED––elementary education). By using this particular configuration of funds and agencies, the selector for Elementary Education, for example, knows at the

Figure 2
Fiscal Record Form

VENDOR #	SOURCE	AGENCY	FUND	PURCHASE ORDER #
6000	Faxon	SUB	NMEX	82185

BOOK # B01234567

ENTRY: New Mexico historical review

SER-6
3/21/76

DATE OF INV.	INV. #	PERIOD COVERED	AMT.	NOTES	DATE OF INV.	INV. #	PERIOD COVERED	AMT.	NOTES
8/10/79	101213	1/80-12/80	10.00	8/24/79 rec'd					
8/15/80	11302	1/81-12/81	11.00	8/15/80 rec'd					
8/15/81	122135	1/82-12/82	11.00	8/24/80 rec'd					
8/30/82	134872	1/83-12/83	12.00	9/10/82 rec'd					
8/1/83	152873	1/84-12/84	14.00	8/1/83 rec'd					

end of the year how much has been expended for subscriptions and standing orders in the field of elementary education. This had not been possible before the library began to manipulate the BATAB data.

The price listed on the recon form was the amount of the most recent payment and was included to give the selector an accurate idea of the cost of a journal. The date of the last payment and period covered also serves as an aid to the selector. For the most part, the recon team did not supply information on index coverage. If a selector wished this information, it was incumbent on the selector to either check the journal itself or the Ulrich's listing which sometimes gives indexing information.

The fiscal record card (see Figure 2) has become for the Serials Department an accounts payable ledger. Instead of having the ledger in book form, it is filed in the CSR. The fiscal record contains information which connects it to the BATAB system -- the book number, vendor number, and fund to which the payment is charged. It also contains space for actual invoice information – invoice number and date, volume or period covered, amount of payment, and usually the payer's initials and date of payment. Much of this data had been abbreviated in the BATAB system due to field length constraints and so the fiscal record is considered "official" payment information. It also shows a more complete payment history record than BATAB does. This fiscal information has been immeasurably helpful to serials acquisitions staff as well as others who use the CSR. It helps the CSR staff in claiming, as the person who is claiming can quickly see whether or not payment has been made. A fiscal card is prepared for all currently received titles regardless of the source. For gifts, exchange items, and depository items, special vendor numbers are used and the fiscal card contains such information as claim address, "received on deposit," "received as part of membership," "received as gift of publisher."

About the same time that serials reconciliation began, a system was devised that would enable the checklist staff and others to quickly see whether or not a title was current, dead, or cancelled. Although other libraries have used similar systems such as flagging, we found that the best use of the space at the bottom of the check–in card was to place a small colored dot in the lower right corner. All currently received titles received a green dot, ceased titles have a black dot, cancelled titles have a blue dot, and "pur-- chase" and/or approval titles have a brown or tan dot. Staff are then able to concentrate on green dots when claiming and can easily skip the cards with other colors. This procedure has speeded up the claiming process considerably.

32

After checklist, holdings, and fiscal information had been recorded on the recon form, and statistics had been taken, the form was sent to the coordinator who then forwarded it to the appropriate subject selector. It was felt that it was important for the coordinators to review all of the forms so that they would be aware of the amount of the work being distributed and to monitor the work flow.

Once in the hands of the selectors, as can be seen from the form itself, many options were offered for continuance, retention, location, and so forth. Cancellations and withdrawals were co--signed by coordinators and the Assistant Dean for Collection Development in order to assure that there was a concensus and to minimize possible dramatic effects upon other instructional programs and the collection as whole. Whenever a journal crossed interdisciplinary lines, selectors ordinarily conferred and both signed the form.

Location notations (section I) on the reconciliation form was noteworthy because any change of location had to be justified as it usually meant re--cataloging. Unless deemed absolutely neces--sary, location changes were given a lower priority by serials cata--loging. In section II, currently received subscriptions and standing orders were reviewed. Although there was an option listed to fill in gaps and order duplicate subscriptions, this was rarely done. Because the UNM General Library was and is on a tight budget, there was not enough money to pursue this. However, it did give the selector an option of keeping a list (or card file, or Xerox of the recon form) of gaps and missing issues which could be ordered at a later date when funds were available. It was felt that the important consideration was that the selector was made aware of the gaps for possible future selection purposes. It became apparent that this was indeed the case, as many selectors returned the form noting that the subscription would be reinstated or back issues purchased when money was forthcoming.

Section III, retention decisions, gave the selectors many op--tions, including binding instructions. Again, selector awareness by actually looking at the pieces on the shelf was vital. Several of the selectors have said that when looking at a particular title for reconciliation, they would find other titles nearby which needed re--binding or withdrawal, for example. Thus a form of weeding the serial collection was brought about by the serials reconciliation project.

Section IV, cancelled or inactive title decisions, was probably the most misunderstood and misused section of the form. As all serial titles, regardless of source, had been placed on the serials check--in record, some selectors thought that a recon form for a title which had been either purchased on a one--time only basis or perhaps had come on an approval plan, was a continuing com-mitment and would note to continue the subscription or standing order in Section II. In these cases, the form was returned to the selector with the explanation that an order must be submitted. This is a rather fuzzy area for almost anyone who does not work with serials on a regular, frequent basis. People tend to think that if a title is on the check--in record, then we must be committed to continuing it forever and, as all serials librarians are aware, this is just not the case. Most selectors became more aware of the distinctions as the project progressed, and it became less of a problem.

For cancellations, selectors were asked to fill out a separate cancellation sheet stating the reasons for cancellation and whether or not any faculty members had been consulted. Copies of the cancellation form are kept in the serials department along with the letter sent to the publisher or vendor. These have been helpful when questions as to the appropriateness of a cancellation have arisen.

The distinctions between widely scattered holdings and fairly complete runs were most often helpful in deciding whether to retain or withdraw a title. Except for unusually unique titles, those with very few or widely scattered issues were often with-drawn. The selectors were most helpful in justifying their decisions in this area by noting that certain issues had pieces by important authors or were unique and valuable in other ways. Several pieces were found to be rare enough to be relocated to the special collec-tions area of the library for better preservation. There were some instances when no pieces of a title could be found nor was there any indication that the title was circulating. Most of the time, these were withdrawn and could be evaluated and reinstated if they turned up in the future.

Due to the length of time which has passed over the life of the project, selectors have come and gone. There have been times when it has been impossible to track down a recon form and duplicates have had to be generated. Early on, it was hoped that, once all reconciliation work was completed, the recon forms could be destroyed. However, mostly due to the fact that bibliog-raphic reconciliation has taken so much time, we have found that keeping the forms is most desirable. Although we will even-tually have to toss them, it is certainly helpful to be able to tell the new social science selector that his predecessor recommended cancellation and/or withdrawal of a particular title. The file has also aided checklist personnel when a patron wants to know why a title was cancelled. Usually the patron is referred to the selector to discuss possible reinstatement. Thus a certain accountability factor was built into the project.

After the selector finished with the form, it was returned to the serials reconciliation team. Statistics were taken, fiscal records were either originated or clarified, orders were forwarded to serials acquisitions, and the form was sent to Serials Cataloging. Up to the point of return of the recon form, titles which were coming to the library via gift, exchange, or deposit had no BATAB records, per se, as they were not paid for. At the beginning of the project a decision was made to enter all current titles into the BATAB system regardless of whether or not they were a cost to the library's acquisition budget. It was hoped that the BATAB system could be manipulated to give each selector a list of all currently received titles in their subject area. The listing would include paid subscriptions and standing orders as well as gifts, exchanges, deposits, and others. Serials recon personnel were responsible for entering these titles after the selector decided to continue and retain the titles. A green fiscal card was also made with information pertinent to the title -- name and address of publisher or donor, whether the title could be claimed or not, and reference to correspondence if such existed.

Another part of the process which was both time--consuming and frustrating was that of writing to publishers to ascertain how we were receiving the titles. Often, a selector would ask that we write and inquire if a title were still being published and if we would continue to receive it. Form letters were devised for these titles and if possible we tried to call the publisher to confirm receipt. We found that phone calls were the fastest and most effi-cient means of securing information about a title (a letter might just sit in an "in" box endlessly, or worse, get tossed in the round file). Some letters were returned as undeliverable, addressee un-known, not forwardable. For these titles, we notified the selector and a final decision could be made. Serials recon team members became quite familiar with various reference tools to find pub-lisher's names and addresses. *Encyclopedia of Associations* and *The World of Learning* were the primary sources. We also heavily utilized the library's collection of telephone books, both domestic and foreign. For some Latin American titles, we wrote to dealers asking if they knew the status of a particular title. The selectors in the Latin American field were very cooperative in advising how to ascertain the status of a title published in Central or South America.

One selector of Latin American materials chose to group together her recon sheets by type of material, and a whole folder concerning national bibliographies from Latin American countries was done at one time. This method proved to be very efficient for serials reconciliation purposes. As most of the bibliographies were available on exchange, form letters were sent out in Spanish or Portuguese.

A major type of serial which caused problems was documents of any jurisdiction. From local all the way through international agencies, many titles were almost impossible to identify as to the appropriate issuing agency (their names and designations had changed often) and addresses were often out–of–state. If the material was arriving regularly and currently, we arbitrarily entered it as "depository" or "gift of publisher–unconfirmed." As the UNM General Library is a full regional depository for all U.S. documents, the only decision to be made was location. This project did not include materials in Su Docs, primarily because they are not checked in on the serial record and thus did not qualify for inclusion.

Recently, a questionnaire was sent out to the thirty–two librarians who act as subject selectors. The questionnaire concerned the serials reconciliation project and whethey they, as selectors, felt that it had been successful. Of fifteen respondents, eleven felt that the project had been extremely successful. Four answered "Don't know." The latter responses were from new staff members who did not think that they could evaluate the project. In answer to a question about whether the project had helped them to be–come more familiar with the serials collection in their areas of expertise, the selectors responded with an enthusiastic "yes, defi–nitely." A question regarding teaching faculty involvement elicited the expected response -- faculty were conferred with concerning current paid subscriptions primarily and hardly ever in decisions concerning gift, exchange, and ceased titles. Most of the comments offered by the selectors indicated that a majority thought that it had been valuable and worthwhile.

Summary

This has been a detailed history and presentation of procedures for the serials reconciliation project at the University of New Mexico General Library. Bibliographic reconciliation looks as though it will be the next major hurdle. If the library intends to have an on–line catalog, bib recon must somehow be completed at least for currently received serial titles.

On–line receipt, claiming, and accounting functions for serials may become possible before an on–line catalog. Reading through the literature concerning on–line serials control systems has given us great encouragement to realize that, due to the serials recon project, we have already performed the clean--up and groundwork which must precede an on-line system. The data which will be entered will be accurate, current, and complete. Due to the collection development inclusion in the process, we are also assured that we will be entering serials which have been evaluated for continuation and retention.

The review and evaluation aspects of the serials reconciliation project have made it ultimately unique. The original concept called for a reconciliation of records into a central file, including inventory and bibliographic up--dating. The original concept alone was commendable and mammoth in scope. Evaluation and review by selectors resulted in a total analysis of the serials collection. In continuing the process of analysis, selectors must now justify new subscriptions and standing orders as well as justify cancellations and withdrawals. Each selector receives, on an annual basis, a listing of current subscriptions, standing orders, gifts, exchanges, in their subject field for review.

After five years, the serials reconciliation project has completed recon forms and has fiscally reconciled approximately 18,000 serial titles. Seven thousand have been bibliographically reconciled. The number of titles on the Central Serial Record has been reduced from 25,000 in 1978 when the project began to 23,000 in June of 1983. This decrease is largely due to withdrawals coupled with the fact that such tight restrictions have been placed on new sub--scriptions and standing orders. There are about 5,000 titles (inactive) yet to be reconciled. The University of New Mexico General Library will probably never again embark upon a total review of its serial collection. Our goal will be, in accordance with Osborne's suggestion, " . . . once every three years, all titles on the current checking records should be scrutinized . . . "[4] Whatever the time period chosen for re--evaluation, we will continue to view the serial collection as dynamic and truly serving the needs of the university community.

REFERENCES

1. Susan Brynteson and Mary E. Sauer, *Review of the Serials Department — The General Library — The University of New Mexico*, February 27, 1978, p. 1.

2. Brynteson and Sauer, p. 17.

3. Benita M. Weber. *Memorandum to Library Executive Council,* October 16, 1978, p. 1.

4. Andrew D. Osborne, *Serial Publications.* (Chicago: American Library Association, 1980), p. 97.

Serials Workflow in a Library Without
A Centralized Serials Department

Florence M. McKenna and Ruth C. Carter
Assistant Director   Head
for Technical Services   Catalog Department
University of Pittsburgh Libraries

Introduction

What library has not struggled with the question of how to handle serials? The myriad problems associated with this type of publication, e.g. frequency of appearance, title changes, have resulted in libraries often placing serials in a separate department which handled all processing activities from order placement and cataloging to public services. Proponents of this position contend that serials differ in so many respects from monographs that a highly specialized staff must be established in order to effectively deal with the problems.

Opposed to the organization based on form of publication is that of one based on function. The libraries which have this type of organization treat serials along with other types of library materials by function such as acquisitions. Order placement, invoice payment, cataloging are handled in the various departments specializing in specific processing functions.

Movement from one type of organization to another is not uncommon. The University of Pittsburgh has done so over the years with the objective of improving processing and service. The current organization is a functional one. A description of the evolution of the processing organization to its current status follows.

Background

The organization of the University of Pittsburgh libraries has developed from the establishment of a University library of 2500 volumes in 1873 to 2.5 million volumes in 1983. The current organization is composed of twenty libraries in the University

Library System (ULS) and eight independent libraries. The ULS libraries are: Hillman (main library housing collections in the humanities and social sciences), the East Asian library, Buhl Library (social work), Afro--American Library, Special Collections, and Archives, and separate branch libraries in chemistry, computer science, biology and psychology, physics and geology, mathematics, engineering, music, fine arts, public and international affairs, library and information sciences, business, and economics. Prior to 1982 the libraries in the areas of business, library and information sciences, and public and international affairs were autonomous units. Presently, independent libraries serve the areas of medicine, public health, psychiatry, and law. In addition, there are four regional libraries serving campuses located up to 165 miles from the main campus.

This discussion will apply only to the operation of the present Technical Services Department located on the main campus in Hillman Library which provides order services to all of the ULS libraries. Several of the ULS libraries do cataloging for their own collections.

Support services for the processing of materials have varied over the years. The early growth of the Pitt library system followed the pattern of many libraries and a structure based on form of material was formed within the technical services operations. By the 1970's a separate serials department (Central Serials) had been established with the supervisor of the unit reporting directly to the head of Technical Services. It handled the placement of serial orders, renewals, prepared invoices for payment, and main-- tained central financial records for all system libraries, as well as maintaining the union list of serials. It also acted as receiver for all continuation and standing orders and for the periodicals and newspapers housed in the stacks of the central library (Hillman Library). The branch libraries received all periodicals and news- papers directly. They maintained their own checkin records in- cluding any necessary claiming. Cataloging was done by the central cataloging department. However, periodicals and newspapers received only a brief entry in the union list. Cards were not placed in the catalog.

In July 1972, a reorganization of technical services functions took place. A new unit, the Processing Department, was estab- lished. It consisted of order services, copy cataloging, card and book processing, catalog maintenance, and serials. Original cata- loging was organized as a separate independent department and responsibility for the union list of serials was placed in the collections development department. The coordinators of these three major departments reported to the Director of Libraries.

This realignment of technical services was undertaken in response to criticism of what appeared to be a lack of communication within technical services units, unclear lines of responsibility, and a lack of response to stated needs of the public service areas. Therefore, the primary objectives of the new processing organization were: expedite the processing of materials, define the lines of authority, and assign responsibility for each of the various technical services functions.

Most of the objectives of the new organization appeared to be met. However, problems with serials processing became apparent soon after the new organization became operational. The placement of the union list of serials outside of the so--called central serial function posed some procedural problems. Where should an order for a new title be searched and verified? Who should notify whom and when in the case of a problem, title change, frequency change? To whom did the catalogers go when a question arose in the cata--loging process? It all came down to the question of which unit had responsibility for serials processing. As a partial solution, the union list function was returned to the Central Serials Unit in late 1974.

In the meantime, the University libraries had been participating in OCLC since 1970 when it was still in a batch mode. The possi--bility of using the database for union list production developed with OCLC's purchase of the union lists of the Pittsburgh Regional Library Center and the University of Pittsburgh in the spring of 1974. Up to that time the Pitt union list records, which were in--tended for internal use only, had been brief in nature. The need for more complete cataloging of serials became apparent. At that point, a full time cataloger position was added to the serials unit and a second position was established in October 1978. With these two new positions, all cataloging of serials was transferred to Central Serials, and the paraprofessional positions which handled serial "adds" were transferred to Central Serials soon afterward. Parallel operations for serials and monographs were maintained and the organization based on form was given greater emphasis.

Current Organization

The above organization remained in place until January 1981. At that time the Processing and Original Cataloging Departments were merged to form a new Technical Services Department. Once again the reasons for the reorganization included expedition of processing of materials and clarification of the lines of responsibility for the various technical services functions. For example, the num-- ber of departments working directly with OCLC input was reduced from three to two. In addition, although the serials operation was largely centralized, it excluded the key function of ordering for classified serials and therefore could not provide optimal service. With the opportunity presented by the requirement for reorganizing to incorporate original monographic catalogers into a new Technical Services Department, it seemed a good time to introduce a new approach to handling all aspects of serials. Therefore, in March 1981, all serials order functions were transferred to Order Services along with receipt of serials for the main library. Prior to this, only the serial standing orders for classed items were handled by the Order Unit. This new functional approach centralized order place-- ment and invoice processing in one area. Bibliographers as well as library users could consult one department for all serial order information. Other benefits were improved interaction with many vendors since many of the same vendors serviced both monograph and serial orders, as one department head became responsible for all invoice processing.

A new Catalog Department was formed with the merger of the Original Cataloging Department and the serials cataloging opera-- tions. The union list function because of its bibliographic nature was included in this department. Binding was assigned to the Card and Book Services Department along with the mending operation so that all end processing activities were centered in one area.

Physical rearrangement of Technical Services was necessary. The original catalogers and the serials cataloging unit were brought together. This arrangement encourages exchange of opinions among the catalogers and provides an atmosphere of collegiality rather than the monograph versus serials attitudes which were fostered by the old organization.

The checkin and subscription payment units were united with the monograph and standing order/continuations order unit to form Order Services. Gift and Exchange remained as a separate unit. However, it is immediately adjacent to Order Services so that interaction is easy.

Procedures which had involved only one department prior to the reorganization had to be refined. Actually, the forms which had been used were satisfactory, and all that was needed was a different routing.

As has been described previously, serial materials receive a variety of treatments in the University of Pittsburgh library system. Although there are a number of different breakdowns, the two major categories for the purposes of this discussion are classified serials and periodicals.

Classed serials at Pitt are those items which receive full cataloging and are included in the public catalog. Most commonly those items include publications such as annuals, yearbooks, statistical reports, and, in general, titles published annually or less frequently. Classed serials may be received on a one by one basis or they may be re--ceived as a continuation or standing order. They also include many titles received via gift or exchange. Unless otherwise specified, remarks describing the workflow of both classed serials and periodi-cals are limited to the libraries included in the University Library System.

Selection of classed serials for the collection is made by a bib--liographer or departmental librarian. Classed serials are requested for order through the submission of a Book Request Form (BRF). When an item is ordered on a Book Request Form, an entry is made for the In Process List which is used to track monographic items and classed serials from the time of order until they are sent to the shelves. Items are updated at each step during the processing flow to reflect the location/status of the item and the date of the most recent action. For classed serials this includes first time orders, back orders, and added volumes. The In Process List has been available at Pitt since 1967 in the form of a printed list based on eighty columns of data. At present, the file provides for only fifteen characters of the author and twelve characters of the title. It is in the process of being converted to an online system which will permit expanded data as an interim measure prior to selection and implementation of a fully integrated library automation system. For classed serials, the addition of more author and title information is particularly important.

After completion, a BRF is sent to the Bibliographic Control Department (BCD) for pre--order searching. BCD forwards searched BRF's to Order Services for assignment of a vendor. The actual order is produced in the Library Systems Department where all of the library's computer equipment is located. At the same time that orders are keyed, accounting records are prepared along with a key punch card. This card is maintained with the order record until the item is received. At that point, it is attached to the item and is used to update it at each step of processing until the item is sent to the shelves. An IBM 1031 terminal is used for this func-tion. The system provides for maintaining the item in the In Process file for eight weeks following its release to the shelves.

All orders for classed serials are received in Order Services whe--ther or not the cataloging will be done by the central Technical Services. If a title was ordered centrally but will be cataloged outside

of Technical Services, it will be checked in by Order Services, up--
dated out of the In Process File and sent to the requesting library.
Those first issues of classed serials to be cataloged in Technical
Services are sent to BCD along with new books. When BCD identi-
fies the item as a serial it is immediately transferred to the Catalog
Department where it will be handled by the Classed Serials Team.

Added volumes for classed serials follow a similar work flow.
They are checked in by Order Services and either routed to a cataloging agency outside of Technical Services or sent to BCD. BCD
separates added serial volumes from added copies of monographs
(including sets) and forwards added volumes to the Classed Serials
Team. Added volumes are accompanied by an order slip containing
the call number. The shelf list and public catalog records are then
updated by the Classed Serials Assistant and revised by the Classed
Serials Team Chief. The latter notifies union list personnel if the
added volume is a back issue which will change the holdings record
or a new issue for an entry previously considered closed.

New classed serials are searched by the Classed Serials Associate.
If acceptable copy is found on OCLC, the Classed Serials Associate
completes the cataloging of the item for Pitt including the ordering
of cards. That individual also notifies union list personnel of the
new title for inclusion in the University's union list of serials. If
the new classed serial has no catalog copy or copy that is clearly
unacceptable in terms of completeness, quality of cataloging, adherence to current rules it is sent to the serials cataloger who is the
Classed Serials Team Chief. That librarian provides necessary original
cataloging or upgrading of the copy. Because the University of
Pittsburgh had been accepted as a CONSER participant in 1983,
upgrading of records will include upgrading records online with
OCLC unless those records have been authenticated by a CONSER
Center of Responsibility and the records are locked.

Following cataloging of the first issue of a classed serial or
the shelf listing of an added volume, the physical piece along with
an Editor's Sheet is sent to the Card & Book Services Department.
Card & Book puts in a book pocket, adds a book label and provides
any other necessary end processing. Then the serial volume is
sent to the keypunch section of Library Systems Development
where the book card for the automated circulation system is prepared from the information on the Editor's Sheet and the book
is released to the shelves.

Many classed serials are received through gift or exchange rather
than purchase. In those cases, they enter the system through the
Gift and Exchange Department. As new gift serials are received,
they are placed on shelves in G & E for evaluation by the appropriate
bibliographer or departmental librarian. If they are accepted to

be added to the collection, a Book Request Form is completed and sent to the Library Systems Department for entry into the In Process File. Individual items will follow the same route through Technical Services as those items which are purchased.

Consistency among the various Pitt records is provided by feed--back of the catalog entry to G & E or the Standing Order/Continua--tion section of Order Services. This will occur whether the classed serial is new to Pitt or whether it is being recataloged for some reason, e.g. a title change.

At the same time that feedback is provided to Order Services or Gift & Exchange on the correct entry for each serial, the infor--mation on new serials or changes in holdings is forwarded for union list updating. As of the date of the writing of this article, the Uni--versity maintains its union list data in two formats: online with OCLC and locally on tape updated by batch input in the library. That input is prepared on coding sheets and keypunched by Library Systems Development. The Serials Printout Team (the Pitt in--house union list team) is headed by the Serial Records Librarian. The locally maintained union list includes a sequence number which is assigned by the Serials Printout Team Chief. It is then used as well in the Subscription File for periodical materials.

After the local union list update has been prepared, the informa--tion is forwarded to the Online Union List and Periodicals Team which is headed by a serials cataloger. The members of the Team update the union list on OCLC with the same information. If the item is a classed serial, presumably that completes the processing of an item. Sometimes, however, items which will be bound to--gether later are sent to the shelves unbound. In those instances, after binding the volumes must re--enter the process with the Classed Serials Assistant who updates the shelf list to indicate which pieces are now bound together. A new Editor's Sheet is prepared for the bound volume. Keypunch will prepare a new book card and destroy those for the previously separate pieces.

Periodicals Workflow

A bibliographer or departmental librarian ordering a new period--ical title, newspaper, or back order of a periodical completes a Periodicals Request Form. It is sent to the Catalog Department for pre–order searching by the Online Union List and Periodicals Team. If the title is new to Pitt, it is sent to the Serials Printout Team for preliminary coding for the local union list including the assignment of a sequence number. A copy of the coding sheet and any OCLC copy accompanies the Periodicals Request Form to Order Services.

45

The two copies of the Periodicals Request Form going to Order Services are separated. One copy is used by the Subscription staff and the second copy is used by the Check--In staff. The Subscription staff prepares a purchase order. At the present time, this is a form on which the order information is typed. A copy of the form is used by Library Systems Department to update the library's accounting records. A coding sheet is prepared and used to key--punch the entry for the new title into the subscription list.

A computer based subscription list has been available at Pitt since 1974. Although it is expected that within a few years it will be replaced by an online system, it has been a valuable tool. The subscription file includes main entry/title, purchase order num--ber, invoice number, term of the subscription, date paid, amount paid, library location, and library account used. It provides for added charges, cross reference notes, and the like. One of the helpful features is the ability to list all subscriptions by either library location or fund account. These lists are often used by bibliogra--phers or departmental librarians in conjunction with their respective faculties to review existing subscriptions. The file carries both current and past payment information.

As the order is being prepared, the Check--In staff prepares the kardex card if it is for the main library. A notification card to be returned when the first issue arrives is sent to the departmental libraries. Periodical ordering is done centrally for all libraries in the University Library System. Receipt, however, is decentralized. This has many advantages in getting periodical materials to library users rapidly.

When the first issue is received, a surrogate of the title page and/or cover is provided to the Catalog Department via Order Ser--vices. If the periodical subscription is located in a departmental library, the surrogate is sent with the notification card to the Check--In staff so that the order records can be cleared. Or, if the periodical is for a location within the main library, the Check--In staff receives it directly. In either case, the Check--In staff notes the holdings and sends the copy of the serials printout coding sheet to the Online Union List and Periodicals Team for verification of the entry. If no acceptable OCLC copy is found, full cataloging records are created for all periodicals. In some cases, existing OCLC records are upgraded with the Pitt CONSER authorization. That informa--tion is sent to the Serials Printout Team which will make any neces--sary corrections for the local union list and add the holdings. The original of the coding sheet is forwarded to Library Systems for keypunching and the carbon is returned along with the OCLC worksheet for entry of Pitt holdings into the online union list. The last step is to return the copy of the coding sheet to Order

Services. Any discrepancies in the entry between the time it was received and what now exists in the catalog and union list records will be corrected in both the subscription and check--in records.

Both claiming of issues not received and update of holdings information is done decentrally. In other words, after receipt of the initial issue, the library which receives the periodical is re--sponsible for claiming it. Order Services only becomes involved in a claim if the first issue has not been received or if it is very complicated and/or proof of payment is required. The receiving library is also responsible for reporting any changes in holdings, title changes, and the like directly to the Catalog Department for union list maintenance. If it was a title change or other action which will affect the Subscription File, the necessary information is forwarded to Order Services when union list maintenance has been completed.

Periodicals received through gift or exchange are first evaluated by the appropriate bibliographer or departmental librarian. Those selected for addition to the collection are sent to Order Services for initial record making. Order Services then sends the first issue received or surrogate of the title page and/or cover to the Online Union List and Periodicals Team in the Catalog Department. Stan--dard routines described above are then followed for cataloging and entry into the two union lists. Back orders for periodicals enter the system via a Serial Request Form and follow essentially the same procedures described above except that they are not entered in the subscription file nor do they enter the In Process file. In addition, as cancellation decisions for serials are made, this information is forwarded by subscription or standing order/ continuations staff to the union list personnel for entry in both the local and online lists.

It is important to note that although Pitt is currently maintaining two union lists, it expects to phase out one soon. It is hoped that in the near future, OCLC will actually produce the offline union list products it has promised for so long. The University specifically requires the tape product. The current local union list includes special coding for area studies programs among other elements which are used to produce special lists on demand. The local union list also provides the primary source for statistics on serials at Pitt, both open and closed. Both union lists include information on all Pitt libraries on the main campus including those for the four pro--fessional schools which are not part of the University Library System. It is planned to add holdings for the four regional campuses in late 1983.

Problems in Decentralizing Serials

On the whole, there have been very few problems following the reorganization which divided the Serials Department into its functional parts. The first problem, if it can be considered such, is that the former Serials Department functioned well. As could be expected, there was some concern about breaking up something that actually worked. There was also some concern, particularly on the part of members of the Serials Department, about separating the various serials activities.

Fortunately, the change to a functional organizational structure has been very positive. In general, any problems existing today are the same ones which existed when more of the serials activities were together in one department. The major problem area continues to be assuring adequate timely communication between four points: the subscription or standing order/continuations staff, the check--in staff, the cataloging and online union list staff, and the in--house union list staff. Even when most of the serials activities except ordering for classed serials were together, it was almost impossible to keep everyone informed of everything at the time that they thought they should be informed. This is particularly true of title changes and ceased publications. One factor is that title changes are often discovered at different points. Sometimes a journal may be received by check--in staff with no record of the title. At other times, the periodical can be cited on an invoice under a new title for which the subscription staff member has no record. Whoever encounters the change first must notify the others and must be sure to go through cataloging and union list procedures. Except for the fact that on occasion two department heads are now in--volved rather than one, there is no noticeable increase in problems in this area.

Another area which can be a problem is the fact that orders are centralized in Technical Services but receipt is decentralized. However, decentralized receipt for periodicals was in place prior to organization by function and any problems in communication it poses are not new to the functional organization. The decen--tralized receipt of periodicals in the departmental libraries which provides users with faster access to new issues outweighs any minor difficulties which may occur.

Classed serials were affected relatively slightly by the reorganiza-tion because the order function for them was already part of the Order Services. Problems which exist are the same as always such as determining whether an item should be treated as a monograph or a serial. If anything, putting all the catalogers together has heightened sensitivities on this question and more time is spent making decisions on the correct treatment. As a result, more items are getting the most appropriate treatment in the beginning and it is to be hoped that recataloging for titles processed from the point of the functional reorganization forward will be minimal.

Benefits of the Functional Organization

We believe that there are a number of benefits in the present organizational structure regarding the processing of serials at the University of Pittsburgh. One obvious benefit is that like functions are brought together. Thus, individuals dealing with acquisitions problems can find common ground with other staff also dealing with acquisitions problems. The same is true for cataloging staff. Many functional issues such as use of a vendor, accounting proce-- dures, or policies for name authority and series authority files are of interest to a functional group regardless of format.

Bringing like functions together to facilitate mutual considera-- tion of policies has been particularly helpful to the catalogers. Because the organizational change at Pitt coincided closely with the introduction of AACR2 all catalogers were concerned with the development of local policies regarding the introduction of AACR2, handling variant headings in the catalog, and the like. It has been a definite plus to have the serial and monographic catalogers together in one department, particularly at this particular point in time.

The union list of serials activities were specifically associated with the Catalog Department when the former Serials Department was abandoned. This was a clear recognition that a union list is a bibliographic tool and that its natural affiliation is with other bibliographic activities, in this case cataloging. The union listing capability on OCLC emphasizes this fact because all local data records containing union list information are tied to a bibliographic record. Correct selection of the bibliographic record for any par-- ticular title is a crucial element in the construction of a union list.

Another benefit of the functional organization is the fact of the change itself from an organization by format to an organization by function. Change of any type, including organizational change, can be revitalizing. It was a positive factor at Pitt. It forced a fresh look at existing policies and procedures as well as provided the opportunity for closer discussions with staff previously encountered only rarely. Department heads were given new challenges as they had to get in depth knowledge of formats and areas that they knew less well. Even the writing of the current article is forcing review of procedures.

One of the probable benefits from the functional organization will come with more automation. Many automated systems lend themselves to a functional organization as serials are handled as integral parts of the online catalog, acquisitions, and circulation.

And, it is anticipated that more comprehensive automation will simplify procedures, reduce paper shuffling, and in general, eliminate redundant processing step.

Conclusion

The functional organization has been working well now for over two years. Procedures, as can be expected, are being contin-- ually fine tuned, but this would be true in any event. The preceding discussion has attempted to present an overview of the general workflow for broad categories of serial materials in the University Library System at the University of Pittsburgh as they exist in mid 1983.

We believe that the current functional organizational structure anticipates automation, presumably an integrated automated system in the libraries. Nevertheless, such a system will undoubtedly bring more organizational change. It is impossible now to predict the exact nature of such change. In the meantime, we can only reiterate that the current functional organization has met and in most cases exceeded expectations for its success. In truth, however, to satisfy the most dedicated serialists, it must be noted that existing speciali-- zations in serials processing have been continued, albeit in a func-- tional organization. In other words, there is still a clear distinction between individuals doing serial or monographic processing. Where the change is most evident is at the department head and policy level where issues based on function are most frequently en-- countered.

Every library has a unique organizational structure because there are always minor variations within several general themes. At present we are very satisfied with the one at Pitt which meets existing needs very well.

Automated Exchanges Control: An Interim Report

Herbert Jones
Margaret McKinley
Serials Department
University Research Library
University of California
Los Angeles

In the past, technical processing operations and procedures in large research libraries have often appeared to be rigid and immutable, incapable of alteration by even the strongest will. Nevertheless, they have undergone transformations over time, apparently unobserved by those most closely involved. In contrast, current economic stresses acting upon research libraries call for planned, radical changes in traditional methods, procedures, and, particularly, in attitudes. What follows, then, is a description of a serial operation in planned transition in one academic library. It is an operation which surely is among those most adorned with myths and heavily weighted by traditional practices. It is a scene captured through a window in time with a known past, an observable present, and an uncertain future.

Acquisitions by means of exchange of publications has long been well regarded by research libraries and other public and private institutions as a method of acquiring monographs and serials. Library exchange programs usually involve exchange of the library's or parent institution's publications for those of other libraries or institutions. Less frequently, a library may purchase trade publications for exchange purposes. In some stances, national exchange centers may act as central depositories for publications of academic institutions which are then distributed to exchange partners in foreign countries.[1]

Exchanges have been favored as a means of acquisition when a library has access to publications at little or no cost which it can exchange for similar publications. Some smaller institutions may prefer to acquire library materials through exchange and will not permit direct purchase of their own publications. In addition, there may be currency or import restrictions in some countries which make direct purchase an unreliable method of acquisition. In some countries, the political situation is unsettled, bibliographic control uneven, and marketing and distributions channels not well established. In these countries, exchange may be a more certain method of acquiring books and serials than direct purchase. Finally, exchange partners may provide special services for one another that a bookdealer would not consider offering. These are standard reasons cited by exchanges librarians for employing this mode of acquisition.

There are, however, additional, often–cited reasons of questionable merit in the present day economic climate. Exchange agreements have long been regarded as excellent means to cement scholarly relations among institutions and as a means of publicizing an institution's own accomplishments. Even when a library must purchase the publications sent to its exchange partners or when exchange is no longer a cost effective method of acquiring material, institutional and library administrators may still insist on the continued maintenance of an exchange program. It is common knowledge among exchanges librarians that an established exchange agreement may be extraordinarily difficult to terminate for many reasons, among them, institutional politics, a partner's reluctance to discontinue an agreement, or inadequate information about the original agreement.

Acquisitions Problems Unique to Exchanges

Library acquisitions, in its many aspects, is always complex. Maintenance of an exchanges program adds several additional elements whose complexity is directly proportional to the age and size of the exchanges program in question.

A library, in acquiring purchased material, is a customer. A library with an exchanges program becomes a vendor. It will probably be a direct shipper and may also be a drop shipper. That is, it may handle its own shipping operation, but may also provide instructions to shipping offices. It should maintain records of individual items sent. If it purchases trade publications or otherwise acquires publications from institutional publishers for exchange purposes, it also becomes an agent acting on behalf of its partners. The library will place orders, make claims, pay bills, and replace missing and defective issues for its partners.

There is agreement that an exchanges operation requires large daily feedings of correspondence for its continued good health.[2] Much of it can be accomplished by a series of form letters but a certain percentage must be original. Records of publications sent to exchange partners must be maintained. Payment records, partners' mailing addresses, receipt records, and balance sheets or their equivalent should be current and accurate. Requests for new serial titles, claims, replacement requests, and cancellation requests to and from partners must be recorded and acted upon.

While no payments among institutions are involved, each partner in an exchange agreement must concur on a method of balancing that exchange. That is, how will each partner determine if publications of equivalent value have been exchanged? Balance may be evaluated by tallying individual issues of serials or monographs received. It may be determined by comparing serial titles sent and adding a certain amount of credit for monographs sent or received. Occasionally, libraries will exchange copies of invoices and balance on exchange by comparing dollar amounts expended. It's important to note, however, that in spite of recent efforts to assess the value of exchanges according to objective criteria[3], assigning values to publications exchanged between libraries has been an inexact art rather than an exact science. Moreover, in even the most diligent evaluation of an exchange agreement, exchange librarians will try to achieve balance in an exchange over two or three years rather than a single year.[4]

The Exchanges Program at UCLA

Exchange has, for the past 50 years, been a major method of acquisition in the UCLA Library, replete with the myths and traditions which impede modification and modernization of any exchanges operation.

In 1932, the scope of the exchanges program at U C Berkeley was expanded to include UCLA. Initially, offers were made to exchange scholarly series of the University of California with publications issued by 25 American universities. There was steady expansion in the following years so that by 1944, UCLA was exchanging publications with 1,016 institutions. In 1983, in spite of deliberate efforts at containment, the total number of partners was near 3,000. In 1946, 29% of the Library's current subscriptions were received on exchange. Today, 23% of the titles in the Serials Department's subscription files are received on exchange.

In addition to purchasing University of California publications for exchange purposes, the Library purchases U.S. trade monographs and serials which are shipped to partner institutions. In all, the Serials Department ships 47 serial titles published by the University to exchange partners. A few of the publications are gratis, but the Library is charged for most of them. The department is an agent in arranging to have 350 commercially published serial titles shipped.

University of California publications and the publications of various centers and institutes within the University are generally received in the Serials Department where they are counted, receipt is recorded, and any invoices are posted and passed for payment.

For large mailings, sometimes exceeding 300 copies, shipping in-
structions are prepared for UCLA's Mail and Messenger Service.
The Serials Department and the Mail and Messenger Service each
maintain mailing lists which should be exact replicas of one another.
Small mailings of 30 or fewer copies are processed by staff in the
Serials Department.

In supplying commercial publications and a few of the institutional publications, the department places new orders, posts billing
information, passes invoices for payment, and corresponds on service
and billing problems. The department does not ship issues except
in a few instances,when publishers are unable or unwilling to ship
to certain countries. In those cases, material is received from publishers and reshipped to institutions in those countries. In brief,
the Serials department may be a drop shipper or reshipper for the
Library's exchange partners.

The Library has traditionally balanced its exchanges serial
title for serial title but also considers monographs received or sent
as well as items selected from duplicate exchange lists in balancing
exchange agreements. Balance lists are maintained in manila folders
also containing correspondence. There is usually one manila folder
per partner although there will be more folders for partners of
long standing. These folders now fill eight filing cabinets to capacity.

As at other U.S. institutions, exchange agreements may be initiated through academic departments or by the central campus
administration. Restrictions may be imposed by donors or publishers when publications are offered gratis to the Library to use
for exchange purposes. If publishers are primarily interested in
having their publications disseminated to publicize scholarly achieve-
ment, they may be reluctant to reduce the number of copies of a
title mailed to exchange partners.

Some arrangements have the weight of legislative pronouncement
behind them. There are, in addition, a number of special arrangements made with publishers or distributors of publications offered
on exchange by the UCLA Library whose origins are undocumented.

Organization

Presently, at UCLA, responsibility for gifts lies with the Technical Services Department, while the Exchanges Section is in the
Serials Department. Prior to 1983, the Exchanges Section was
staffed by a librarian with competency in Spanish correspondence
and by a library assistant with competency in Russian correspondence. In other sections of the department, 5% of the time of
one staff member was devoted to shipping activities and maintaining
mailing lists, and 10% of the time of another was devoted to distri-

bution of samples of new titles and construction of address files. Other tasks such as mail sorting, check--in, claiming, acnowledging receipt, and bibliographic checking are integrated into departmental procedures for other kinds of material.

In 1983, the exchanges librarian's position was vacated through retirement of the incumbent and has not been filled. The lack of adequate staff to maintain this labor--intensive operation has dramatically increased the urgency of defining the exchanges pro--gram as narrowly as possible and converting all files to machine--readable form so that the program can be managed by the meager staff remaining. The library can no longer afford the luxury of monitoring and maintaining an elaborate exchanges program.

Automation's Advent

In 1980, UCLA entered a new era of machine--readable files. The library developed its own computer--assisted processing system for acquiring and cataloging monographs and serials. This system provides automated support for technical services operations in a large research library but was not designed to meet the requirements for maintenance of an exchanges program.

There were two hypotheses in system design which had serious implications for future exchanges control. First, that processing of monographs and serials could always be distinguished from one another and that files for the two types of formats could be separate with no links. Secondly, system developers maintained that the UCLA Library would always be a customer, never a vendor.

In addition, there were two restructions in developing the system which limited its applicability to automation of an exchanges operation. First, billing and shipping addresses should always be identical, and second, all printed purchase order forms were to include billing instructions. These restrictions meant that the auto--mated system could not be used in ordering monographs or serials from partners or from publishers to be sent to partners. It could not be used to claim missing issues for serials titles ordered on behalf of partners. The system could not produce many of the form letters used in corresponding with partners or on behalf of partners. Final--ly, it is difficult to include all information relevant to the payment of invoices for serials ordered for exchange partners.

Computer--Assisted Serials Processing

The UCLA Library has been engaged in a rolling conversion of its manual serials records to machine--readable form in all libraries since 1978. During this conversion, a no--activity time limit of three years has been observed to select records eligible for conver--sion. That is, if the check--in record for a serial title showed no issues had been received for the past three years, conversion of that title was deferred in favor of more active titles. This procedure was adopted to hasten full implementation of on--line processing.

By the summer of 1982, two disturbing developments were apparent. First, a disproportionately large number of the inactive titles remaining in the manual files were exchange titles -- titles which, needless to say, were still being counted in the balancing of exchange agreements. Second, with so many of the exchange titles lying inactive, the master exchange records (manila folders for each partner mentioned earlier) could no longer be relied upon to furnish an accurate basis for review of the entire program.

It became clear to the staff of the Serials Department that a realistic assessment of any given exchange partnership could only be made from records of active exchange titles with machine--readable records placed side by side with current data from our mailing lists of titles sent by UCLA. If a balance sheet for each exchange agreement could be produced by the automated system, the first step toward a complete review of the program would be accomplished. Before they could be produced, however, some enhancements to the original system design were necessary.

Each processing record for a purchased title contains either a code for its vendor or the full name and address of the vendor in a separate field. The automated library system interfaces with a separate vendor file which contains names and addresses of the Library's book vendors along with three--letter codes carried in machine--readable processing records. This vendor file already contains the addresses of some of the larger exchange partners, but addresses of most partners are carried in individual records. There has not been, therefore, any efficient means of manipulating the machine--readable file to obtain balance lists.

A separate parallel file of names and addresses of exchange partners, structured somewhat differently from the vendor file, seemed to be essential to automated control of exchanges. The department is now well along in the creation of such a parallel file. Each partner's name and current address is followed by a line of numeric codes representing the serial titles sent to that partner by UCLA. When the file is complete, three or four--character codes will be assigned to each partner and added to machine--read--able records for exchange titles currently received. The Serials Department will then have the capability of requesting balance sheets showing titles sent and received from each exchange partner. The staff will also be able to produce mailing labels for shipments of University of California publications to partners as they become available.

Computer--produced exchange balance sheets, while offering a possible first step toward automated control of exchanges, would also force the library to examine some other problems inherent in any large exchange program. The first of these problems to arise at UCLA is that of accounting for monographs recieved on exchange. The exchange of serials has always been the primary concern of the exchanges program, and the program is maintained in the Serials Department using serials files. But in a cataloging and processing system consisting of separate files for monographs and serials, dictated by their differing MARC record formats, it would be impos--sible to account fully for exchange monographs in the serials file.

Another problem connected with the production of balance sheets for 3,000 exchange partners is the question of staff time required for reviewing them. Optimistically estimating an average of half an hour for review per partner, 1500 hours or approximately 38 weeks of full--time work would be required to determine what adjustments would still have to hammered out through time--con--suming correspondence, and the entire project would need to be repeated annually. This is impracticable. Machine capabilities must be called in to assist human judgment.

The criteria for judging balance or imbalance when reviewing exchange agreements must be carefully considered. In order to make maximum use of the capabilities of the automated system, exchanges should be balanced on a strict serial title for serial title basis, excluding monographs. The automated system could then be programmed to produce balance sheets only for those exchange agreements where the number of titles from one partner failed to match those of the other. The system would in fact produce "im--balance sheets" after having performed the larger portion of the exchanges review.

The effectiveness of this "imbalance alert" approach to auto--mated exchanges control would depend on prior decisions to ex--clude monographs from exchange agreements and to adhere to a strict serial title for serial title accounting, but most importantly, on a revised policy governing the selection of titles to be received on exchanges. In the past, many new titles offered by exchange partners have not been submitted to the selection process at all, but were simply added to the collection. Those that were submitted to selection officers for evaluation were regarded as more or less gratis, and accepted if they had any discernible value at all. There have even been cases where exchanges staff have politely accepted a title offered through exchange, and then made records directing check--in staff to discard any issues received.

Clearly, an automated exchange review program which allows

to stand as balanced an exchange agreement wherein UCLA supplies its relatively expensive *Statistical Abstract of Latin America* in exchange for a small museum's annual financial report is not much help. But the failure is not one of systems design but rather a reflection of selection policy. An exchanges control system based on title for title accounting must presume each title received through exchange to be a carefully selected addition to the research collec--tion, and this presumption is at present unwarranted at UCLA.

The Library administration, aware of the urgent need for cost accountability in the exchanges program, and mindful of the neces--sity to reduce the size of the program, has now requested selection officers to conduct a careful review of titles received on exchange. To facilitate this review, the Serails Department is producing lists of exchange titles arranged by country of publication. Selectors have been asked to indicate those titles valuable enough in their areas of responsibility to warrant expenditure from their book funds for purchase. The Serials Department will first cancel those titles not selected for purchase, and second, place purchase orders for the selected titles through vendors in country of publication. Those titles definitely not available for purchase will remain on the exchanges lists.

Conclusion

The exchanges program has served the UCLA Library well in the past and can continue to do so. Nevertheless, staffing reductions, the rising prices of serials subscriptions, and costs of shipping have made an intensive, ruthless review of the entire program a necessity. Such a review, given the size of the program in relation to the staff devoted to its operation, can be accomplshed only through harness--ing the capabilities of UCLA's computer–assisted processing system to bring about a coherent and accurate description of the exchanges file. An objective and disciplined evaluation of each individual exchange agreement is an economic necessity and can best be achieved through the dispassionate manipulation of elements of machine--readable records.

When all cancellations have been effected, and as many paid subscriptions established as possible, the UCLA Library should find itself in possession of a list of serial titles of real importance to the research collection, and a reduced number of exchange part--ners whose transactions can be efficiently monitored through an automated exchanges control system.

After the large collection policy issues have been examined, modified to fit the world of the late twentieth century, and exe--cuted in balancing each exchange agreement, the matter of im--

proved efficiency in correspondence and in posting payments can be addressed.

NOTES

1. Kovacic, Mark, "Acquisition by Gift and Exchange," *Acquisition of Foreign Materials for U.S. Libraries,* ed. Theodore Samore (Metuchen, N.J.: Scarecrow Press, 1982), p. 37.

2. Lane, Alfred H., *Gifts and Exchange Manual* (Westport, Conn.: Greenwood Press, 1980), p. 15.

3. Yu, Priscilla C., "Cost Analysis: Domestic Serials Exchange," *Serials Review* 8 (Fall 1982): 79. Also see Pamela Bluh and Virginia C. Haines, "The Exchange of Publications; an Alternative to Acquisitions," *Serials Review* 5 (April/June 1979): 103, for a "strictly monetary approach" to exchange balancing.

4. Lane, *Gifts and Exchange Manual,* p. 13.

Serials De–Acquisition

Barbara P. Pinzelik
General Services Librarian
Purdue University Libraries

When a library system undertakes a serials weeding program there must be very strong reasons: a need for space, the changing focus of the library, the availability of storage space, or a desire to improve access to the collection. At Purdue University's General Library, all of those reasons prompted a major weeding and storage project. Of the 18,000 serial titles in the collection, over 6000 titles were reviewed and withdrawn or relocated.

In this paper, I will discuss the serials weeding process as it evolved at Purdue. Purdue has a de–centralized system with many school/departmental libraries and without a central serials processing unit. My task was to reduce the size of the serials collection in the largest and oldest library in the system. A reduction of approximately 20% was needed so that a major rearrangement could take place. It had to be done in a limited period of time, which meant keeping the number of consultations with faculty and library subject specialists to a minimum. A new and relatively accessible storage area was available. Decisions could be made to retain, store, transfer, or withdraw for each title up for review.

The information we gained from the review of our serials collec-tion should be of value to other libraries contemplating a similar project. When collections continue to increase in size but shelving space cannot expand to fit shelving needs, libraries must look for the best solution to the problem. Although one knows intuitively that serials de–acquisition will be costly and time–consuming, there comes a time when it is a necessity.

While library literature abounds with articles on weeding mono-graphs, articles on weeding serials are not as numerous. Many of them deal with the process of de–selection, reflecting the serials cancellation projects many libraries experienced in the past decade.

Criteria used for cancelling serials and the effort needed to evaluate them can seem overwhelming. In the literature, Bourne and Gregor outline a methodology based on language, cost, duplica-tion, coverage by indexing and abstracting services, frequency of citation, use, record--keeping costs, storage costs, microfilm avail--ability, scope, and usefulness.[1] Broude used the variables of price, use, impact, indexes and abstracting, local availability, publisher reliability, and curriculum--relatedness which he put into a weighted formula.[2]

Wood and Coppel reviewed a seminar on periodicals de--acquisition in academic libraries which reported various methods including using collection development guidelines as a basis for de--selection, turning the responsibility over to the deans of the university, and conducting in--depth use studies.[3] Windsor used productivity/cost rankings.[4] Scholman and Alhl found that a questionnaire sent to the faculty was useful.[5] Feller coded titles in six categories and had them reviewed by faculty and library staff.[6]

Papers on selecting serial titles for withdrawal or storage include Fussler and Simon, who depended on use patterns to send materials to storage.[7] Taylor relied on a reshelving survey.[8] Lawrence pre--sented a cost model which required obtaining expected average number of years between circulations, a value factor, annual cost of housing the volume, the cost of weeding, and the cost per circu--lation.[9] In the weeding program at Yale, Ash found that there was disagreement on the best serial candidates for storage. Faculty objected to storing long runs of complete sets, but incomplete serial files did not meet initial guidelines for storage candidates.[10] Urquehart used the criteria of currency, use, local availability, con--dition, special features, and regional availability.[11]

A review of the literature makes it clear that there is no easy way to cancel or withdraw serials. The amount of information that must be collected to make informed decisions seems limitless. Additionally, these decisions must be made in full view of library users, who may be hostile to any changes, no matter how necessary or well informed.

The Selection Procedure

At Purdue, our review of 40,000 running feet of serials, with a deadline of a year to complete the project, required an efficient way to evaluate each title. The records available were computer print--outs of the serials catalog in call number order. Working from these records, the project staff reviewed only those categories of material that seemed most likely to produce results, which en--abled us to use the time available for the project efficiently.

We further refined the process by dividing the titles into four categories: current unique, current duplicate, ceased unique, and ceased duplicate. Our printed records made these categories imme--diately obvious. Working with each category as a separate entity allowed assumptions to be made and material handled in batches. This permitted considerable mass handling of materials and auto--matic decision making.

The Evaluation Process

The Serials Evaluation Tree (Figure 1) shows how retention tests can be applied to the title under review and indicates an appro--priate outcome. On the tree, twenty different categories are identi--fied. The current titles are tested for uniqueness to the system, use, scope, and origin of the subscription. The ceased titles are tested for duplication in the system, use, scope, size of run, and regional availability. There are nine possible outcomes: keep; re--evaluate; cancel, then transfer and store; transfer; cancel, then withdraw or transfer; discard; withdraw; store; or offer to a regional depository.

Definitions of the retential tests applied at the branching points of the chart are:

Current -- Any title currently received by the library. The public serials records are used to identify titles in this category.

Unique -- Only one set of this title is in the library system. Public serials records are the source of this information.

Use -- Determining serials use can be very difficult. If there is a policy that serials may not circulate, or if the circulation system does not include marking the material at the time of circulation, more subtle indication of usage must be found. Condition of the binding, whether in mint condition or of ex--treme fragility are helpful signs, as is a coating of dust. Deter--mining present or future use can include investigating such factors as language of the publication, indexing, and frequency of citation.

Scope -- Titles that are appropriate to the collection, based on collection development guidelines. The title or the cataloging of various issues or volumes may sometimes be misleading. When there is doubt, it is necessary to examine the contents or refer to the subject specialist.

Gift -- Library fiscal records should be used to determine the source of a title. While gifts can be useful, allowing donors to determine appropriateness is not the best way to build a good collection.

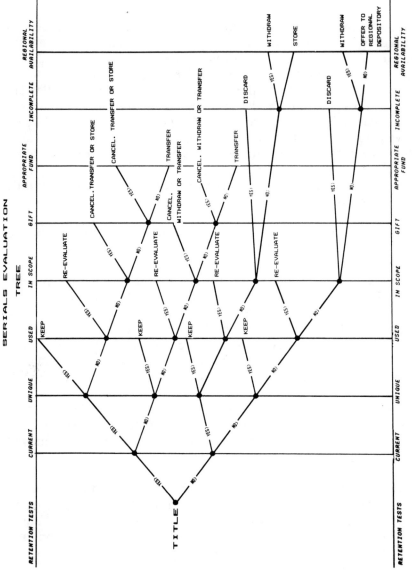

SERIALS EVALUATION TREE

FIGURE 1

64

Appropriate Fund -- Libraries that keep fund records by depart-ments may find this helpful in determining if the serial is reach-ing the proper destination.

Incomplete -- Can be defined as deemed appropriate, based on the size of holdings and completeness of individual volumes.

Regional Availability -- Defined as convenient, based on consortia agreements, shared cataloging, or regional services available.

At the beginning of a serials reduction project it may seem that every title is a unique case. Eventually, however, a pattern similar to the one shown in the serials evaluation tree should emerge. The retention tests need not be exhaustively followed in every case. For example, if a serial is current and unique, it is presumed to be used. Depending on the pressures to complete the project, efforts to verify use can be fairly superficial. On the other hand, ceased duplicate titles can be presumed to be unused. Without substantial evidence to the contrary, lack of use can usually be assumed. The disposition decisions need not be rigidly followed, but common sense dictates following a standard such as that suggested by the illustration. In actual application, every decision to remove a title from the collection should be made by an appropriate subject spe-cialist. The outcome requiring the fewest steps, retaining the title, can be decided without input from the subject specialist.

Current Unique

If a serial title is current, unique, and used, it should be retained without further question. If the title is not used and seems appro--priate to the collection, consultation with a subject specialist is needed. If it is considered inappropriate, it could be the result of a gift. In any case, it can now be cancelled and transferred to a more appropriate library or to storage. In a decentralized library system, if an inappropriate fund is the source of the material, it can be transferred to the funding library. If appropriately funded but not used or not in scope, it most probably can be cancelled and removed from the collection. Although there may be very few cases to cancel and transfer in this category, those few may make significant cost and space savings. Because the titles are unique, it would be unusual to remove them from the system entirely.

Current Duplicate

Current duplicate titles are a slightly more rewarding area for discard. Because the library system already contains the title, the evaluator can feel fewer constraints against a decision to cancel and withdraw. If the title is not used and not in scope, checking the funding information may provide some useful money and space-- saving opportunities.

Ceased Unique

Although a title is no longer current, if it is still used there is reason enough to retain it. If not used and not appropriate to the collection, the size of the run may be a factor in its disposition. If the run is very small, broken, or consists of only one or two issues or volumes it requires special treatment. The presence in a collection of a large number of "unique scraps" is usually the result of a faulty gift acceptance policy. These titles can be collected for examination by a subject specialist.

Identifying and removing a library's scraps will improve the appearance of the shelves, remove deadwood from the public records, and perhaps help to change the gift acceptance policy. The amount of work necessary to withdraw titles, however, may seem disproportionate to the space gained.

Titles which have longer runs but meet no retention criteria can be stored.

Ceased Duplicate

The most rewarding category for a de--acquisition project is the ceased duplicate. Many libraries have titles in this category because of serials cancellations of the past decade. Whether the title was cancelled or ceased on its own, chances are that most titles can be withdrawn. Evidence of use of these materials may be rare.

The Withdrawal Procedure

The decision to keep, withdraw, store, or transfer is part of the larger withdrawal process. (See Serials De--Acquisition Flow Chart, Figure 2 and Serials Review Form, Figure 3.)

Keeping a title requires only one action, recording the decision so the title will not inadvertently be involved in re--evaluation. The project coordinator should keep a copy of the serials shelf list for this purpose, and note the decision made for each title. The record will be useful for monitoring progress, verifying decisions, and compiling statistics at the conclusion of the project.

If the serial records and a brief examination of the materials

SERIALS DE-ACQUISITION
FLOW CHART

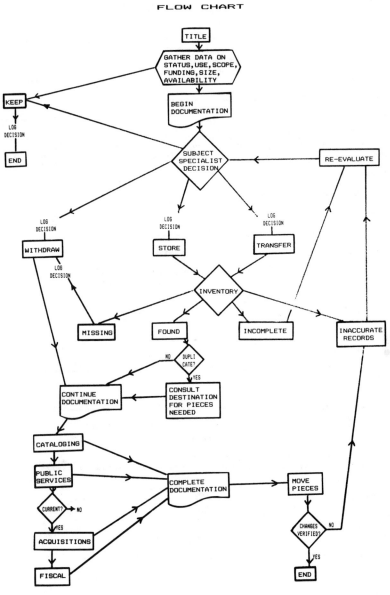

FIGURE 2

ID Number   Date of Request

_____

                          SERIALS REVIEW FORM
                       Purdue University Libraries

Title _____

Call number/set number_____ Present Location _____

Current Fund Name _____ Cost Per Year _____

Reason(s) for Request _____
****
HOLDINGS: Location   Holdings   Subscription/Gift
                                                           Depository/Other
Set to be
withdrawn or
transferred: _____   _____   _____

Other sets: _____   _____   _____

                  _____   _____   _____

****
DISPOSITION: Complete   Partial
                       Holdings?   Holdings?
                       yes/no   (please list volumes)

Withdraw and
send to G & E   _____   _____

Transfer to: _____   _____
_____
Keep in present
Location   _____   _____

Other (please
specify)   _____   _____

****
AUTHORIZATION:

Librarian authorizing withdrawal/transfer_____

Librarian receiving volumes(if a transfer)_____
****
ACTION: Date   Initials

   Cataloging   _____   _____

   Acquisitions   _____   _____

   Fiscal   _____   _____

   Public Services   _____   _____

   Remove Volumes   _____   _____

   Verify   _____   _____

                          FIGURE 3

68

on the shelf show that there is a possibility of discarding the title, documentation (the Serials Review Form) is prepared for the information of the subject specialist.

The forms, prepared in call number oder, are put in batches as shown on the Serials Evaluation Tree, and sent to the appropriate subject specialist. The specialists make decisions based on the documentation, if possible. If not, they may request further clarification or information, or they may inspect the holdings. The forms are then returned to the project coordinator with decisions noted.

If the decision is to withdraw, copies of the Serials Review Form, appropriately marked, are sent to the Public Services, Cata--loging, and (if current) the Acquisitions and Fiscal departments. Each unit changes the records it has on the title. Project personnel move the materials, following the disposition instructions on the form.

Only if the decision is to store or transfer is an inventory taken. Although there was a temptation to inventory the materials earlier in the project, it would have consumed valuable time and not have contributed to the goals of the project. The results of the inventory, however, may change some of the earlier decisions. If a title is missing in inventory it will be withdrawn. If holdings are incom--plete, they are returned to the subject specialist for re--evaluation. If the records are inaccurate and the title has a longer run than indicated, re--evaluation is also necessary.

If titles to be withdrawn are duplicates, consulting with other libraries for pieces needed can be a lengthy step. Eventually, the documentation is completed and sent to Public Services, Cataloging, and, if the titles are current, Acquisitions and Fiscal. Records are changed and pieces are removed from the shelves and shipped to their new destination.

Finally, the project coordinator should verify that the shelves have been cleared and the records changed as stipulated. Not until this final step can the project be considered completed.

Personnel Needed

Personnel are needed to:

1. Coordinate the project. The project coordinator should have an overview of the collection in order to select the most pro--ductive areas for weeding candidates. Familiarity with the subject specialization of the professional librarians, knowledge of systems and procedures in technical services, and supervisory experience are needed.

Duties include setting up procedures, training clerical personnel, initiating and distributing documentation, logging decisions, and monitoring the work flow. The coordinator is also responsible for verifying the accuracy of the results and dealing with problems.

2. Gather information on each title. Requires the ability to interpret serial records and knowledge of collection development guidelines, circulation procedures, and funding sources.

3. Prepare Serials Review form. One form must be prepared for each title to be investigated. For accuracy, these forms should be reviewed by another person.

4. Evaluate material. The subject specialist librarians are given information on currency, uniqueness, use, scope, completeness, source of funds, and regional availability. Their responsibility is to translate this information into disposition decisions to keep, store, transfer, or withdraw.

5. Take inventory. This task requires knowledge of bibliog--raphical eccentricities, language facility, and physical stamina.

6. Change records. Changing records is a nomal routine of the technical services units affected, so it is assumed that it can be worked into regular procedures. However, the quantity of materials to be changed may seriously affect the work flow. If a special goal has been set, it will be helpful in making a realistic assessment of the need for additional personnel or a change in priorities.

In public services, the staff responsible for the current periodical room must pull binding records, change periodical room labels, change or remove stack dummies, and revise visible files and lists. Circulation must check its location file for material in temporary locations or in circulation. Information about unusual locations will be helpful in inventory. Records should also be modified to show the status of the materials if library patrons request them while they are in motion. Reference will need the information to interpret the catalog while the records are in a state of change.

7. Remove volumes. This is a dirty and exacting job. All the volumes must be pulled regardless of where they may be lurking. Supplements, title changes, added copies, and other irregularities must be dealt with appropriately. Once the titles are pulled, sending them to their appropriate destinations cannot be taken for granted, nor can proper handling once received at those destinations be assumed without the enclosure of a packing slip, preferably a copy

of the Serials Review Form, prominently located in the packing box.

8. Dispose of volumes. If materials are not sent to storage or transferred to another library, another unit of the library such as the Gifts and Exhange department or Acquisitions will have the responsibility for the final disposition. Offering the materials for sale, sending to a regional depository, or to USBE requires corres-- pondence, typing of lists, fiscal activity, and packing and shipping.

Conclusion

Reducing the size of the serials collection involves two major processes. The first is evaluating the collection for appropriateness, a responsibility of subject specialists. Gathering sufficient data to assist them in their decisions requires considerable investigation and documentation by project personnel. The second is the actual withdrawal process; disposing of the proper volumes and changing the records as recommended. As can be seen in the Serials De-- Acquisition Flow Chart, this is a multi--step process that offers many opportunities to make errors and lose volumes.

While these processes are going on, there is a constant need to reevaluate each title based on changing information. Errors in records, title changes, sudden patron demand, and inventory dis-- coveries may change decisions at any point. The complexity of serial records and the likelihood that various internal records have been created throughout the system slow the process. Errors are usually difficult to find. A withdrawal project can easily become bogged down by these records and merely become an unsuccessful inventory and record correction project.

Unless patrons consistently have difficulty locating materials, librarians assume that records are correct. This can mean that records for lesser--used materials are the worst in the system -- unused, unrevised, and inaccurate. Working with such records over long periods of time can be dispiriting.

If a withdrawal project is based on the serials records, only cataloged titles can be reviewed. At the end of the project, an examination of the shelves may reveal more titles to be evaluated. The inventory project will have identified cataloging lacking volumes, and, finally, it will identify serials lacking cataloging. A review of the serials collection is not complete without this last step. It is possible that some very interesting titles will be discovered on the shelves at the end, when all the records have been reviewed and materials moved. This may be the result of an earlier project in which the final step of disposition was handled carelessly, or it may reflect several decades of cumulating errors

The task of weeding the serials collection reflects the complexity of serials. The amount of information that must be collected to make an informed decision on each title takes time, effort, and experience. The many areas of the library that deal with serials must be involved and informed of the procedures throughout the project. These tasks will require a substantial committment in personnel.

The work load in technical services will increase by an amount that should be easy to predict, based on the goals of the project. Committments of time by subject specialists throughout the system must be insured by stressing the value of the project to the entire library system. Public Services personnel who are responsible for work during the beginning and ending parts of the project must be in adequate numbers and have sufficient motivation and training.

The work of these groups must be coordinated so that the increase in the work load does not become a bottleneck at any point. Adding extra personnel to manage a large project is useless if they are idle while waiting for another unit to process materials.

There is no simple way to make major changes in a library's serials collection. Weeding serials with their many parts, title changes, and irregularities is difficult. The rewards of accomplishing the task are a better collection, improved bibliographic access to the collection, a staff with pride in its accomplishments, and better service to library users.

REFERENCES

1. Charles P. Bourne and Dorothy Gregor, "Planning Serials Can--cellations and Cooperative Collection Development in the Health Sciences: Methodology and Background Information," *Bulletin of the Medical Library Association* 63 (October 1973): 366--377.

2. Jeffrey Broude, "Journal Deselection in an Academic Environ--ment: a Comparison of Faculty and Librarian Choices," *The Serials Librarian* 3 (Winter 1978): 147--166.

3. John B. Wood and Lynn M. Coppel, "Drowning our Kittens: Deselection of Periodicals in Academic Libraries," *The Serials Librarian* 3 (Spring 1979): 317--331.

4. Donald K. Windsor, "De--acquisitioning Journals using Pro--ductivity/Cost Rankings," *De--Acquisitions Librarian* 1 (Spring 1976): 1, 8--13.

5. Barbara Frick Schloman and Ruth E. Alhl, "Retention Periods for Journals in a Small Academic Library." *Special Libraries,* 70 (September 1979): 377–382.

6. Siegfried, Feller, "Library Serial Cancellectomies at the University of Massachusetts, Amherst," *The Serials Librarian* 1 (Winter 1976--77): 140--152.

7. Herman H. Fussler and Julian L. Simon, *Patterns in the Use of Books in Large Research Libraries* (Chicago, University of Chicago Press) 1969, 93--106.

8. Colin R. Taylor, "A Practical Solution to Weeding University Library Periodicals Collections," *Collection Management* 1 (Fall–Winter 1976--77): 27–45.

9. Gary S. Lawrence, "A Cost Model for Storage and Weeding Programs," *College and Research Libraries* 42 (March 1981): 139--147.

10. Lee Ash, *Yale's Selective Book Retirement Program* (Archon Books, 1973), 10--16.

11. John Urquehart, "Relegation." in *Periodicals Administration in Libraries,* edited by Paul Mayes. (London, Clive Bingley, 1978), 116--125.

Periodicals Inventory as a Library Event

Mitsuko Collver
Head, Serials Department, Main Library
State University of New York at Stony Brook

Accurate cataloging and holdings records are the foundation of good public service in a library. It is hard enough for library users to cope with such problems as the fact that a needed publication was never acquired or that since being acquired it has been stolen[1] or misshelved or pages have been torn out. On top of these obstacles, the patron does not need the frustrations, aggravation, and delays that are caused by incorrect information in the holdings record.

Consider the all--too--familiar story of the hopes and disappointments of a researcher looking for a journal article in the library. He first checks the catalog and finds the title of the periodical, then checks the holdings record to ascertain that the library has the volume in which the article appears. With a sense of satisfaction and pleasant anticipation, he jots down the call number and takes the elevator to the book stacks. When he arrives at the designated shelf, however, the volume is missing. At the circulation counter, a helpful and sympathetic clerk spends some time searching among the ready--to--shelve book trucks at the depot but cannot locate it there either. Since the library does not circulate any periodicals, the volume is now considered to be missing. He is advised to go to the interlibrary loan office to request the article. There he is told that it will take at least a few weeks. If the holdings record had informed him in the first place that the volume was missing, he could have gone directly to the interlibrary loan office, and his frustration would have been much less.

No less frustration will be experienced by the library staff who assist the patron and by the interlibrary loan personnel who search among inaccurate records for the volume in response to requests by other libraries.

There can be two kinds of errors in the catalog. In one type, as in the above case, the volume is missing but the record indicates that the library has it. In the other type, the library actually has a volume, but it does not appear in the catalog. In the latter case, the patron usually will not go to the stacks to look for the volume.

These errors can be substantially reduced by a serials inventory, which is a check of the stock on hand of serials publications, under--taken in order to correct discrepancies between actual holdings and cataloged holdings and other bibliographical information. Only through an inventory can a library be assured that serials that were reportedly received years before are still present in the collection and that all volumes received have been noted in the catalog. By reducing the patrons' frustration experienced in trying to locate volumes in the stacks, a library can improve the quality of its public services. Other benefits that can be gained as byproducts of the serials inventory are, for example, weeding, locating misplaced volumes, and filling gaps in the collection.

Inventories of monographs are equally as desirable as those of serials, but differences in circulation policy, cataloging, and inventory procedures make it advisable to inventory them separately. After a case study in systems analysis of the University of Michigan Library, Beck and McKinnon concluded " . . . the authors now believe that serials will have to handled separately from the rest of the inventory by workers with considerable bibliographic skill."[2]

Experiences of Several Libraries

In the last fifteen years, there have been only a few published articles on inventory taking, perhaps because inventories themselves are rare. In one library, forty years had elapsed since the last inven--tory.[3] In another, it had taken half a century for staff and user complaints about inaccuracies in the public card catalog to accumu--late to the level where an inventory was deemed necessary.[4]

The majority of published reports describe inventories of general collections or monographs only, and only one reported an inventory specifically of serials.[5] While two of the libraries[6] were closed to the public for a few days to take inventory, the rest remained open. In one large library it was estimated that it would take ten years to complete the project.[7] In another instance, an inventory of circulated materials (mainly monographs) was obtained rather easily as a byproduct of computerization of circulation.[8]

The statistical data published as the results of inventories of various libraries are not uniform and are sometimes vague and diffi--cult to compare. For example, some libraries report the number of volumes inventoried per hour, but one reports the cost per volume in manpower at the then--current wage. Since wages are not constant over the years, information of this kind is not easily compared. The number of problems identified is sometimes given in terms of volumes and sometimes in terms of titles.

In any event, the costs reported by other libraries would only be useful as a rough estimate for planning purposes. The efficiency and quality of the inventory performance depend on various factors other than the number of persons involved and the size of the collec-- tion. The thoroughness of planning and the effectiveness of a pro-- ject's organization both can make big differences in the costs. Other factors are the types of employees, their experience and expertise, physical conditions of the work area, and whether the inventory is done with the participation of all staff members in a few days or is a long range project involving only a few people.

The published quantitative information concerns only the physi-- cal inventory of general collections. Costs of post--inventory follow-- ups such as correcting the catalog, updating holdings information, and pulling cards from the files are considered to be almost impos-- sible to estimate. One library reported that an average of forty--two volumes were inventoried per hour,[9] while another reported a rate of sixty--three books per hour.[10] Missing volumes statistics vary over a wide range, from 0.3% and 1.8% in two serials inventories[11] to 6% of circulated materials in a relatively new university library[12] and to as high as 31% in a library that had not had an inventory for fifty years.[13] A great deal of followup work is generated by the inventory, but only one author ventured to estimate its cost. Bluh, in 1969, calculated a figure of sixty cents per error for follow-- up processing, in contrast to the inventory's cost of four cents per volume.[14]

Almost unanimously, the authors recommend partial inventories of selected problems areas in case a full inventory is felt to be in-- feasible. Clark recommends pilot inventories as a guide to the collections most in need of inventory, to be followed as feasible by selective inventories of these problem areas.[15] Various ways to identify the needy areas have been suggested,[16] including a method of predicting from circulation data.[17] One library used a random sampling of 1% of the collection to locate problem areas.[18] Some libraries took volume count inventories to measure losses as a test of the effectiveness of book detection systems.[19]

Is an inventory necessary? Is it worth the trouble? That depends on the library's goals and priorities, the availability of staff time, and money. The inventory is physically exhausting labor. The authors reviewed, nevertheless, all agree that their efforts and time have been well spent.

Making it a Big Event

The term "inventory" carries with it the connotation of a tedi-- ous, time--consuming task, conducive to backache, headache, and eyestrain. This is why it tends to be put off year after year, and this is why no one volunteers to do it. There never seems to be a convenient time or enough resources for an inventory until pro--blems accumulate to the breaking point. Yet, there are many good and sufficient reasons for taking periodic inventories, and some way should be found to mobilize resources to accomplish the task.

The answer, for me at least, is to be found in a simple but effec--tive principle of management: if something must be done and no one wants to do it, then let everyone pitch in together and get it over with. The way to handle an inventory is to close the library for a few days and organize the entire staff to conduct the inventory. The entire project can be done in a few days and everyone comes out of it with a feeling of accomplishment and camaraderie. This paper discusses how to plan and carry out such an event in order to correct and update a library's records of serials holdings.

During a season when the library' services are the least in de--mand, it can close the doors to the public for a few days for the purpose of taking an inventory of serials holdings. Then the entire library staff, administrators, librarians in both public and technical services, clerks and secretaries, whose daily responsibilities differ greatly, can all engage in the same task of serials inventory. The project can be made into something exciting and fun, a memorable event that will boost the morale of the entire library staff. To realize this, there are a few points to remember, including human factors.

At the State University of New York at Stony Brook, the momentum to continue inventory of the Main Library stacks was strong in the summer of 1975, since the library had just completed an inventory of all circulated materials by use of keypunched book cards.[20] Accordingly, it was decided that periodicals, which were not circulated but were always heavily used, should be inventoried. For two days in August of that year, the library was closed to the public and the entire staff participated in the inventory. An announcement of the planned closing was issued to the campus community in advance. The director appointed the head of the Serials Department as the coordinator for the project and requested that all of the staff participate. The inventory was successfully completed in two days. The planning, organization, and actual inventory procedures were carried out so smoothly that we expect to use the same basic organization and procedures in future inven--tories. The following is a description of the inventory with an emphasis on the organizational and human aspects of the project rather than the resultant statistics.

The goals for the two day inventory were (1) to complete an inventory of all identifiable periodical titles in the stacks and refer--

ence room of the Main Library; (2) to update holdings information in the central serials record in the Serials Department and complete refiling of all updated holdings cards in the public serials file; and (3) to submit search requests for all missing volumes to the circula--tion department for further search to be conducted in the future. Cataloging was to be revised in the light of new information produced by the inventory, and all holdings cards were to be stamped with the date of inventory before filing, regardless of whether any changes were made on them. All errors found were to be corrected, and problems found were to be resolved within these two days with the help of all staff members.

An inventory involving a large number of participants requires extensive and careful planning. Poor planning will waste personnel time or participants will find the task too difficult and unpleasant. Three stages are involved: the planning, the actual inventory, and the follow--up stage. Among them, the planning and preparation are the most important, and many of the serials personnel devoted their time to this stage.

Planning

In the planning and preparations stage, our first major task was to create a periodical shelf list. The library had a shelf list for monographs, serials, and other materials, but it was decided that it would be too time consuming to identify periodical shelf list cards among thousands of others and remove them temporarily. As a safety precaution, we did not want to remove the catalog cards from the public serials file or the central serials records in the Serials Department. Since our periodicals reading room had a small file containing only periodical catalog cards without holdings cards, we refiled them by call number order to make a temporary shelf list. We then removed the corresponding holdings cards from the public serials file in the reference room and attached them to these shelf list cards. We duplicated the cards for those titles which were shelved in more than one location, as indicated by such notations as, "Latest edition in reference," and "Some vols. in X (oversize) section."

Test runs made us aware of some of the types of problems that inventory takers would encounter. We identified a variety of these problems and incorporated answers to them in the instruc--tions. One important question settled by the test runs was whether to take the holdings cards to the shelf and compare them with the volumes on the shelf, or to write a complete new list of holdings on blank cards. The test runs proved that reading holdings cards and making corrections on them was much easier and more efficient.

79

The time required to take inventory was calculated according to the test runs, and we estimated the appropriate division of personnel between the physical inventory in the stacks and the card processing section where all the results of the inventory and the follow--up work were to be processed.

A list of names of participants containing their assignments, names of partners, names of captains, and work locations was compiled and issued. Instructions and procedures were written, and all the captains received a briefing and instructions. A package containing a batch of shelf list cards with holdings records, pencils, pads, and envelopes labeled with types of problems into which the inventoried shelf list cards were to be deposited, was prepared to be handed out at the beginning of the two--day project.

A statistical form was designed and given to the floor captains. Before the inventory, the Circulation Department had reshelved all of the books and serials completely. Since no periodicals were circulated, all existing volumes were then supposed to be on their proper shelves.

Organization

The project was divided into two parts: inventory taking in the stacks and reference room, and card processing. For the inventory taking, three levels of personnel were designated: floor captains, section captains, and inventory takers. A floor captain was appointed for each floor of the stacks and the reference room to be responsible for coordination of work on the entire floor, and to communicate between the section captains and the personnel in card processing. A floor captain was to help section captains with their problems, coordinate personnel changes, redistribute workloads among section captains as needed, and keep statistics of the number of titles and volumes by type of problems using the forms provided.

A section captain was assigned to work closely with six to eight inventory takers, assist them with problems, and revise their work. Three section captains reported to a floor captain in the stacks. Those who were most familiar with serials and periodicals were selected to be be the section captains. Their duties included (1) assistance to inventory takers with problems; (2) confirming missing volumes or adding newly discovered volumes to the holdings cards; (3) redistributing the work according to the speed of the different teams; (4) communicating with the floor captain concerning work and personnel problems; (5) coordinating lunch and coffee breaks; (6) spot checking inventory takers' work; (7) giving instructions for spine label changes; and (8) gathering all the finished and unfinished work of their teams at the end of the day.

Two persons took inventory together as a team, one reading the shelf while the other checked the holdings cards and noted differences between the observed volumes and the bibliographic record. Usually a librarian or technical assistant was paired with a clerk. Each team was given seven pages of directions with examples of the different types of problems and instructed to classify the inventoried cards according to the types of problems encountered.

Three members of the book processing section circulated in the stacks with tools and labels to correct the spine labels, and a team from the Circulation Department gathered misshelved volumes and reshelved them.

The spacious current periodicals reading room with its large tables located in the central area of the first floor of the library was chosen for the card processing headquarters. Card processing required forty--one people, all of whom were from the technical services departments. Serials catalogers, who supervised the entire operation, required no special instructions. Card processing opera-- tions were divided and assigned to several stations.

After recording statistics at the end of each hour, floor captains brought the cards with missing information to the missing volumes station, located in the Circulation Department. Here the cards were xeroxed and sent down to the card receiving station in the periodicals reading room. Floor captains deposited all other inven-- tory cards hourly at the card receiving station, where receiving boxes were marked "no problems," "title not found," "location pro-- blems," "cataloging problems," and so forth.

All cataloging problems from the card receiving station were brought to the cataloging station in the reading room for recataloging or for attention to such matters as adding, titles not found, location, or no shelf list.

All precataloging and miscellaneous searching, including reinven-- torying, were done at the searching station in the reading room.

The typing station, located in the Cataloging Department, received typing work requested by cataloging and other stations. Work completed there was passed on to the stamping station in the reading room, where the date of the inventory was stamped on all cards.

After being stamped, cards were sent to the alphabetizing station, also in the reading room, where they were alphabetized by title and sent to the central serials record station in the Serials Depart-- ment. This station updated information according to the results of the inventory, using the completed holdings cards and shelf list cards and also stamped the date of the inventory on the periodicals cards in this file.

Questions regarding Kardex file information was referred to the Kardex station in the Serials Department.

The bindery station in the Serials Department stood ready to bind issues as requested, using an inhouse binding machine, and also answered questions regarding binding and related records.

A public serials file station in the reference room was in charge of refiling cards as the final step of the inventory project.

The Event

A few days before the inventory date, all inventory participants were given written instructions describing their duties. They were also informed of the identity of their assigned teammates and floor captains. The coordinator met with all captains and went over the instructions. Section captains were assigned the responsibility for training their inventory takers during the first hour of the inven--tory.

On the morning of the first day of the inventory, all participants came to the reporting place. There they signed their names upon receipt of a prepared package. Inventory takers met with their section captains for an orientation and instructions, and left to--gether for their assigned stations.

One member of each two--person team read aloud the volumes of periodicals on the shelf while the other carefully checked the holdings cards to see whether they were correct.

The inventoried shelf lists and holdings cards were gathered every hour by the floor captains and brought down to the card receiving station. Personnel at the card processing area tried to solve discrepancies and problems and complete changes and updating including minor cataloging revisions, retyping and refiling of holding cards into the public serials file within the two day inventory period.

Results

The overall organization of workflow and the pattern of the distribution of personnel were efficient and successful. The shelf inventory of periodicals was completed on time in two days, and no unexpected problems were encountered.

The inventory project resulted in a complete check of bibliog--raphic and holdings information on 5,770 identifiable periodical titles in the stacks and reference room of the Main Library, of which about 40% were in some way updated and corrected to give more accurate information. It took the card processing stations an additional day to process over 4,000 titles. About 1700 titles were left with the Serials Department to be taken care of at a later time. A small portion of the titles had to be reinventoried simply because the information received did not make sense.

We began the inventory with shelf list cards representing 5,349 titles, of which 3,033 had no problems. In the course of the inven-- tory, 421 additional titles for which we did not have shelf list cards, were found on the shelves. Of the 2,316 titles that were found to have problems, 388 were missing one or more volumes for a total of 964 volumes, 223 could not be located, 105 had discrepancies in location information, 851 needed a variety of changes on catalog cards, and 749 required adding of volumes. About 200 of the latter had accumulated immediately prior to the inventory when adding was postponed as serials staff worked on preparations for the inventory.

During the inventory, many misshelved items were immediately reshelved in the right locations. Often this reshelving led to the discovery of volumes that had been inventoried as "missing."

One surprising discovery in the course of this project was that 1,369 volumes in the stacks had not been entered on the holdings cards. The only explanation that we can offer for most of these discrepancies is human error and carelessness in the recording of holdings. Also many involved second copies that had been ordered to replace missing volumes. When the lost volumes reappeared at a later time, the replacements became duplicate copies without any notation of this fact on the holdings cards. A similar finding is reported by Cook: "most of the inaccuracies in the records reflected volumes not recorded, but found on the shelf."[21]

While the project demonstrates the effectiveness of the "big event" approach to inventory taking, it also brings out the impor-- tance of attention to human factors. Since the work of inventory is tedious and highly labor intensive, human aspects have to be considered with care in assigning responsibilities.

An average of 114 employees from all departments of the library signed up to participate in each day of the event. The majority of the participants had no prior experience in the handling of periodicals. Some had never been in the stacks. For the two--person team, the partners were selected so that a clerk and a professional or paraprofessional member would be combined, with care being taken to avoid matching individuals who would not be compatible with one another. If someone insisted upon certain duties, as long as the person was qualified for the job, the request was granted. One status--conscious individual told the coordinator that he would participate only if he could be assigned as a floor captain. Actually he turned out to be one of the hardest working participants in the project. Everyone participated willingly and worked very hard. Today, several years later, the inventory project is still remembered as an enjoyable and successful event.

REFERENCES

1. J.W. Griffith, "Library Thefts: A Problem That Won't Go Away," *American Libraries* 9 (April 1978): 224--27.

2. R.E. Beck and J.R. McKinnon, "Development of Methods and Time Standards for Large Scale Library Inventory," in *Case Studies in Systems Analysis in a University Library* ed. Barton R. Burkhalter. (Metuchen, N.J.: Scarecrow, 1968), p. 47--75 (p. 68).

3. Arlene Mangion, "Inventory: Luxury or Necessity?" *Wilson Library Bulletin* 52 (March 1978): 574--75.

4. Jay B. Clark, "An Approach to Collection Inventory," *College & Research Libraries* 35 (Sept. 1974): 350–53.

5. Colleen Cook, "Serials Inventory: A Case Study," *Serials Librarian* 5 (Winter, 1980): 25--30.

6. Hardin E. Smith, "Taking Inventory," *Library Journal* 87 (Sept. 1962): 2847--48; Thomas L. Welch, "An Approach to an Inventory of the Collections," *Library Resources & Technical Services* 21 (Winter 1977): 77--80.

7. Pamela Bluh, "A Study of an Inventory," *Library Resources & Technical Services* 13 (Summer 1969): 367--71.

8. Catherine V. von Schon, "Inventory by Computer," *College & Research Libraries* 38 (March 1977): 147--52.

9. Clark, "An Approach to Collection Inventory."

10. Smith, "Taking Inventory."

11. Bluh, "A Study of an Inventory"; Cook, "Serials Inventory: A Case Study."

12. von Schon, "Inventory by Computer."

13. Clark, "An Approach to Collection Inventory."

14. Bluh, "A Study of an Inventory."

15. Clark, "An Approach to Collection Inventory."

16. Irene A. Braden, "Pilot Inventory of Library Holdings," *ALA Bulletin* 62 (Oct. 1968): 1129--31; David F. Kohl, "High Effi--ciency Inventorying Through Predictive Data," *Journal of Academic Librarianship* 8 (May 1982): 82–84; Clark, "An Approach to Collection Inventory"; Robert N. Sheridan, "Mea--suring Book Disappearance," *Library Journal* 99 (Sept. 1974): 2040--43.

17. Kohl, "High Efficiency Inventorying."

18. Braden, "Pilot Inventory of Library Holdings."

19. Vera Cunliffe, "Inventory of Monographs in a University Li--brary," *Library Resources & Technical Services* 21 (Winter 1977): 72--6; Sheridan, "Measuring Book Disappearance."

20. von Schon, "Inventory by Computer."

21. Cook, "Serials Inventory," p. 29.

University of Washington "Online" Serials Catalog

Linda Woo
WLN Records Management Unit Supervisor
Serials Division
University of Washington Libraries

Introduction

The University of Washington Libraries (WaU) system is com--posed of several collections housed in the Suzzallo Library, the Odegaard Undergraduate Library, the Health Sciences Library, and eighteen branch libraries. The serials collection of the Libraries are centrally cataloged and fully represented in its Main Catalog located in the Suzzallo Library. The Libraries maintains the Central Serials Record (CSR) which is a single main entry internal card cata--log with check--in information of all cataloged serials in the Libraries system. The Libraries also maintains machine readable records for its serials collection stored online in the Washington Library Network (WLN). The database is used to generate a computer output micro--form (COM) catalog on a regular basis.

Records are created and updated daily online by the staff of the Libraries' Serials Division. Institutions participating in the WLN Bibliographic Subsystem have online access to the Libraries' bibliographic and holdings records. The University of Washington Libraries uses the Anglo--American Cataloguing Rules, 2nd Edition (AACR2) and follows Library of Congress (LC) practice. The Libraries is a participant in the CONversion of SERials (CONSER) and the Name Authority Cooperative (NACO) projects and con--forms to project guidelines for creating bibliographic records and establishing headings.

The printed CSR grew out of the List of Current Serials Holdings of the University of Washington published between 1971 and 1972. There were four editions of the CSR published between April 1973 and September 1979. The September 1979 edition was produced simultaneously as the first microfiche edition of CSR.

The tenth edition of the CSR has just been produced. It is a complete cumulation of the WaU's serial holdings current as of August 1983 and supersedes all previous editions. The CSR con--tinues to grow both in terms of unique records as more of the cataloged serials collection is added to the database and in terms of access points for individual records as existing data is upgraded. The following table provides detailed statistics of the tenth edition, including number of unique records, number of index entries or access points generated by these records, number of references, and number of fiche.

TOTAL unique titles		75,660
Access points	Author	63,184
	Title	88,235
	Subject	62,844
	TOTAL	214,263
References	See references	4,589
	See also references	4,332
	Information references	451
	TOTAL	9,372
No. of Fiche	Author index	18
	Title index	21
	Subject index	19
	Register	36
	TOTAL	94

Beginning with the ninth edition, the CSR is being produced in a new physical format in addition to the regular cut microfiche. A master negative for roll microfiche containing the Title, Author, and Subject indexes has been created for each edition from which roll fiche copies may be produced as required for use in the Micro-max Rollfiche Reader. At present this format is in use in the Suz-zallo Library and several branch libraries.

Scope

The Central Serials Record contains bibliographic and holdings records for the following types of publications:

All cataloged journals (periodicals)

All cataloged serials, including annuals, directories, proceedings, and series

All monographic series classed together and all separately classed monographic series for which the Libraries has s standing order

Loose leaf services

Retrospective newspaper holdings in microform and printed newspapers on subscription

Most government documents, the holdings of the Law Library, and all uncataloged materials are not included in this catalog.

Contents of the Catalog

1. Bibliographic records.
Cataloging entries and authority headings in the CSR COM catalog are generated from records in the WLN database: LC MARC records and bibliographic records added locally by WLN participants. The locally input records include LC cataloging not distributed on the MARC tapes by LC but found in the National Union Catalog, and original cataloging using AACR2 and following LC rule interpretations.

2. Authority headings, cross references, and notes.
Authority headings and related cross references and notes are based on AACR2, the current edition of the LC Subject Headings (LCSH) and its supplements, and LC rule interpretations as published in the LC *Cataloging Service Bulletin*. LC MARC and local cataloging records are the source of all headings appearing in the CSR COM catalog. The great number of references and notes found in the CSR is invaluable in providing easy access to serials. Headings in the WLN Authority File are linked to the records in the Bibliographic File which use them. This linkage provides not only expanded searching capabilities, but also supports maintenance of the bibliographic database through "global" changes of cancelled or changed authority headings – all bibliographic records containing an authority heading that has been changed and changed automatically. With AACR2 heading changes and revised LCSH heading changes popping up constantly, the WLN authority control functions constitute an indispensable aspect of quality bibliographic control.

The following types of references and notes are manually keyed into the database by WLN Bibliographic Maintenance staff:

"See" references for use with personal, corporate, and meeting names, with uniform title headings, series headings, and for subject headings

"See also" references for use with geographic and topical sub–

jects, uniform titles headings, and personal names

"Former name/later name see also" references for use with corporate and meeting or conference names

Scope notes providing general information regarding the usage or coverage of subject headings and explaining changes of per-- sonal, corporate, and meeting/conference names

General reference notes for use with topical and geographic subject headings referring to a general type or category of head-- ings rather than specifically listing all cross references

3. Holdings statements.
The holdings statements include abbreviations representing the primary and secondary locations of the serial, the call number for the serial, and a statement of what portion of the title is part of the Libraries collections. All holdings statements are derived from WaU summary holdings information stored in the Standing Order File (STO) of the WLN Acquisitions Subsystem, although WaU does not utilize the WLN Acquisitions Subsystem in any other way.

Organization of the Catalog

The CSR COM catalog is organized into three indexes: Title Index, Author Index, Subject Index, and the Register. The Title Index is an alphabetical list of WaU's serial holdings by title, whether main or added entry, including earlier titles, variant titles, and series titles. The Author Index is an alphabetical list by author of all serials for which there is an author or issuing body, whether main or added entry, including both corporate and personal authors and author/title series. The Subject Index contains entries arranged alphabetically by subject heading for all subject headings assigned to each title. In all Indexes the bibliographic citation appears under every entry for a given title, together with the location, call number, and holdings statements. The Author and Subject Indexes contain references from unused forms of headings. The Register is a sequen- tial listing of the entire bibliographic record as it exists online in the WLN database for each serial cited in the Indexes.

Format of Entries

1. Indexes.
Indexes entries contain the following types of information:

Bibliographic information relating to the publication itself including title, issuing body, volumes, numbers and/or dates of publication, publisher, collation, frequency, and notes concerning numbering peculiarities, variant titles, and other related publications.

Holdings information relating to the specific copy owned by WaU including location symbols, the call number for the serial, and a statement of what portions of the title are part of WaU's collection

Control numbers relating to the specific machine--readable record including the LC card number or the WLN record identification number and the Resiter entry sequence number. The LC card number or the WLN record identification number constitutes the Record IDentifier (RID) and may be used to retrieve records online in the WLN database. The Register sequence number is used to locate bibliographic entries in the Register, which are arranged numerically by sequence number.

SAMPLE ENTRY

```
                              Title

Science news. v. 89, no. 11-   Mar. 12 ◄──── Publication information
   1966- Science Service  Continues:
      Science news letter ISSN 0096-4018 ◄──── Related title note
┌OUGL   Q1.S76  v. 89, no. 11-  Mar.
│    12, 1966-
│NAT-SCI   505SN  v. 89, no. 11-  Mar. ◄──┐ Call numbers and
│    12, 1966- LATEST ISSUES IN: DISPLAY ─┘ holdings statements
└ENGRG   Q1.S76  v. 97-  1970-
                         sc76-000923 ◄──── Record IDentifier (RID)
                         (00023165) ◄──── Register sequence no.
Locations
```

2. Register.

Each Register entry contains all bibliographic data present in the MARC record as it exists in the WLN database at the time the catalog is produced. This includes all information usually found on a printed catalog card. Locations, local call numbers, and hold-ings statements are not included in the Register record. Records in the Register are arranged in numerical order by an arbitrarily assigned sequence number. Access to the bibliographic records contained in the Register is provided through the sequence number which is part of the information provided with each citation in the Title, Author, and Subject Indexes.

Figure A.
SERIAL FLOW CHART

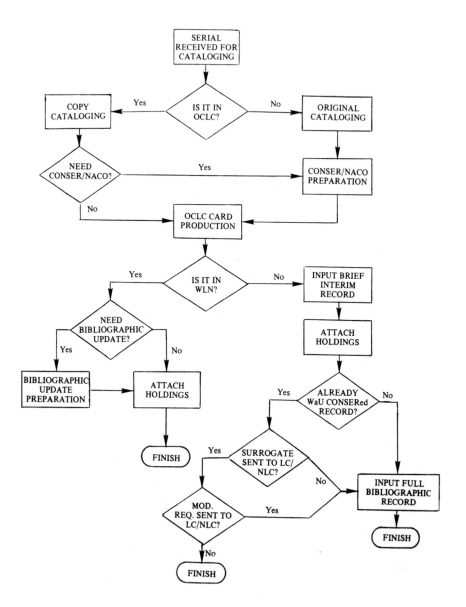

SAMPLE ENTRY

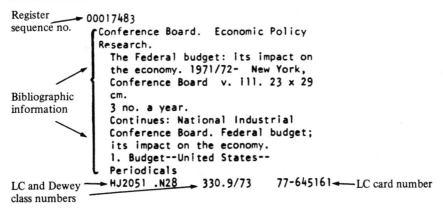

Register sequence no. ——▶ 00017483

Conference Board. Economic Policy Research.
The Federal budget: Its impact on the economy. 1971/72- New York, Conference Board v. ill. 23 x 29 cm.
3 no. a year.
Continues: National Industrial Conference Board. Federal budget; its impact on the economy.
1. Budget--United States--Periodicals

Bibliographic information

LC and Dewey class numbers ——▶ HJ2051 .N28 ——▶ 330.9/73   77-645161 ◀——LC card number

The LC and Dewey classification numbers appearing in the Register record are those assigned by the cataloging agency and are not necessarily those used by the Libraries. Local UW Libraries call numbers must be obtained from the index entry.

Database Maintenance for the Production of CSR

When a serial title is received for cataloging (see Figure A), it is searched on OCLC. If there is no record for it, original cataloging data will be prepared and input into OCLC. All name head-ings used in the record are checked against the LC Name Authority File (NAF) available online on OCLC. If the name is not found in NAF, it will be established according to AACR2 with required cross references and submitted to LC's NACO project. The surrogate and the NACO forms are sent together to LC for authentication. If there is an already authenticated record, it will be used for card production with minimum local modifications for WaU public catalogs.

If the record found is incomplete and not yet CONSERed, modification will be made online and treated as original cataloging. A surrogate will be sent to LC or the National Library of Canada (NLC) as appropriate for authentication; NACO forms, if required, will be sent to LC. If it is necessary to modify or correct a CONSERed record, a Modification Request will be prepared and sent with proper surrogate to LC for authentication.

After OCLC card production, WaU inputs serial bibliographic and holdings data into WLN for the production of CSR. If the title is not found in WLN, a brief interim level record is input into WLN. An interim record is an abbreviated bibliographic record which functions as a place holder in the bibliographic file until a full record is available to replace it. It provides a link among records in various WLN computer system files (see Figure B) in the absence of complete cataloging information. Based on the interim record, a Standing Order File screen can be established for attaching WaU summary holdings. The holdings information can be updated online.

Last year the record input routines were changed to restrict full input for bibliographic records into WLN to those records which had not been CONSERed by WaU, instead relying on full record replace of interim records by tape load of LC authenticated MARC--S records. Records with Modification Requests sent to LC, however, are fully input into WLN because of the long delay involved in LC's authentication. Microforms cataloged also are input fully into WLN because WaU does not send surrogates to LC/NLC for microforms for authentication.

When WaU is ready to enter full cataloging data into WLN, it is done in the appropriate online serials input workscreen. Whenever a full bibliographic record is added to the database, it replaces the interim record that was input earlier. All Acquisitions, Holdings, or Waiting File records which were linked to the interim record are automatically relinked to the full bibliographic record. This link is established by inputting the RID number of the interim record in the REPLACE RID field in the full record input screen.

If the title is found in WLN, the existing bibliographic record is compared with our cataloging. By using the Criteria for Screening Cataloging Copy for Changes to WLN Records (see Figure C), it is determined if the record needs bibliographic updating. If no updating is required, WaU holdings are attached to the bibliographic record. If updating is required, the record is then called into one of the WaU working files of the WLN Bibliographic Subsystem for modification. The WLN Bibliographic Subsystem can support multiple working files for each participant. WaU uses four working files defined for separate input and review purposes. A special symbol is fabricated for each alternate working file, e.g., WaU–2 for the second working file. Upon input of a record into an alternate working file, the alternate WaU symbol will be displayed on the record and will be associated with it for the duration of its existence on the working file. Upon entry of the record to the database, the alternate symbol will be replaced by our master symbol, WaU.

All changes will be done online and the modified record will be then routed online to WLN's Bibliographic Maintenance Section for network level review and verification. While a record is being changed, and before the changed record replaces the original record, no other participant can work on the record. However, the original

WLN FILE STRUCTURE

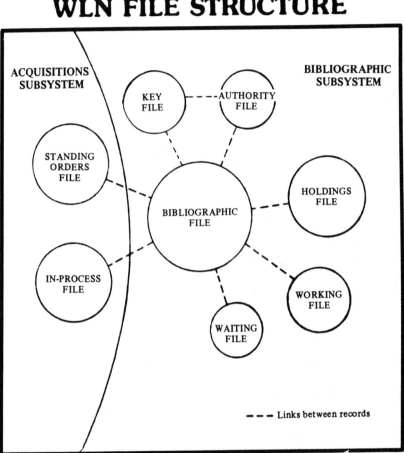

Figure C. CRITERIA FOR SCREENING CATALOGING COPY FOR CHANGES TO WLN RECORDS

FUNCTION	MANDATORY	MANDATORY IF MAKING OTHER CHANGES TO RECORD	NOT MADE
Changes within field	Form of access points: AE]Authority File change SET SA TIL PRE LAT Errors in significant subfields of above fields	DAT IMP NO FFD: PUB STAT, BEG DT END DT, SL ENTRY CAS COL Typographical errors	SU only ↑w in any field ISBD punctuation COL only
Addition of fields	AE SET SA VAT FOR PRE LAT	DAT SSN LCN SCN MOF NOY LON SU	SU only ↑w in any field NO only COL
Changes of field (tagging changes)	Choice of entry if: OCLC 590 = analyzed; OCLC 78X present Tagging errors for access points or linking entry fields		

All records identified during holdings input/adjustment as having the potential to generate changes to WLN bibliographic records will be screened by the WLN Database Supervisor using the above criteria and any special instructions added to the cataloging copy by the cataloger. Changes/additions/corrections are NOT made to acceptable records which will subsequently be loaded into WLN as part of the MARC-S Subscription Service.

MOST COMMONLY USED NUMERIC/MNEMONIC TAGS

010	LCN	310	FRQ
022	SSN	362	DAT
040	CAS	4xx	SEx
050	CAL	5xx	NOx
090	SCN	6xx	SUx
1xx	MEx	700	AEP
222	KEY	710	AEC
245	TIL	711	AEM
246	VAT	730	AEU
247	FOR	780	PRE
260	IMP	785	LAT
300	COL	8xx	SAx

version of the bibliographic record is available for inquiry during the change process. The working version of the record is also available to any participant who wishes to find out what is being changed and by whom.

Because of the increase in the number of records CONSERed by WaU, the decision of restricting input of full bibliographic records to those records which had not been CONSERed resulted in providing the staff time needed for inputting those authorities prepared for the NACO project directly into the WLN Authority File. Staff time spent updating authorities and adding cross references improves the reference structure of the CSR as all cross references are included in the indexes. Now that all NACO forms have a pre-assigned number which will be used for identification in the NAF, this feature can also be retained with the WLN authority heading in a note field.

Conclusion

The introduction of the CSR, is a campus union list of serials, resulted in a new way of retrieving bibliographic information for serials at the WaU Libraries. It has given librarians an opportunity to examine the ways in which patrons use catalogs and to provide a better tool to meet the patrons' needs. The CSR COM catalog has more than adequately fulfilled the need for complete, accurate, and accessible serial bibliographic information. The constant increase in the quality and quantity of data contained in this catalog and the online database from which it is generated is decreasing our dependence on incomplete and labor-intensive manual card catalogs.

Copies of the CSR are available in all WaU libraries. Copies may also be purchased from the WaU Library Publications Officer. This wide distribution of the CSR on and off campus assures maximum access. Besides being the most complete record of cataloged serials information the Libraries has, the CSR provides other benefits as well. The information can be used to create various lists of subsets of the database on demand for special projects and programs. It has now been possible to eliminate several partial card files in both the Serials Division and other branch units and the associated staff time required for their maintenance. This catalog has, in part, been responsible for Serials Division's ability to respond successively to an increased demand for service with a decreased staff. Because of the wide distribution, interlibrary loan requests for WaU serials are coming to the Libraries accompanied by complete citations found in the CSR, including call numbers and locations. This saves considerable turn-around time in handling these requests.

There is still no clear answer to whether, or if, an online catalog is the solution for every library. As with other areas of the computer industry, library automation is growing at an accelerating pace. It will not take long to develop mature online catalogs or integrated systems. The CSR are being issued two or three times every year. With multiple access to records and holdings in the CSR and the WLN database, the serials records at the WaU Libraries have become a *de facto* online serials catalog. Improving the quality and expand- ing the scope of the WLN serials database will increase the effective- ness of the CSR, will decrease dependence on manual files, and will contribute to the upgrading of the machine--readable file of serials records to the point where it can replace the Card CSR as the official repository of authoritative bibliographic and holdings records for the WaU Libraries' serial collections. Eventually, the serials card production activities could be discontinued and full reliance on the CSR be achieved. The saving would enable the Libraries to purchase and install more terminals to assist patrons. The usefulness of the CSR would be facilitated immensely by in- creased online access by patrons to the WLN or an in--house database where bibliographic data and holdings information are updated constantly.

"Serials as a Project" at Vanderbilt,
an Early Library Computer Utilization

Jean Acker Wright
Vanderbilt University Library

Introduction

Contributing one chapter to a volume on serials is a bit like attending a pot–luck dinner and finding that everyone has included tomatoes in their appetizers, salads, and other dishes. Since bib-- liographic control, inventory management, access to information for resource sharing, and financial accountability form part of the menu related to the role and treatment of serials in libraries, some redundancy is to be expected. My particular subject has applications to many of the topics mentioned, and is an example of the ways in which all aspects of serials are inter–related.

In any library, there are special problems and local situations which have required unique solutions. The number of branch loca-- tions, the age of the collection, its size, and the places and form in which information on library holdings is available all have an effect on the quality of service which we are able to provide and the manner in which we do it. Anyone who handles serials realizes that each title presents its own potential for presenting a "challenge" and adding a dimension to collections management problems. Since serials are "dynamic" both in nature and extent of holdings, dis-- tributed access to information about them is difficult to maintain in manual files which must be updated and kept consistent. Organi-- zational structure may vary among institutions, but there is a pattern to many of our operations, based on logical approaches to meet similar needs.

Many libraries have developed machine--readable data bases covering part or all of their collections, and it is possible that more of these relate to serials than to other special categories. The history and uses of the Vanderbilt University Library serials data base may closely parallel situations with which the reader has had experi-- ence. As an example of this type of tool and its uses, the following case history is offered.

Background

In the preface to the first edition of *Scientific Serial Publications in the Joint University Libraries,* the background of the Vanderbilt serials data base is described by Eleanor F. Morrissey, originator of our "Serials Project." "The Joint University Libraries were established in 1936 to meet the needs of George Peabody College, Scarritt College and Vanderbilt University. A pioneering venture in inter--institutional cooperation in higher education, the JUL system has grown to include more than a million volumes in eleven book collections. . . . For a number of years there has been a need for a central listing of serial holdings of the entire JUL system. Such a list could be produced by manual methods, but keeping it up to date would be most difficult. The advent of the computer and its use in libraries has changed the situation, and with this preliminary edition a first step is taken toward the goal of one consolidated list, capable of frequent revisions."[1] It is important to observe that the preliminary edition is dated January 1968, before most librarians were aware of the impact that technology would have on their operations. Assisted by Medical Library Re--source Grants made to the School of Medicine, Vanderbilt Univer--sity, the list included "holdings of the Medical Library, Science Library (including collections in chemistry, geology, and physics), Biology Library, General Science (including mathematics) and engi--neering titles now located in the General Library."[2] Exceptions to the coverage were carefully explained, and plans for the future were stated. "Regular supplement to the JUL serials list are planned. At first these will consist of corrections to the present list and the addition of science titles not now included. After the scientific collections have been covered, other subjects will be added as quickly as possible until the goal is reached of one consolidated list of holdings of the entire system."[3]

Record Structure Development

When one considers that the MARC Pilot Project was completed in June 1968, and that this edition of our list was dated January of the same year, it is apparent that the elusive "full MARC tagging" was not an option in the development of the formats. In fact, the preliminary edition of *Serials: a MARC Format* was issued as a working document in August 1969. Tracing the history of the "Serials Project" presents an interesting case history of the evolution of computer utilization in libraries.

The 1968 version of the local list included 5,286 bibliographic records and additional entries for cross references. A manually assigned identification number provided for the alphabetical arrangement of the printed list. The first lists and supplements were hard copy, but we converted to microfiche with the December 1978 list. The growth of the coverage is reflected by the September 1983 set of microfiche, which contains 32,192 records, 27,558 of which are bibliographic.

The record structure has gone through several stages of development since its inception. Originally the information was blocked, with terminators added after the bibliographic portion and before the notes. The holding library and call number were separated by operator input devices. Refinement of the records has been an ongoing process, and enhancements are being made to the format and the programs at the present time. Currently defined fields contain information closely parelleling the fixed fields of the MARC serials format, and numeric codes are assigned to authors, titles, imprints (locally defined as a combination of the existing MARC 260 and 362 fields), and notes. The tags are not subfielded. Cross references are distinguished from bibliographic records by using an assigned code in a portion of the fixed fields. Obviously, many other parts of the fixed fields are not applicable to cross references, but both types of records are in one file at this time. Information related to the individual copies of the title, giving the library, receipt status, discipline, classification, and summary level holdings statement, is in a separate portion of the record. More than one copyrelated record may be attached to any bibliographic record. With the advent of the ISSN, space was provided, and they were added to titles in the data base as a special project. When the library began cataloging serials on OCLC, the format was upgraded to include the OCLC control number to which the "TJC" symbol has been attached through cataloging or retrospective conversion.

The transfer of data from computer to computer has been a serial of the "Soap Opera" variety. There have been two transfers. The Vanderbilt University Computing Center housed the file on the campus mainframe until the University's Sigma was replaced in 1980. At that time, the decision was made to transfer the Library's computing to the administrative computer system. "Siggy" was kept in operation, with the Library's serials file as the only "tenant" while the necessary programming for the "dump" could be completed. Tension was high until the conversion was successfully done, which served for the implementation of AACR2 which was occurring simultaneously. There *are* silver linings to every cloud. Because of time constraints, some of the features which we would like to have had were postponed, but we were grateful that Administrative Systems performed our miracle before "all was lost."

Another factor which has affected the "Serials Project" is the merging of George Peabody College for Teachers and Vanderbilt University. This has required the redefinition of the scope of coverage. Library reorganization, including the combination of some collections and the additions of new ones, has been reflected over the years. In the 1968 listing there were six collections represented; in the current version there are twenty–four. Only two of the original six remain in the current organizational structure in the same form. Obviously, this has required handling many records in all catalogs as well as in the data base. Part of these changes are the result of adding coverage of components not listed originally, as was the stated plan; others are caused by the establishment of new units. Even now, our on–campus data base does not include all Vanderbilt serials holdings.

Products and Benefits of Local System

As the record structure has been developed, the data base provides a number of products and reports. In addition to the micro–fiche listing which is updated regularly and still serves as the largest system–wide catalog for serials, we can produce lists or counts of portions of the collection. Subsets which can be extracted are: current purchases, current gifts, particular collections, titles by discipline, publications from a given country or in a particular language, and titles by type (such as periodicals, newspapers, or monographic series). It is possible to combine more than one of these subsets. As acquisition and cataloging for some of the libraries were centralized, "target lists" from the serials data base provided the basis for planning and preparation for required reclassification and merging of files. These special reports are used extensively in collections development and evaluation. As more subject codes are added, additional use for preparation of bibliographies for public service is anticipated. The average user of the microfiche is not aware of the data which is included in the file since only a portion of the information, which is really the "tip of the iceberg," is used in the display format. An example of one frame is shown at the end of the chapter.

Access

Careful consideration has been given to the practicality of continuing the building of a local machine readable file, since online cataloging and retrospective conversion of information on the library's holdings on OCLC has been implemented.

For the present, it has been determined that the local data

base has capabilities which are not available elsewhere and which we are not willing to lose. Conversion of currently received titles on OCLC has been emphasized for resource sharing and serials control, but it will be many years before the coverage is comprehen--sive. Even now, not all parts of the library have their processing done by General Technical Services, and not all of the cataloging is done on the OCLC system. When all General Technical Services locations have had total serials holdings converted, we will still require the reporting features which currently exist only through our local system. In addition to the originally planned addition of portions of the collection to the coverage, all current cataloging by General Technical Services or the Medical Library are reported to the "Project." Any title which changes acquisitions status, is recataloged, or reclassified is reported, as well. Since 1968, re--classification from Dewey to the Library of Congress scheme has been underway, and as this reclassification is based on receipt status and use, the coverage in our data base is quite comprehensive. Records are deleted when titles are withdrawn, and modified so that when transfers are made the holdings information and location are kept current. For several locations, the microfiche serves as the only catalog at the periodicals location, since the public service areas are removed from the card catalogs. In fact, at the Education and Medical Libraries periodicals have not appeared in the card catalogs at all.

Maintenance of Data Base

The effort involved in changing records to be compatible with cataloging entries, and in the assigning of the alpha--sequence num-bers became aggravated with the adoption of AACR2 and the post--poned changes to many authority forms which were postponed when the Anglo--American rules were put into effect. It became evident that the deletion and re--entering of records to relocate records in the file could no longer be supported. The entire file was machine sorted, for the first time, in an experimental version, during the summer of 1983. A standard character by character sort of the first 150 characters of each of the first two tags, either Author/Title or Title/Imprint, with programming to read all groups of spaces as single spaces, was so successful that we have been able to discontinue the manual alphabetizing. It was particularly inter--esting to note that the Title/Imprint sort gave a logical result when combined with the constructed "unique" or "uniform" titles which had been entered in the file under AACR2, when there were multiple entries with the identical title. We asked the public service staff to look at the trial version, but not to put it out for public use, since punctuation was considered in the sorting and there was quite a variation from the assigned alphabetical arrangement of the same records. With the ASCII sort, numerals, which had been alphabetized as if spelled out in the language of the title, came to the front of the file. By error, one set was put in public use, and no comments were made, nor was there any difficulty in inter--preting it. Perhaps "computer literacy" is with us now! Some edit--ing was done before the next version, such as regularizing or elimi--nating some punctuation and standardizing abbreviations, but the quality of input over the years was remarkable. Consistency had been sought and attained even through many changes in personnel and format. This is a tribute to Mrs. Morrissey's meticulous editing and to the diligence of the staff who contributed to the work.

It is difficult for those of us who work with serials to believe, but some records have remained "undisturbed" since 1968, because there has been no change required for the title since it was entered. These have the entire "tag detail" as a "245." Any record which is handled for any reason is edited to bring it to the current standard.

The activity which takes place in maintaining the data base reflects the functions performed by technical processing staffs in handling serial publications, especially in a centralized unit which supports multiple public service locations. In the period from January 1981 through January 1982, nearly 7,500 of the records were altered in some manner. This total does not include records which were deleted, or which had only an OCLC number or ISSN added. The percentage of the 32,000 records which had changed made during this period is impressive, but it even more noteworthy that, after planning for the machine sorting capability was under--taken, again 7,500 of the total records had changes made between February and September of 1983. Changes which involved only alteration of punctuation to accommodate the machine sorting are not included in this total.

Originals of reports which had been input were held for a two year period, 1981--1983, and typical types of transaction were assigned values. Categories which were identified were:

A. New titles (added to the data base for the first time)

B. New successive titles (title changes which continue a title already in the file)

C. New successive titles, retrospective (titles which result from recataloging of an existing title and breaking it into successive entry, often replacing a previous cross reference)

D. Changing a holdings reference to a cross reference

E. Upgrade of format, caused by changes in our own internal record structure

F. Cease and close without successive entry

G. Cease and close, with an associated continuing entry

H. Recataloging (routine)

I. Recataloging caused by an authority change, not changing alphabetical sequence in the listing

J. Recataloging caused by an authority change, and requiring that the record be moved (This category includes such entries as the famous "University of . . . " and supported the need for the machine sorting enhancement. Just as in shifting cards in a catalog, moving records in a machine readable file by delet--ing and re--entering is time consuming and creates space pro--blems)

K. AACR2 recataloging (note that the authority changes are sepa--rate, because so many are not the result of AACR2, but of the abandoning of "super--imposition" and reflect earlier changes which had been delayed)

L. Recataloging to successive entry (We used this for the record which *was* in the file, and used "C" for the new portions)

M. Assigning ISSN (dropped because no records were available)

N. Adding OCLC number (same as M, there were not sufficient records)

O. Change in library or location within library

P. Change in classification (used only when this was the sole change)

Q. Holdings change (although the file does not have detailed hold--ings statements, major changes such as completing a file are made)

R. Change fund to which title is charged

S. Change receipt status

T. Change made only to reflect arrangement in the fiche listing (not all of these were recorded)

X. Cross reference

The intention was to study a brief period of activity, but as the potential benefits of capturing this type of information were con--sidered, it was decided to add the codes as a matter of routine. Some of the categories will be changed after studying the results of the test period. The new options being considered are related to acquisitions, cataloging, and data base management, and include some of the test options, while combining or eliminating others. Entering these values into the machine readable file will make it possible to monitor types of changes and identify the various pro--cesses required in serials maintenance. By including them in current input, we will be gathering research data as well as replacing some of manually gathered statistical reporting.

Future Uses

Currently, programming is being done to link the "serials pro--ject" with our institution's acquisitions data base. In the restruc--tured records, the activity codes will be contained in the area related to a specific copy of a title so that changes which affect the records in the acquisitions data base can be triggered for title changes and changes in receipt status. Since the acquisitions data base includes ordering, receiving, tracing, claiming, in--process control, and fund accounting, the records can originate in either system, avoiding duplication in storage and maintenance of records for the same title. Bibliographic information will be stored and maintained only once, and will serve both systems.

In many ways, the local serials system serves as an index to the OCLC serials data base and vice versa. One of our uses of the OCLC serials Local Data Record is as an online authority file for monographic series. Each of our monographic series standing orders has a record in the OCLC Serials Control System. The form for series tagging in cataloging is entered on the record with notes on continuing or earlier forms used in our OCLC cataloging. The established forms are identified by whether they are AACR2 and if there has been more than one form used. At the time we process our tapes for an institutional catalog, we can produce a list of mono--graphic series with OCLC control numbers from our serials data base and regularize the series entries to one standard form. Con-

ID=13310500   OCLC=02431086   (ISSN 0026-2617)
MICROBIOLOGY.
WASHINGTON, AMERICAN INSTITUTE OF BIOLOGICAL SCIENCES.
U.24, 1955-
ENGLISH TRANSLATION OF MIKROBIOLOGIIA AND ASSUMES ITS
VOLUME NUMBERING.
QR1.M653   #SCIP V.26-

ID=13310800   OCLC=
MICROBIOLOGY AND IMMUNOLOGY.
TOKYO, JAPANESE SOCIETY FOR BACTERIOLOGY, SOCIETY OF
JAPANESE VIROLOGISTS, JAPANESE SOCIETY FOR IMMUNOLOGY.
V.21, 1977-
CONTINUES JAPANESE JOURNAL OF MICROBIOLOGY.

ID=13312000   OCLC=
MICROCOSM. ANN ARBOR. V.1, 1955-
778.315 M626   CENP V.1-14

ID=13312300   OCLC=
MICROENTOMOLOGY. STANFORD UNIVERSITY, NATURAL HISTORY
MUSEUM. V.1, 1936-
SCI V.1-21(22-25)

ID=13312450   OCLC=00526991   (ISSN 0733-1355)
MICROFICHE COLLEGE CATALOG COLLECTION.
SAN DIEGO, CA.
CONTINUES: COLLEGE CATALOG COLLECTION.
MIFICHE 16   REDL CURRENT EDITION

- CONTINUED

ID=13312600   OCLC=
MICROFILM ABSTRACTS.
SEE   DISSERTATION ABSTRACTS INTERNATIONAL.

ID=13312900   OCLC=01998426   (ISSN 0362-0999)
MICROFORM MARKET PLACE.
WESTON, CONN. 1974/75-
COVER TITLE MMP. MICROFORM MARKET PLACE.
Z265.M5 M53   #CENP 1974/75-

ID=13313200   OCLC=01757389   (ISSN 0002-6530)
MICROFORM REVIEW.
WESTON, CONN. V.1, 1972-
Z265.M565   #CENP V.2-
                #LS V.1-

ID=13313350   OCLC=
MICRON.
NASHVILLE, TENN. VANDERBILT UNIVERSITY SCHOOL OF
NURSING. V.1, 1927?-1?/?
MED V.(1-3)

ID=13313650   OCLC=01645558   (ISSN 0026-2803)
MICROPALEONTOLOGY.
N.Y., AMERICAN MUSEUM OF NATURAL HISTORY.
V.1, JA 1955-
SUPERSEDES: MICROPALEONTOLOGIST.
QE701.M527   #SCIP V.1-

ID=13313800   OCLC=
MICROSCOPIC JOURNAL AND STRUCTURAL RECORD.
LONDON. V.1-2, 1841-42//
MED V.1-2

ID=13314100   OCLC=   (ISSN 0044-3760)
MICROSCOPICA ACTA.
STUTTGART. V.71, 1971-
CONTINUES ZEITSCHRIFT FUER WISSENSCHAFTLICHE MIKROSKOPIE
UND MIKROSKOPISCHE TECHNIK.
QH201.Z4   SCIP V.71-79

1426

ID=13314400   OCLC=
MICROSCOPICAL BULLETIN AND SCIENCE NEWS.
PHILADELPHIA. V.1-19, 1883-1902//
578 M72   SCI V.1-18

ID=13314700   OCLC=
MICROSCOPICAL SOCIETY OF LONDON.
SEE   ROYAL MICROSCOPICAL SOCIETY, LONDON.

ID=13315000   OCLC=
MICROSTRUCTURAL SCIENCE.
SEE   INTERNATIONAL METALLOGRAPHIC SOCIETY.
MICROSTRUCTURAL SCIENCE.

ID=13315300   OCLC=03817957   (ISSN 0026-2854)
MICROTECNIC.
ZURICH. 1947-
VOLUMES FOR 1947-1973 NUMBERED V.1-28. ABSORBED
MICRO-NEWS, 1975.
QC81.M55   SCIP 1948-72

ID=13315600   OCLC=   (ISSN 0026-2862)
MICROVASCULAR RESEARCH.
N.Y. V.1, 1968-
#MED V.1-

ID=13315800   OCLC=01757398   (ISSN 0026-2927)
MID-AMERICA.
CHICAGO, LOYOLA UNIVERSITY. V.1, 1918-
TITLE VARIES JL 1918-AP 1929 ILLINOIS CATHOLIC
HISTORICAL REVIEW.
BX1415.13 M5   #CENP V.1-

ID=13315850   OCLC=05235296
MID-AMERICA FOLKLORE.
STATE UNIVERSITY, ARK., OZARK STATES FOLKLORE SOCIETY.
V.7, SPRING 1979-
CONTINUES MID-SOUTH FOLKLORE.
GR108.M53   #CENP V.7-

ID=13316065   OCLC=4456407
MID-ATLANTIC RADICAL HISTORIANS' NEWSLETTER.
N.Y. V.1,NO.1-6, 1973//
CONTINUED BY MID-ATLANTIC RADICAL HISTORIANS'

1427

ORGANIZATION. NEWSLETTER. FILMED WITH LATER TITLE.
FILM LACKS V.1,NO.2.
MIFILM 2105   CEN V.1

ID=13316075   OCLC=5306579
MID-ATLANTIC RADICAL HISTORIANS' ORGANIZATION.
MARHO NEWSLETTER.
N.Y. NO.2-, 1974//
CONTINUES MID-ATLANTIC RADICAL HISTORIANS' ORGANIZA-
TION. NEWSLETTER. CONTINUED BY RADICAL HISTORY REVIEW.
FILMED WITH LATER TITLE.
MIFILM 2105   CEN V.2

ID=13316085   OCLC=4456338
MID-ATLANTIC RADICAL HISTORIANS' ORGANIZATION.
NEWSLETTER.
N.Y. V.1,NO.1, 1974//
CONTINUES MID-ATLANTIC RADICAL HISTORIANS' NEWSLETTER.
CONTINUED BY MID-ATLANTIC RADICAL HISTORIANS' ORGANI-
ZATION. MARHO NEWSLETTER. FILMED WITH LATER TITLE.
MIFILM 2105   CEN V.2

- CONTINUED

ID=13316050   OCLC=04077838   (ISSN 0190-7380)
MIDAMERICAN OUTLOOK.
CLEVELAND, CLEVETRUST CORPORATION. SPRING 1978-
SUPERSEDES CLEVETRUST CORPORATION. BUSINESS BULLETIN.
HC101.C533   #CENP 1978-

ID=13316200   OCLC=   (ISSN 0544-0335)
MIDCONTINENT AMERICAN STUDIES JOURNAL.
LAWRENCE, KAN. U.3-11, 1962-70//
CONTINUES CENTRAL MISSISSIPPI VALLEY AMERICAN STUDIES
ASSOCIATION. JOURNAL. ISSUED BY THE MIDCONTINENT
AMERICAN STUDIES ASSOCIATION. CONTINUED BY AMERICAN
STUDIES.
J169.1.M44   CENP V.3-11

ID=13316250   OCLC=02138049   (ISSN 0146-1109)
MIDCONTINENTAL JOURNAL OF ARCHAEOLOGY. M.C.J.A.
KENT, OHIO. V.1, 1976-
E77.8.M43   #CENP V.4-

ID=13316500   OCLC=   (ISSN 0146-5244)
MIDDLE AMERICAN RESEARCH IN THE HISTORY OF ART

sidering the period of time, since 1975, over which we have cata--
loged and done retrospective conversion on OCLC, we expect that
this will prove to be quite helpful. This is merely an example of
the use to which we put our records, in addition to those which
are obvious when looking at the microfiche as a public service
tool.

It is evident that maintenance of our "serials project" is not
an inexpensive operation, but the purposes which it serves make
it worthwhile. Eventually, as integrated systems are developed
within the library, the linked acquisitions/serials/in--process files
will become part of the overall structure. Meanwhile, we appreciate
the vision with which this early automation effort was undertaken
and the support which has been given to it over the years since its
origin. It will remain as a milestone in our advance to the manage--
ment techniques which are made possible by technological develop--
ments.

NOTES

1. Morrisey, Eleanor F., comp., *Scientific Serial Publications in the Joint University Libraries,* Prelim. ed., Nashville, Tenn., January 1968, i.

2. Morrisey, i.

3. Morrisey, i.

Copy Cataloging of Serials

Nancy Romero
Original Cataloging Librarian
University of Illinois--Urbana Library

Background

In Fall, 1979 several units within Technical Services of the University of Illinois at Urbana–Champaign Library underwent a massive reorganization. A result of this reorganization was the dis-- mantling of the Serials Department and the reassigning of all serial functions to units newly formed by the reorganization. For the serial cataloging function this meant reassigning copy cataloging of serials to the OCLC Cataloguing Unit of Automated Records, and combining the original cataloging of serials and monographs to form Original Cataloguing. Each cataloging operation works totally independent of the other. Procedures, work flow, and policies are established separately to suit the individual requirements of each unit.

Pre--Cataloging Routines

The beginning of the cataloging process for both copy cataloging and original cataloging of serial publications begins in Acquisitions where pre--cataloging records are established and filed. Each title sent for cataloging is accompanied by a routing slip, noting location information and any necessary acquisitions data. The pieces are then forwarded to the Searching Unit in Automated Records for searching in the OCLC data base. All titles are searched for matching copy. If matching copy is found, a printout is produced to accom-- pany the pieces. It is also at this point that all personal, corporate body, and geographic names are searched in the OCLC Name Authority File for verification of form, and printouts are made of each entry found. These printouts also accompany the pieces, together with a record of headings searched and not found.

After the searching process, all titles are returned to Acquisitions, where the pre--cataloging records are noted as to whether a title is to be forwarded to the OCLC Cataloguing Unit or to Original

Cataloguing. The purpose for noting the acquisition records is so that the check--in clerks will know where to forward subsequent pieces should the next issue be received before the title is cataloged.

Original Cataloging Routines

Titles without serial copy are forwarded to Original Cataloguing's Bibliographic Verification Section for further authority work. Per-- sonal, corporate body, and geographic name headings, previously searched in the OCLC Name Authority File, are then searched in the in--house Authority File. This file consists of 3 x 5 cards on which headings are established by the *Anglo--American Catalogu-- ing Rules,* 2nd edition (AACR2), either from an OCLC Name Authority File record or independently by cataloging personnel. The file also contains cross references and series authority records. If the heading is located in the in--house Authority File, the card on which the heading is established is Xeroxed and the copy in-- cluded with the pieces for the cataloger's use. Headings searched, but not found, are coded in a prescribed pattern alerting cataloging personnel that the heading must be established. It is at this point in the process that inconsistencies between headings established in the in--house Authority File and in the OCLC Name Authority File are brought to the attention of cataloging personnel.

After the verification process in Original Cataloguing is complete, the titles are distributed to the serial catalogers. For the original cataloging of serials for input into OCLC, complete adherence to all requirements of the *Anglo--American Cataloguing Rules,* 2nd edition, the OCLC *Serials Format,* and the Library of Congress Rule Interpretations are followed. A Level 1 description (enhanced according to LC guidelines) is prepared. In Original Cataloguing, copy for serial titles is prepared by one of two methods. For foreign language titles and titles requiring complex bibliographic descriptions and relationships, complete copy, the class number, and authority work are supplied by a cataloger. For titles in English requiring simple bibliographic descriptions and relationships, the description, added entries, fixed field tagging, and authority work are provided by a Graduate Library Science Assistant trained and supervised by a cataloger. A cataloger reviews the assistant's copy and adds subject headings and the class number.

With the cataloging complete, the pieces, with the accompanying cataloging copy, are forwarded to a finisher who completes the process by assigning the cutter number to the classification, checking it in the online circulation system (LCS), filing the temporary shelflist card, marking pieces, completing holdings cards for depart-- mental locations, and supplying Xerox copies of the complete

110

cataloging copy for Acquisitions and the departmental locations to use as processing records. With the completion of this last stage the pieces are forwarded to the locations and the cataloging copy forwarded to Automated Records for inputting into OCLC.

Copy Cataloging Routines

The processing of serials with copy through the OCLC Cataloguing Unit is very similar to that done in Original Cataloguing even though an OCLC record is already available. Titles with copy come directly from Acquisitions to a paraprofessional who is responsible for editing all serial copy, under the general supervision of a librarian with serial cataloging experience. The first step in OCLC cataloging process is to closely compare the accompanying OCLC record with the pieces in hand to see that the copy is correct for the title. If it is determined that the copy is not correct for the pieces in hand, the title is referred back to Acquisitions for the records to be changed and then forwarded to Original Cataloguing.

All variable fields are reviewed for any needed editing. Main entry (1xx), subject heading (6xx), and added entry (7xx) fields receive close attention to insure that the form of heading conforms to the *Anglo--American Cataloguing Rules,* 2nd edition. Some editing of fixed fields is done, particularly in the frequency, regularity, dates, language, description, serial type, and successive entry fields.

In the main entry field (1xx), attention is not only paid to form of entry but also to choice of main entry. If under *AACR2* main entry would be under title, the 1xx field is converted into a 7xx field. If necessary, either a statement of responsibility is added to the title field or an issuing body is added to justify the added entry. It is at this point in the process that consideration of main entry under uniform title takes place. On the decision of the individual editing the record, the guidelines for establishing a serial uniform title are applied. If a uniform field (130) already exists in the OCLC record, it is retained.

Minor changes are made in the title field(s) (245, 246). Lengthy other title information is deleted from the title field (245) and changed to a general note. If a statement of responsibility is needed, it is added to the 245 field. For a record which also includes an alternative title field (246) to bring out another title carried on the piece, both the title in the 245 field and the title in the 246 field are compared with the piece to determine whether the title used as main entry is the correct one. Occasionally, due to the rules for determining the chief source of information for a serial and the date of the record, the individual editing the record finds it

111

necessary to switch the title used in the 246 field with that used in the 245 field. On those occasions where the title on the piece in hand varies only minutely from the title used in the 245 field, the title in the 245 field will remain unchanged, and a title varies slightly note will be added to account for the variation.

Of all fields in a record, the imprint (260) and physical descrip-- tion (300) fields receive the least editing. Information in these fields is checked against the pieces in hand and very rarely require any editing. Other 3xx fields such as frequency (310, 321) are added if needed and if the data is readily available from the piece. The numbering and date field (362), if present in the record, is retained even if the pieces in hand are later ones. On occasion, numbering and date are supplied if the individual editing the record has the first piece in hand the record is lacking a 362 field. Number-- ing and date information is always supplied if the record being edited is for a title which continues or is continued by another.

Series statement fields are looked at to determine whether those tagged as traced in a different form (490 1) should be converted to 440 fields instead. At this time the series added entry fields (8xx) are reviewed to determine if they should be converted to 830 fields, or deleted altogether, especially if the 490 field is changed to a 440 field. Those series added entries remaining as 830 fields are also checked for *AACR2* form of entry.

In the note fields (5xx), most are left unchanged. Occasional local notes are added when necessary. The linking entry complexity note field (580) receives close scrutiny. Whenever possible, the 580 notes are deleted in favor of using the print constant in the 78x fields. Only complex merger data is described in the 580 field. Another note field receiving a close look is the issuing body field (550). Issuing body fields are changed to reflect changes in issuing body when main entry is under title without a uniform title. Issuing body notes are also added when the choice of main entry is changed from author/title to title by the individual editing the record, and a note is needed to justify the resulting added entry. Should any data supplied in an issuing body field not apply to the piece in hand, the field is deleted completely and a new issuing body note constructed to match the piece in hand.

Subject heading fields (6xx) are always updated to reflect *AACR2* forms, particularly if the heading contains personal, cor-- porate body, or geographic names. However, topical headings are not reviewed for changes in pattern. Subject headings are always added if issues in hand reflect a change in scope from the issues used by the cataloging agency to produce the record, or if the record being used was input without subject headings.

Those fields which receive as much attention as the main entry and title fields are the added entry fields (7xx). All 700, 710, and 711 fields are reviewed thoroughly for possible change to *AACR2* form. The linking entry fields (760–787) are reviewed for general accuracy of information. None of the linking entry fields are deleted even though the information may not apply directly to the library's holdings.

Information in the preceding and succeeding entry fields (780, 785) is reviewed for matching with any linking entry complexity notes (580) that might be present in the record. Whenever possible, 780 and 785 fields are used in preference to the 580/78x combination. The construction of the entry in both the 780 and 785 fields follows the guidelines cited in the OCLC *Serials Format* document.

After all editing to the record is complete, a class number is assigned by the individual editing the record. The pieces and edited copy are forwarded to a processor. The processor assigns a cutter number, checks the call number on the online circulation system (LCS), types a temporary shelflist record, marks the pieces, stamps them with the library ownership stamp, and sends them on to their location. Multiple copies of the temporary shelflist record are made before the slip is filed in the shelflist catalog. One copy accompanies the pieces to the location. The second copy is forwarded to Acquisitions where the information is used to complete the serial order record. A third copy is retained in the OCLC Cataloguing Unit for statistical counting purposes. The fourth copy is filed in the Central Serial Record (a card file available to the public) to serve as a temporary record until a permanent card is filed.

Even though the rapid cataloging of serials and the original cataloging of serials are completely separated both philosophically and administratively, there is still a certain amount of interaction and cooperation which takes place. This cooperation is very evident in the treatment of related serial titles. A serial title which precedes or succeeds another serial title follows the same route as all other serial titles. Those titles with copy are forwarded to the OCLC Cataloguing Unit, while those without copy are forwarded to Original Cataloguing. However, certain adjustments in the routine are made to inform the other unit of the existence of the related serial title. In the case of a preceding title going to the OCLC Cataloguing Unit, Acquisitions notifies the unit that the succeeding title, for which no copy was found, has been routed to Original Cataloguing. Original Cataloguing in turn receives with the pieces for the succeeding title the printout of the OCLC catalog record for the preceding title with a note that the preceding title is in the OCLC Cataloguing Unit. In order to keep the class numbers for both titles the same, the OCLC Cataloguing Unit informs Original Cataloguing of the call number once the preceding title is cataloged. Any changes in the format of the 780 or 785 fields are also noted so that each related record cites the other accurately. The process is reversed when the preceding title is forwarded to Original Cataloguing and the succeeding title to OCLC Cataloguing. Similar serial titles, such as independently issued serial supplements to other serials, are processed in the same manner.

Each month, a meeting is held to discuss general serial cataloging policies and procedures, Library of Congress Rule Interpretations relating to serials, and any changes to the OCLC *Serials Format*. Those attending are serial catalogers from Original Cataloguing, serial cataloging staff from the OCLC Cataloguing Unit, and a repre--sentative from Acquisitions. It is at this meeting that common problems are discussed and solutions determined, proposed changes in general policy are presented, and decisions determined. By in--volving those individuals associated with serials from acquisitions to cataloging in these meetings it is possible to keep everyone at every step aware of the full process.

A major goal in establishing any type of organizational structure like this one and the supporting procedures is to make maximum use of OCLC and of support staff, in order to catalog serials as quickly and as inexpensively as possible, without compromising the integrity and usefulness of the catalog.

Retrospective Conversion of Serials Using OCLC

Patrick F. Callahan
Catalog Supervisor of the Serials
Retrospective Conversion Project
Center for Research Libraries

Retrospective conversion is the process of transforming manual bibliographic records into machine–readable form. By definition, it deals primarily with existing catalog records as opposed to cata-- loging directly from the material. Considerable attention has been paid to the retrospective conversion of monographic records, and there now exist many excellent vendor--supplied conversion packages for this purpose, such as REMARC. Unfortunately, this is not the case with serials, whose complexity discourages the creation of simplified systems for conversion. Therefore, many libraries are forced to develop in--house projects to deal with the conversion of serials.

The following is an attempt to outline possible procedures for an in--house project and to present some of the considerations and pitfalls of which one should be aware before starting a serials conversion. The procedures are primarily based on the experiences of the Center for Research Libraries' serials retrospective conversion project, begun in Oct, 1982, and many of the statistics are also culled from that source. There is no discussion of the desirability of retrospective conversion. It has become a fact of life for librarians whether it is motivated by the impending installation of an online catalog or by resource sharing efforts. The challenge is to accomplish it in a time of financial austerity combined with the upheaval caused by the adoption of AACR 2.

The procedures were designed for use with the OCLC system and while there is some degree of universality, there are also some aspects which are solely applicable to that utility. It is more likely to be of interest to academic libraries than public. Several other dis-- claimers are worth noting. The Center for Research Libraries is unique in many ways. Some of its practices and certainly its collec-- tion are atypical. The Center collects seldom used research materials and as a result a much higher percentage of its serials collection is in foreign languages than the average library's. This should be kept in mind when making statistical comparisons. In addition, CRL does not employ subject headings or assign classification numbers to its serials, so these topics will not be discussed. However, this fact should not radically alter applicability of the approach presented here.

There are four major phases in a retrospective conversion project:

1. Planning

2. Training

3. Implementation

4. Evaluation

Of these, the first two are extremely important. There is a great temptation to start converting records as soon as the project is approved and funded. Without adequate planning and training of staff, however, it is virtually impossible to finish the project on time, within budget, and to have a satisfactory product.

Planning

The first step in the planning process is to specify the goals of the conversion project. The value of this step should not be underestimated since it is against these goals that all future decisions will be weighed. The factors in goal formulation vary from institu‑‑tion to institution because local circumstances are unique. The important thing is to clearly define them before procedures are developed.

There are certain generalized goals which are, in effect, the verbalization of those factors which motivated the conversion in the first place. For example, at CRL a primary goal of the conver‑‑sion project is increasing the accessibility of serial holdings to the membership. It is best to make these goals measurable, if possible, so that they can be translated into quantifiable objectives.

Quantifiable objectives, ultimately, boil down to converting a certain number of records, within a specific time period, with a limited amount of money. It will be a rare situation that is without time or monetary constraints, especially since many of these projects are funded through outside sources (grants) or one‑‑time appropria‑‑tions. Therefore, a vital part of the planning process is estimating how many bibliographic records need to be converted, how many man‑‑hours per record are required, and what the average cost is per title converted.

Estimating the total number of serials can be done several dif‑‑

ferent ways. The figures may already be available, or the serial record can be used as the source for the estimate. Merely count the number of cards to an inch and measure the contents of each drawer. If the serial record is not comprehensive, then a random statistical sampling of the card catalog or shelflist will have to be substituted.

There are four components of the time estimate: identification, searching the data base, cataloging (used here to mean editing the OCLC record or transferring bibliographic information from a cata‑log card to a MARC format worksheet, and inputting. Identification time can vary widely, from being insignificant to taking substantial time, depending upon the method chosen to identify serials to be converted.

A reasonable estimate for searching time is four to five minutes per serial. This includes searching the L.C. Name Authroity File when necessary. It also assumes an adequately trained searcher and an above average degree of difficulty for the serials being searched.

A trained inputter, with typing skills of 40‑‑60 words per minute, should be able to input six to seven records per hour. This assumes a mix of original inputs and edits with a substantial amount of edit‑‑ing. In the structure of the CRL project, clerical staff performed the identification, searching, and inputting of the titles. Including identification time, the average amount of clerical time required per serial was 20‑‑30 minutes. It should be kept in mind that the shorter the duration of the project, the more likely it is that the time will be towards the upper end of the range. This is for the simple reason that the staff will likely be less experienced in using OCLC and with the procedures of the retrospective conversion pro‑‑ject. These estimates may seem high and in fact certain libraries with different circumstances may have to scale down the figures, but it should be remembered that the estimate is based on actual experience and includes time devoted to a variety of miscellaneous duties as well as taking staff leave into account.

Cataloging time averaged 30‑‑40 minutes per title during the CRL project. This figure includes time devoted to error reporting, checking reference sources, and recataloging. Obviously, the esti‑‑mate is relative since the quality of existing cataloging varies widely from library to library thus varying the need for recataloging and verification of data. Elimination of error reporting, or at least severely limiting it, can substantially reduce the average time. Once again, the longer the duration of the project the more likely that the estimate will drop near the bottom of the range.

The preceding time ranges can be used for calculating the total number of clerical and cataloger hours needed to convert a particular number of serials. Staff salaries and fringe benfits make up the largest line in the budget so the number of personnel required is a crucial decision.

Decisions related to staffing levels naturally depend upon the general procedures and structure of the project. Many retrocon projects rely heavily on clerical and student help. This is practical and cost efficient especially when it is primarily monographs that are being converted. It may not be as prudent with serials. CRL decided to have professional catalogers work on each title. The main reason for this decision was the relative complexity of serials cataloging. The variety of problems that arise is mind boggling, and it was thought that clerical staff might not be able to cope with them. CRL's decision was influenced by the nature of its collection which is heavily foreign language and contains many obscure serials.

Many libraries accept uncritically OCLC records input from certain sources, most commonly the Library of Congress and CONSER participants. This allows clerical staff to process these titles without professional intervention. CRL chose not to accept any records without professional review for the reasons mentioned above and for the simple reason that it would not provide any great savings. This is because the number of high quality OCLC records for serials encountered during retrospective conversion is extremely low.

Table 1 gives a breakdown, by type of inputting library, of a sampling of OCLC records encountered by CRL during its conver-- sion. In addition to the source of cataloging, the table gives the percentage of records from each source which have been authenti- cated by the Library of Congress. Records input or authenticated by LC are generally assumed to be of higher quality than the average OCLC record. Thus, they are used here to gauge the overall quality of the data base as it relates to retrospective conversion.

The percentage of records input by the Library of Congress (DLC/DLC) is very small, only 6.6%. This is not particularly sur-- prising given the nature of the MARC data base, but the number of records input via tape load is somewhat shocking. Tape loading here refers not to current OCLC policies involving the loading of libraries' tapes created on other utilities, but rather to the loading of tapes from sources such as the Minnesota Union List of Serials (MULS), Pittsburgh Union List, and others, which was done in the mid--1970's. These can be distinguished by their use of encoding level "L". The tapes were clearly incompatible with MARC format, and the records produced from them are both incomplete and inaccurate. The records need major editing and usually require error reports just to make them findable. Thus, discovering that

38% of the hits from the system come from this source is quite disturbing. Fortunately, about 75% of the tape loads have been upgraded to some extent either by CONSER or through OCLC change requests. However, the extent of upgrading varies widely and only 21.9% of the upgraded records are authenticated by L.C. This still leaves almost 10% of the total number of hits as unmodified level L records, which are the lowest quality records in the data base.

TABLE 1   Source of Cataloging for Retrospective Serial Titles

	DLC/DLC	DLC (copy)	Member	Tape load	Tape load (upgraded)
Percentage of OCLC serials Records from each source	6.6	13.8	41.6	9.9	28.0
Percentage from each source authenticated by LC	---	17	13	0	21.9

Overall, only 14.9% of the non–DLC/DLC records were authenticated by L.C. Inclusion of the DLC/DLC records produces a figure of 20.5%. This means that using Library of Congress authentication or input as the standard for acceptance would eliminate only one fifth of the total from a cataloger's scrutiny. This also assumes that LC authentication implies an acceptable record, which is not always the case.

The average cost of converting a serial bibliographic record is determined mainly by the costs of personnel, equipment, and OCLC activities (i.e. FTU's, processing archival tapes). The personnel costs vary according to staffing requirements and the salary structure at individual institutions. Major equipment needs include OCLC terminals and printers. Some libraries will be able to use previously acquired equipment, wereas others will have to purchase. Assuming approximately ten hours of terminal time a day, one terminal will be needed for approximately every 6,000 serials processed per year.

OCLC activity costs are directly related to a library's hit rate in searching the data base. It is difficult to find published studies of hit rates for serials alone. Studies on whole collections for retro-spective conversion indicate a 90% hit rate.[1] CRL found 80%

1Carolyn A. Johnson, "Retrospective Conversion of Three Library Collections", *Information Technology and Libraries* 1 (June 1982): 137.

of its current serials and 65% of ceased titles in the OCLC data base. However CRL's collection contains a higher percentage of foreign language serials than most libraries, and it is well known that a smaller proportion of foreign language materials are in the data base than English language titles. Thus the average library may well expect a hit rate closer to the 90% rate. Naturally, current cataloging provides some indication of expected hit rates, but retro--spective rates will generally be lower than the current rate. It should be noted that the flurry of retrospective conversion activity over the past few years has significantly increased the likelihood of finding a record for a particular serial. At least 8% of the records encountered in the CRL project were known to be input through retrospective conversion. Undoubtedly the figure would be much higher if it were possible to identify all retrocon records. It indicates that with eash passing year, the gap between retrospective and cur--rent hit rates is likely to narrow.

The hit rate is used to estimate the number of first time uses (FTU's) which will be required for the project. One could multiply that figure by OCLC's retrospective conversion charge, currently $.90 per FTU, and get a reasonable cost estimate. It is worth con--sidering that substantial savings can be realized by utilizing non--prime time (prior to 9 a.m. EST and after 5 p.m. EST, plus rates, soon to be $.25 per FTU. Using non--prime time allows a library to take maximum advantage of its existing OCLC terminals as well as saving money on FTU's. Unfortunately, not all libraries are able to make full use of non--prime time because of difficulty in getting staff to work at night or maintaining supervisory coverage for the extended hours.

It is also necessary to count on there being a certain number of title for which cards will have to be produced. Since the retro--spective conversion discount only applies to updates, these will be billed at the regular price for FTU's. The number of titles which fall into this category depends almost entirely upon the quality--related decisions that are made.

Adding up all the individual costs to arrive at a per title figure is a complicated process. It is influenced by the size and duration of the project. CRL's per title costs approached $20 per title over the first eight months. The extension of the project over another year reduces the figure to $11 per title. The high initial figure is due to fixed start--up costs, such as purchasing equipment, plus the lower productivity rate that is likely during the training period.

There are several issues that must be addressed during the plan--ning phase because of the great influence they have on the duration, cost, and procedures of the conversion. The first concerns applying the provisions of AACR 2. Obviously most of the records to be converted, as well as the majority of OCLC records, are in pre--AACR 2 form. OCLC allows the input of pre--AACR 2 records under retrospective conversion authorization. It is therefore up to the individual library to decide if all or part of its conversion will be governed by AACR 2.

From a strictly qualitative viewpoint, doing everything in AACR 2 form has internal benefits as well as fulfilling the responsibilities inherent in a cooperative venture such as OCLC. Pragmatically, it is considerably less desirable. AACR 2's emphasis on cataloging from the first issue is precisely the opposite of latest issue policies of the past. In order to create an accurate AACR 2 record it is necessary to look at the issues, which is tantamont to recataloging. There will also be a substantial number of serials whose choice of main entry will change under AACR 2. This poses the choice of having the archival tapes vary widely from the card catalog or producing great numbers of cards, which is not really the purpose of retrospective conversion and is considerably more expensive.

A reasonable solution may be to enter all original records using AACR 2 but this too may be a great burden if the percentage of original inputs is high. This was the case at CRL, and it was decided that time and monetary constraints did not allow consulting the issues for every original record. Each serial was input according to the rules under which it was originally cataloged. Exceptions were made if the cataloger had to examine the issues for some other reason. In those instances the cataloging was upgraded to AACR 2. There is no single answer to this problem. It depends upon the relative weight given to factors such as time, money, quality, and numerous local considerations. It should be noted, however, that all headings on original input must be in AACR 2 form. This is an OCLC requirement, and it alone will cause a sufficient amount of difficulty.

The same sort of conflict, qualitative responsibility to fellow OCLC participants versus the need to economize, arises in the second area of concern -- error reporting to OCLC. Meticulous error reporting can sharply increase both the cost and length of a conversion project and thus must be evaluated carefully. CRL adopted a policy of reporting only those errors affecting retrieval or those that would cause substantial confusion to a patron. This limited approach still produced error reports for 6.8% of the current serial titles. This figure could easily double for older serials. Remember that nearly 10% of these earlier titles are unmodified tape loads, the vast majority of which would require error reports. Since CRL is a relatively new OCLC member (Oct. 1981), a much higher percentage of its current serials needed conversion than would be the case for a longer term OCLC participant. Such libraries would likely be converting older serials having mostly lower quality OCLC records. Thus the amount of error reporting is potentially high.

A 1979 study estimated the cost of this activity at $1.10 per error report.[2] This figure would undoubtedly be much higher if all the labor costs could be accurately isolated. In most cases, proof must be assembled to document the report. This means re-trieving the issues for photocopying or doing the same from ref--erence sources. It can be a time consuming chore, and the total cost can run into thousands of dollars.

Of course, it is a great service to other OCLC members to correct mistakes in the data base, and in a certain number of cases an error report will be virtually mandatory. It seems of dubious value to bother editing a record and adding one's holding symbol if errors in the record make it almost impossible to locate in the data base. At the same time, excessive error reporting can jeopardize timely completion of the conversion. Clear cut guidelines should be estab--lished as to what particular elements in a record necessitate comple-tion of a change request form. This should serve to standardize the practice and reduce the possibility of having excessive costs generated by this activity.

A final planning consideration worth mentioning concerns the impact of the conversion on other departments in the library. Circu-lation and reference will be affected by the changes in the card catalog. Serials sections will have to deal with the title changes and ceased titles discovered during the project. Of course, cataloging will be greatly disrupted even if the conversion is done by all new staff. It is best to make these other departments aware of what is going to happen and solicit their advice as to how ill effects can be minimized. This will not make them happy, but it should make them less angry.

Training

The level of training of the staff handling the conversion obvi-ously bears heavily on the quality of the final product. It would seem that having adequately trained personnel would be something of a given, but a conversion project of any magnitude usually entails hiring new staff, on a temporary basis. There is also time pressure, which means that the temporary staff must be able to function competently more quickly than the average new employee. This

----

[2] Judith J. Johnson and Clair S. Josel, "Quality Control and the OCLC Data Base: A Report on Error Reporting," *Library Resources & Technical Services* 25 (January/March 1981): 45.

consideration has great influence on the establishment of procedures, as will be seen later, as well as upon the training techniques to be employed.

If experienced staff is handling the bulk of the conversion, training becomes less critical. It involves familiarization with conversion procedures and breaking out of some of the habits of everyday cataloging. Even if the conversion staff is composed mostly of new people, it is helpful to get the permanent staff thoroughly involved. They have the experience and the knowledge of both the catalog and the collection. The most complex problems will most likely be referred to them in any case and they can also fill in gaps in particular areas of expertise such as language specializations. Naturally, there is a competing desire to minimize disruption of daily cataloging operations. To some extent upheaval is unavoidable, but it may be possible to minimize it by having permanent staff work on the conversion on an overtime basis.

The problem of training new staff is considerably more difficult. The problems start during the hiring stage. Since retrospective conversion is necessarily a temporary proposition (it only seems never ending) it is difficult to attract experienced catalogers and clerks. The most likely candidate is someone recently graduated from library school and with limited experience in serials cataloging. This fact makes formulation of simple procedures and comprehensive documentation important elements in the success of the project. This topic is discussed in the next section concerning implementation.

Assuming that catalogers will handle the actual editing, the most difficult area of clerical training is searching the OCLC data base. It is insufficient to merely give them the OCLC searching manual, *Searching the On-Line Union Catalog,* and tell them to start searching. That manual is not designed as a training document, but as more of a reference source where answers to specific problems can be found. It seems more effective to use some form of programmed instruction as an introduction to OCLC. There are several good choices, *Monographic Searching on the OCLC Terminal* by Jinnie Davis and Josefa B. Abrera, *Self-instructional Introduction to the OCLC models 100 and 105 terminal* by Bonnie Juergens, and *Self-instructional introduction to searching the OCLC On-Line Union Catalog* by Michele Duffy (the latter two are part of the AMIGOS training series). While they do not specifically deal with serials, they provide a hands--on introduction to using the terminal and the search keys. The one problem with programmed instruction books is that they become dated rather quickly since the data base expands so rapidly. They do, however, deal with a person's hesitancy or aversion to using the terminals.

Once searchers are familiar with the basics, they can start actual searching but their progress must be monitored carefully. It is worthwhile to have them keep a record of search keys they have attempted either by printing out the results or writing down the search keys and attaching them to the card or photocopy being used, i.e. = medi,off,o ame,jo,of,m. This allows the supervisor or trainer to see where the searcher is having problems and what areas they should emphasize in the training. It is usually easier to make this determination on items that are not found because a searcher may find the correct record without following the most efficient route. This is an ongoing process which should be maintained to some degree throughout the conversion. There is always room for more sophistication in searching techniques and as the project progresses, searchers may be able to absorb more subtle points.

It is useful to try anticipating common problem areas. For example, inexperienced searchers often fail to anticipate possible variations in a title that can affect searching, such as hyphenated words or use of the ampersand instead of "and." A few written examples of what to be on the lookout for can save considerable time.

It takes a relatively short time to become a proficient inputter once a person is comfortable using the terminal. Of course, edited records should be put in the save file and checked carefully prior to updating, at least during the training period. Beyond that time, it is up to the individual project manager as to how much checking of input there should be.

One final suggestion is that it might be desirable to have the clerical staff hired prior to the catalogers. This allows those doing the training to concentrate on the clerical procedures and not be swamped by having a large group of new people to cope with simultaneously. Also, if the catalogers are dependent upon the searchers to supply material to be edited, it is a good idea to have a certain amount of searched titles stockpiled so the catalogers have something with which to work.

The fastest way to train new catalogers is to have clearly written procedures for them to follow. This is discussed in more detail in the next section. All work should be reviewed prior to inputting and the cataloger should receive constant feedback. The trainees can then learn from their mistakes.

Implementation

This stage is the actual conversion of the records. It consists of four general phases:

1. Identification of titles to be converted

2. Searching OCLC

3. Cataloging (editing OCLC records or transferring information from cards to OCLC workforms)

4. Inputting

Fig 1 diagrams one possible configuration for the work flow. It is the one used in the Center for Research Libraries project and will serve here as the basis for discussion. Naturally, there are equally plausible variations. The method selected depends upon the decisions made in the planning stage.

Identification

Identification is the process of selecting the local bibliographic records that are to be converted to machine readable form. The first step is deciding which manual file to use for this purpose. Most libraries prefer to use their shelflist since it does not interfere with patron use of the public catalog. CRL used a microfiche copy of its card catalog, filmed during a previous grant project, as the basis for its conversion. This also had the advantage of not involving the main card catalog but had the disadvantage of not being completely up to date. Since the catalog was filmed in Aug. 1982 and the actual conversion didn't get under way until Feb. 1983, there was an intervening six month period during which changes were made to the main catalog. This proved to be a minor inconvenience but it could be significant if the time differential is greater.

There also can be problems with using the shelflist, the major one being that some shelflists lack complete bibliographic description of the items. This is tolerable provided there is enough information to identify the item and that the hit rate is fairly high, 90% range. The hit rate is significant because it is undesirable to create original records based on substantially incomplete information. Therefore, it could be necessary to photocopy the card(s) from the public catalog prior to completing an original workform. If the hit rate is low, this may become a burden or it might be simpler to just use the public catalog as the basis for the conversion.

Regardless of the file being used, a clerk must be able to distinguish the serials from the other entries in the catalog. There may be a simple distinguishing characteristic such as each serial card having "For Holdings See Serial Record" or "Periodicals" stamped on it. CRL used its holdings statement, a "Center has" note (fig. 2),

125

Figure 1
IMPLEMENTATION FLOWCHART

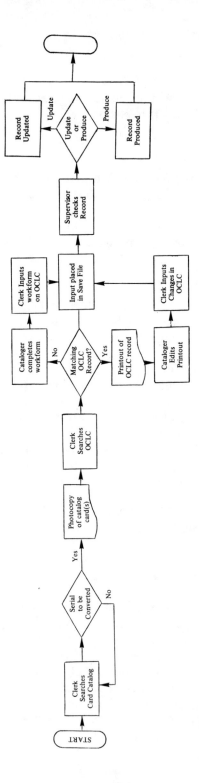

Figure 2
In-House Card — AACR 1

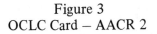

Title ------- Journal of neurosurgical sciences. v.17 ──┐ Numerical and
              1973 ──────────────────────────── } Chronological
Imprint --------- Turin, Edizioni Minerva medica. ──────────┘ Designation
Collation -------------- v. ill. quarterly. ---------------------Frequency

           Continues: Minerva neurochirurgica.
           Supplement to Minerva chirurgica.
Notes   "The official journal of the Italian Society
          of Neurosurgery."
     Center has note Center has:
                 v.17-   1973

                              Hyphen or plus sign indicating
                              current subscription

Imprint = Place of Publication + Publisher + Publication dates (AACR 2)

Figure 3
OCLC Card — AACR 2

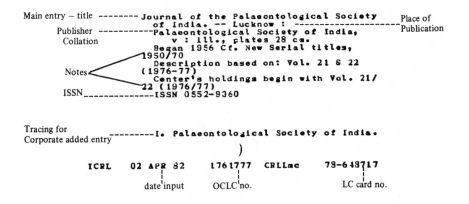

Main entry — title -------- Journal of the Palaeontological Society   Place of
                    of India. -- Lucknow : --------------------- Publication
      Publisher ----------- Palaeontological Society of India,
      Collation   v : ill., plates 28 cm.
                Began 1956 Cf. New Serial titles,
         1950/70
               Description based on: Vol. 21 & 22
      Notes   (1976-77)
               Center's holdings begin with Vol. 21/
         22 (1976/77)
      ISSN _____ISSN 0552-9360

Tracing for
Corporate added entry ---------I. Palaeontological Society of India.

ICRL   02 APR 82   1761777   CRLLmc   78-643717
           date input   OCLC no.   LC card no.

for identification purposes. Clerks were told to print out, from the microfiche, any bibliographic record containing a "Center has" note.

If the file lacks a reliable identifier, clerks will have to be instructed in separating serials from monographs, etc. One way is to think of those features which only apply to serials. These include frequency, ISSN, numeric and chronological designations, "Began" notes, "Ceased" notes, "Description based on" notes, and a "v." in the collation. Some of these elements are not foolproof indicators, i.e., multivolume monographs also have a "v." in the collation, but the selection of some nonserial items is probably inevitable in any event. Mistakes can be caught at a later stage. It is best to provide concrete examples of what to look for, such as copies of serial cards with the significant elements indicated (fig. 3).

Searching

After being identified as representing a serial within the scope of the project, the card or photocopy is then searched in the OCLC data base. At the end of the searching process, the material will go to a cataloger, and there is a certain amount of information that the cataloger will need to know. A cataloger either must know that there is a matching record in the data base or know with certainty that there is no record in the system. If there is a record, the cataloger will need a printout of it. It will also be helpful if the LC Name Authority File has been searched for relevant corporate bodies or personal names. It will be necessary for the searcher to make quite a number of judgments in providing this information. To facilitate this process the searching procedures should be as systematic as possible. The searcher should be guided stepbystep by a searching manual. This helps the training process as well as standardizing the output which the catalogers receive. The manual developed at CRL is really a fleshed out, written version of the flowchart in fig. 4 combined with examples illustrating each step. Fig. 5 is a sample page from the manual.

The searcher is conducting a process of elimination. First, all OCLC records that cannot possibly be matches are eliminated. Then each possible match is evaluated in terms of certain key elements. The universal ones are listed in Decision Table 1. Does your library's holding symbol already appear on the record? Does a "Do Not Use" note appear in the 043 field? Is the record latest entry cataloging (S/L ent code = 1)? Is the reproduction code in the fixed field (Repr) different from the format of the item in your collection? If the answer is yes to any of these questions, then the record cannot be edited and must be eliminated from

128

Figure 4
SEARCHING FLOWCHART

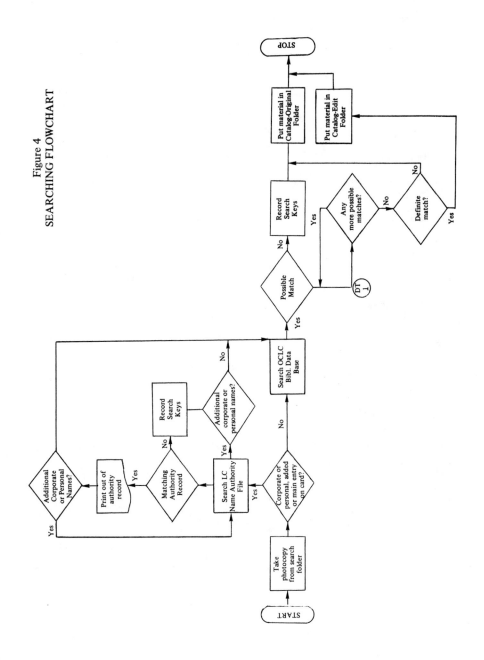

Figure 5

Variable Field	Original	Edit
010 L.C. Card Number	Record per Serials Format if it is available. Do not search for it in reference sources.	Add to record if it is available. Do not delete if it is already in the record. Do not search for it in reference sources.
011 Linking LCCN	Do not use	Do not add or delete
012 Terminal Display	Do not use	Do not add or delete
015 National Bibliographic Number	Do not use	Do not add or delete
019 OCLC Control Number	Do not use	Do not add or delete
022 ISSN	Use if available. Do not search for it in reference sources.	Add if available. Do not delete. Do not search reference sources.
025 Overseas Acquisitions Number	Do not use	Do not add or delete
030 CODEN Designation	Do not use	Do not add or delete
035 Local System Number	Do not use	Do not add or delete
037 Stock Number	Do not use	Do not add or delete
039 Level of Bibliographic Control	Do not use	Do not add or delete
040 Cataloging Source	CRL ≠c CRL	Cannot change
041 Languages	Use when more than one language is associated with the serial. There should be a corresponding language note (546) Assign codes based on Serials Format and List of Language Codes.	Same as Original. If OCLC and CRL language notes conflict, code for all languages mentioned in either record, and change OCLC record as needed.

1st indicator Ø Not a translation (Most common for serials)
   1 Translation (Seldom used for serials,
          requires ≠h if it is used)
2nd indicator ƀ

| 042 Authentication Center | Do not use | Do not add or delete |

Decision Table 1 (DT 1)

Decision		1	2	3	4	5	6	7	8
1	Library Holding Symbol on Record?	Y	Y	Y	N	N	N	N	N
2	"Do Not Use" in 043?	Y	N	N	Y	Y	N	N	N
3	Repr Code Differs from Format of Serial?	—	Y	N	Y	N	Y	N	N
4	S/L ent Code?	—	—	—	—	—	—	1	0

Action		1	2	3	4	5	6	7	8
1	Discard Material	x		x					
2	Print Out Record	x			x	x	x	x	x
3	Give to Supervisor	x							
4	Circle Code on Printout						x	x	
5	Return to Flowchart		x		x	x	x	x	x

consideration. It becomes apparent when using the system that some libraries are still using latest entry records, but the OCLC serials format expressly forbids their use and instructs you to input an original record, if additional successive entry records are lacking. Of course, other decisions can be added to the table depending upon the scope of the individual conversion project. For example, at CRL, newspapers were not to be converted, so any newspaper record (ser tp = n) would be removed from the process.

From an efficiency standpoint, it is important that searchers consistently make the proper judgements during this phase. If they select the wrong record or one that has already been converted, then the cataloger must catch these mistakes. Unfortunately it is easy for a cataloger to get in the bad habit of accepting a searcher's work uncritically, and there is a distinct possibility that unnecessary or duplicate work will be done. The more frequently this occurs, the more expensive the conversion becomes.

The most difficult step in the searching process is checking the Library of Congress Name Authority File. Non--librarians in par--ticular have trouble understanding its purpose and how to use it. However, since every personal or corporate, main or added, entry must be checked against this file, it is very helpful to have this done before the cataloger receives the material.

Corporate bodies, especially those in foreign languages, cause the most difficulty, and there is often an initial problem in merely identifying them in the catalog card. The less experience a searcher has in using libraries, the more likely that this problem will arise. It seems most successful to get a searcher used to the format of the catalog card so that the corporate body can be spotted by its posi--tion on the card. This eliminates the necessity of understanding the language.

There is, also, the question of which or how many authority searches to perform. The choice of added entries on the local bibliographic record often will differ from those on the matching OCLC record. One answer is to search for any main or added entry that appears in either place. This has the drawback of potentially wasting a substantial amount of searching time since a cataloger may not want that many access points. CRL selected the option of performing authority searches for those corporate or personal authors appearing as main or added entries on the CRL card. The cataloger then decides if additional access points are needed and does the necessary authority searches. This proved to be generally satisfactory. There is always the possibility of allowing catalogers to do all authority work, but this increases the amount of cataloger per title. A certain amount of this searching will always fall to the cataloger, in any case, since there are some extremely complex situations.

It should be noted that the flowchart places authority searching before searching the main database. If a corporate search is required in order to locate the bibliographic record, it is more sensible to execute the authority search prior to the corporate search. Other--wise, the wrong search key will be formulated when the entry in the card catalog differs from the form established by the Library of Congress.

There may be some questions concerning the wisdom of printing out a copy of every record. Why not just do the editing online? Aside from the fact that in this structure searching and editing are performed by two different individuals, it is actually more efficient to print out the records and edit off--line. The CRL experi--ence showed that major editing was required on the majority of records. In addition, conflicts between data on the local bibliogra--phic record and the matching OCLC record were so frequent that a substantial amount of time was spent verifying information in reference sources. It is obviously an inefficient use of terminal time to have the operator jumping up to consult a reference book. Editing on a printout also allows more efficient quality control. A supervisor can review the material prior to inputting thus prevent--ing a waste of inputting time.

One final observation on searching: the difficulty in selecting the proper OCLC record should not be underestimated. There are many cases where the local or OCLC record overlooks a title change that the other considered valid. Naturally, this alters the dates and linking entries associated with the serial and a searcher must be alert in order to figure out the situation. There also seems to be a disturbing tendency for a searcher to stop once one seeming match is located rather than examining all the possibilities before making a selection. This must constantly be guarded against be--cause a cataloger cannot always know if something has been over-looked and a lot of unnecessary effort can be expended.

It is helpful to the cataloger if the searcher keeps a written record of the actual searches performed. At least in cases where a matching record is not located, the cataloger can evaluate the thoroughness and accuracy of the search strategy. This also allows constant reinforcement of searching techniques.

Cataloging

Cataloging is used here for lack of a better phrase but it is some--thing of a misnomer. The actual duties of the cataloger are to edit OCLC records in terms of the local bibliographic record or, alter-natively, to transfer information from the catalog card to an OCLC workform in order to create a new OCLC record. Actual cataloging from the item should be avoided whenever possible since it is really beyond the scope of retrospective conversion. A certain amount of recataloging is inevitable but it should be limited to those titles with severe problems.

The cataloging procedures can be designed in the same fashion as the searching procedures, a sort of verbal flowchart, but the actual editing decisions are much more numerous and involved than in searcing. Fig. 6 shows the workflow for this section of the pro--ject. The first step is to evaluate the work done by the searcher. If the preparation is inadequate, the situation should be rectified before going any further. It is easy to forget to look closely at the search keys that were employed and merely assume they are accurate. In addition, double--check all the elements in decision table 1. It is safer to be skeptical although not to the point of retracing every step the searcher has followed.

Unlike normal cataloging, it is actually simpler to create an original record than to edit an OCLC record. This assumes that the local records being used are relatively accurate and complete. If they are, it is merely a matter of assigning the correct MARC tags. If they are not, it is wise to verify certain key data in reference sources. This includes beginning dates, linking entries, and fre--quency. Some may have the luxury of examining the first issue for each original record but, as mentioned previously, this may be more time--consuming than timetables and budgets allow.

In any case, it is on the problems of editing which most of this section will focus. The reason it is more complex is the incom--patibility of OCLC and local records. This includes not only dis--crepancies involving specific pieces of information, but also major disagreements involving choices of entry, selection of title, and changes in title. Often the most difficult problems arise due to changes in cataloging rules or differences in interpretation, rather than actual errors.

One such problem involves titles which have been split in the data base due to a change in name of the corporate body main entry. When the local record has been cataloged according to AACR 2, it may very well have a title main entry instead of a cor--porate one. If the title of the serial has remained constant, then the issues described by the two OCLC records are consolidated into one catalog entry. The library is then faced with an unsavory choice. It can choose one of the OCLC records and edit so that it conforms to the AACR 2 catalog entry. Unfortunately, OCLC will not up--grade the record in this way even if an error report is submitted. Their reasoning is that the inputting library was correct to enter two separate records according to the rules in effect at the time of

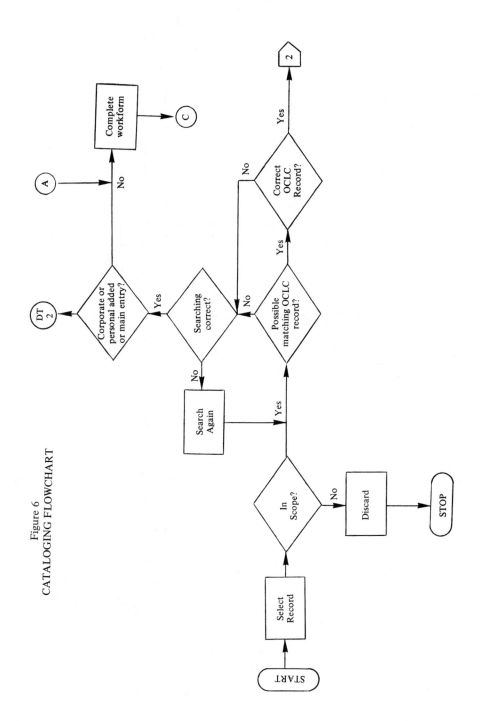

Figure 6
CATALOGING FLOWCHART

135

Figure 6 (cont.)

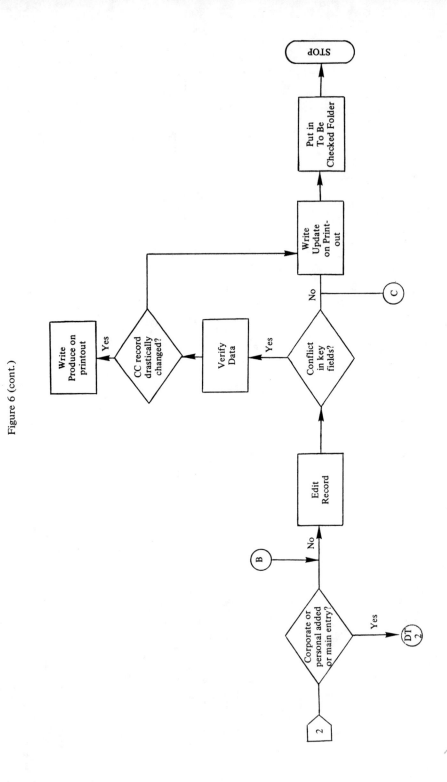

cataloging and institutions who have used those records are unlikely to have uniformly upgraded to AACR 2. Thus, editing one record makes it appear that only the issues represented by that permanent record are held. This obviously misleads potential patrons. Inputting a new AACR 2 record is not allowed. This leaves two options:

a. Produce cards for both OCLC records to replace the current AACR 2 catalog cards thus downgrading the cataloging.

b. Edit one record to AACR 2 standards and just update on the other OCLC record to communicate that those issues are held. This leaves an unedited record on the archival tapes unless some sort of explanatory note is included referring to the edited record.

Neither situation is completely satisfactory, but these are the kind of choices often encountered in a serials conversion.

Before looking at the problems of editing, it is nesessary to discuss the other major component of the cataloging process -- authority work. This applies to both originals and edits, although there is room for laxity when editing. For original input, there is no option. All headings must be in AACR 2 form. It is an OCLC requirement. Choice of entry can be pre--AACR 2 but not the form. Obviously OCLC has a mixture of AACR 2 and pre--AACR 2 headings, and it is likely, unless there has been systematic upgrading to AACR 2, that the local card catalog will also have a mixture, although not the same one. The ultimate goal is to have the AACR 2 form of heading appear on both the OCLC record and the catalog card. It may provide short--term savings not to worry about having the headings match, but it will drastically diminish the usefulness of the archival tapes generated by the conversion project. (Decision Table 2)

OCLC participants are compelled to use the form of name in the Library of Congress Name Authority File when it has been designated as AACR 2 (denoted by a "c" in the 13th position of =w in the 1xx field of the authority record). When an AACR 2 authority record is available, the decision is clearcut: use the form of name found in the authority file and reconcile the OCLC record and/or the catalog card to it. Obviously, there is no problem when the heading is the same in all three places.

CRL and probably many other academic libraries dealt with AACR 2 by upgrading headings to AACR 2 as they were encountered in daily cataloging. Thus retrospective conversion provides an opportunity, if one looks at this optimistically, to upgrade a substantial number of headings. Unfortunately, it involves a tremendous amount of catalog maintenance in the form of changing

137

Decision Table 2 (DT 2)

Decision		1	2	3	4	5	6	7	8	9	10	11	12	13	14	15	16	17
1	Is There Authority File Record?	N	N	N	N	N	Y	Y	Y	Y	Y	Y	Y	Y	Y	Y	Y	Y
2	Is Authority Record AACR 2?	–	–	–	–	–	N	N	N	N	N	N	Y	Y	Y	Y	Y	Y
3	Is There an OCLC Record?	N	N	Y	Y	Y	N	N	Y	Y	Y	Y	N	N	Y	Y	Y	Y
4	Is OCLC Record Heading AACR 2?	–	–	N	N	Y	–	–	N	N	Y	Y	–	–	N	N	Y	Y
5	Is Card Catalog Heading AACR 2?	N	Y	N	Y	N	N	Y	N	Y	N	Y	N	Y	N	Y	N	Y

Action		1	2	3	4	5	6	7	8	9	10	11	12	13	14	15	16	17
1	Establish AACR 2 Form of Heading	x	x	x	x	x	x	x	x	x	x	x						
2	Use Authority File Heading												x	x	x	x	x	x
3	Use AACR 2 Heading on Record	x	x	x	x	x	x	x	x	x	x	x	x		x	x	x	x
4	Fill Out Change Slip	x					x		x		x		x		x		x	
5	Fill Out Change Request Form							x						x		x		
6	Go to A	x	x				x							x				
7	Go to B			x	x	x			x	x	x	x	x		x	x	x	x

headings, tracings, authority cards, and cross–references. The time involved caused CRL to decide to have this work performed by non--conversion cataloging department staff. Whenever a cataloger encounters a heading that needs to be changed, a form is filled out giving the old and new headings along with instructions as to what action to take (fig. 7). The slips are then forwarded to non--conver--sion staff and the changes made as time allows. At CRL this was necessary for less than 5% of the converted serials. This figure is probably low due to the fact that CRL, doing most of its business through inter--library loan, needs fewer added entries than a library with mostly walk--in patrons. Also, many of the headings requiring changes, such as those of Soviet academies and institutes, had already been upgraded. These slips are also used to notify the serials depart--ment of changes in title or entry for current serials. CRL's current serials are arranged alphabetically by main entry so it is imperative that serial record entries match those in the catalog.

When the form of heading in the OCLC record varies from that in the authority file, an error report is completed and sent to OCLC. A printout from the authority file serves as the proof for the change. Caution should be exercised in using an authority record; it cannot be blindly accepted. One vexing problem is that many valid name changes for corporate bodies are entered in 410 (see reference) fields thus indicating that the headings in 110 should be used in their stead. This would actually be incorrect. L.C.'s policy has been not to put valid name changes in 510 (see also) fields unless L.C. has used the headings internally. This is symptomatic of the general difficulty, that of taking a file intended for internal L.C. purposes and using it in an entirely different fashion.

Figure 7

CHANGE   U.S. Library of Congress
_____

_____

1. Main entry heading.
2. Added entry heading.
3. Qualifier.
4. Tracing.
5. Authority and x-ref. cards.
6. Make x-ref. (from the form to be changed to the new
   form) and authority cards.
TO:
          Library of Congress_____

_____

_____

The situation is more muddled when there is no authority record or the heading on the authority record has not been established as AACR 2. It is probably best to leave well enough alone if the OCLC heading is the same as that in the card catalog. When they differ, a choice must be made. The most expedient solution is to change the OCLC heading, but it should be remembered that an error report cannot be filed in this circumstance. OCLC will only change the form of heading if LC proof can be supplied. CRL chose, for the sake of consistency, to establish an AACR 2 form of heading and change the OCLC and/or card catalog records, as necessary. The catalog maintenance resulting from these reconciliations can be both tedious and time consuming. Allowances should be made for it when calculating the total cost of the project.

This still leaves the bulk of the actual editing process. A general decision must be made concerning standards. It may be advisable to adopt standards below those used in everyday cataloging. The standards decided upon should not be so minimal so as to impair the usefulness of the final product. It is also necessary to consider the responsibility to other data base users in regard to the quality of original records. All CRL cataloging is done at encoding level "k," mainly to allow omission of call numbers and subject headings, so this already allowed sufficient flexibility. The general standard applied is that all information on the CRL catalog card must be represented in the edited OCLC record. Data in the OCLC record that is not on the CRL card is usually left in the record, provided that is not contradictory. A holdings statement is always added in a 590 field, and the holdings are also represented in the 049 field.

The important thing is to establish consistency among the catalogers as to the degree of editing. This was accomplished at CRL through a compilation of decisions regarding individual MARC fields (fig. 5). This section of the cataloging manual instructs the cataloger as to which variable fields to omit or include in editing and in creating an original record. It also codifies internal decisions concerning each field and illuminates unclear sections of the serials format. It is not intended to supplant the serials format but is used as a supplement to it.

A major function of the manual is to give instruction on what to do when there is a conflict between the OCLC record and the catalog card. It tells when and how much to search in order to resolve the conflict. For instance, in the case of preceding or succeeding titles it was considered essential to search all possible sources to resolve a discrepancy. On the other hand, a discrepancy about which languages a journal had summaries in is relatively trivial, and time should not be wasted checking on it. Instead an arbitrary

Figure 8

CRL Card	MARC Tag	

Series (contd.)
    Not Traced   490   1st indicator = 0
        ISSN   ≠x
        Numbering   ≠v

Notes[1] (enter in numerical order)
    Language Note   546   (should agree with Lang code)
                                    Multiple languages should have
                                    corresponding 041 ≠a

        Language of summaries   546   Appropriate codes in 041 ≠b

    Title varies slightly   500

    Title varies: [title]   500   Repeat in 246   1st ind. = 3
    Sometimes published as [title] 500   2nd ind. = 0
    At head of title: [   ]   500   Repeat in 246   1st ind. = 2 or 3
                                                    2nd ind. = 0

    Cover title.   500
    Caption title.   500
    Running title.   500
    Spine title.   500
    Masthead title.   500

Distinctive title: [title]   246   2nd ind. = 2   1st indicator
Other title: [title]   246   2nd ind. = 3   will be 0 or
Cover title: [title]   246   2nd ind. = 4   1 depending
Added title page title: [title] 246   2nd ind. = 5   on whether or
Caption title: [title]   246   2nd ind. = 6   not an added
Running title: [title]   246   2nd ind. = 7   entry is
Spine title: [title]   246   2nd ind. = 8   necessary

    Quotations   500

    Began with: [no. or date]   362   1st ind. = 1
    Ceased with: [no. or date]   362   1st ind. = 1
    Ceased publication.   500
    Published: [dates]   362   1st ind. = 1

    Suspended [dates]   515
    Suspended publication.   515

    Numbering irregular   515   Use 515 for any note concerning
                                      numbering peculiarities

    Report year ends [date]   515

    Supplement: [title]   580
    Supplement to: [title]   580

----

[1] All sources go in ≠z following Cf.

decision can be made, i.e. include in the OCLC record all summary languages mentioned on either the catalog card or the OCLC record. There will be elements of the record which will be difficult to evalu-- ate without having the item in hand. How does one select a "Cont" code for the fixed field without looking at the contents? To sim-- plify matters, the cataloger could be instructed not to change the "Cont" code when editing a record and to use the default value when doing an original. This is the kind of information that should be in the manual, so that the editing can be almost mechanical for those areas of relative insignificance.

There are three important areas where conflicts are likely to occur: dates, linking entries, and frequency. CRL chose to exhaust all possible avenues in order to verify the first two. This involved searching available reference sources and consulting the issues. There were so many conflicts involving frequency that it became impractical to follow this same standard. It was up to the cataloger to try to decide which frequency was the latest and edit the record accordingly. Only in cases where an error was apparent, as opposed to just a change in frequency, was the information verified. The change slip (fig. 7) was also modified for the purpose of correcting errors on the CRL card regarding dates, holdings, "Continues" notes, and the like, provided that the change did not necessitate a major alteration of the card.

This sort of manual also aids the inexperienced cataloger during the training period. To increase this benefit, an additional table can be used (fig. 8) to translate a catalog card into the MARC for-- mat. This table guides the catalogers to the proper place in the serials format rather than having them search for the right slot for each bit of information on the catalog card. This approach not only encourages consistency, but also forces the planners to antici-- pate situations that will occur during the actual editing. The more problems that can be dealt with in advance, the less trouble there will be getting the conversion off the ground. No matter how careful the planning, there will be unanticipated problems, and these can be concentrated on if the obvious ones have been dealt with already.

The decisions made concerning editing comprise the heart of the conversion process. It is impossible to go into sufficient detail in this setting. In general, though, it is necessary to communicate to the catalogers the proper priorities as to how to spend their time. They should not get bogged down in trivia, but at the same time should avoid glossing over important points. It is tempting to take a lax approach in the interest of saving time. Whether this is advisable depends upon the goals of the project and how the tapes resulting from the conversion are going to be employed in the future.

There is one final decision for the catalogers to make before their work is passed on to an inputter. That is whether to produce cards or update holdings for the record. Retrospective conversion, by nature, implies that all the records will be updated, but there will certainly be cases where new cards need to be produced. The most obvious is when a local record has overlooked a change in title, but the records in OCLC reflect the title change. In most cases it will be desirable to split the titles in the card catalog. There will also be cases when the local record is woefully inadequate and should be replaced. A decision should be made in advance as to when it is allowable to produce cards and these guidelines should be distributed to the staff. This must be monitored carefully since producing cards results in being charged at the full FTU rate rather than the cheaper retrospective rate.

Inputting and Quality Control

After cataloging, the records are passed on to a clerk for input-- ting. There is not anything startling to say about inputting except as it relates to quality control. How much quality control is enough? In the CRL project, catalogers submit their work to a supervisor so that it can be checked prior to inputting. During the training period, a supervisor also checks all input. Inputters save every record and the supervisor does the actual updating after the work is checked.

Quality control efforts should not cease when staff is considered adequately trained. There can be modifications, however, in the way it is done. One method is to have inputters check each other's work. This way they learn from each other in addition to correcting inputting errors. Certainly a supervisor should continue to spot check and all original inputs should be checked carefully. Here, as in much of the conversion process, there is a trade--off between quality and speed. Constant checking and rechecking may guarantee perfect records but not a great quantity of records.

CRL includes an extra step in the inputting process by entering local data records into the OCLC serials subsystem. This makes exact serial holdings available online as part of a union list. It causes a slight increase in cataloging and inputting time but is worth it as a service to Center members. It is more efficient to do the union listing as part of conversion process, so it is worth considering if participation in a union list is contemplated in the future.

Evaluation

Evaluation is an ongoing process. It does not chronologically follow implementation, but instead is done concurrently, just as training and implementation overlap. Procedures need to be con-- stantly re--evaluated and compared to the goals and timetable of the project. Progress must be carefully monitored to see if more speed is necessary. It is a good idea to plan ahead as to which activities can be modified or discontinued if the conversion is falling behind schedule. There will also always be those unexpected problems to deal with as the project progresses. So as not to be too discourag-- ing, there is also the possibility of things going better than antici-- pated, which is in fact what happened during the first phase of the CRL project. This takes off the pressure and allows more time to be spent on some of those quality concerns that were previously sacrificed.

Retrospective conversion of serials is a complicated undertaking. It requires the balancing of many contradictory concerns and often necessitates making arbitrary decisions. The likelihood of smooth execution is directly related to the care taken in the planning process and the extent to which potential snags are anticipated. It need not be an ordeal but it remains a considerable challenge.

Series Authority Control

Susan Matson
Head, Serials Cataloging
Southern Illinois University at Carbondale

Serials and Series

Many works which come into a library bear some kind of collective title which indicates that the work is part of a larger group of works. Phrases like "annual report," "journal of," "series on," "fourth report on," "proceedings of the ninth conference" suggest that other works bearing the same or similar titles probably exist. It is a matter of judgement to decide how such works should be cataloged for the greatest usefulness to the library process and the library users.

When there is a suspicion that the title may be that of a serial, many libraries submit such pieces to a serials cataloger, following the unwritten dictum that a serial is anything a serials cataloger says is a serial, with the corollary that anything that is not handled as a serial will be handled in the context of a monographic record. The serials department may keep a decision file on some titles, recording the decision that a particular set or proceedings run is not be treated as a serial. It may also either catalog or at least create holdings records for certain sets, monographic series, or "made--up" series which are purchased on standing order. With the exception of such record--keeping, however, the participation of the serials department in handling collective titles such as series often ceases. The majority of series occur on monographs, and the decisions regarding them are viewed as the responsibility of those who are experts in cataloging monographs.

However, even though the majority of series occur on monographs, the series themselves are more akin to serials than to monographs. The very fact that in many instances someone has to make a decision about whether a collective title is a serial or not indicates the hazy line between the two. Series are subject to the same rules for form of entry and the construction of uniform titles as serials. It is not unreasonable to think that people familiar with the peculiarities of serials should also handle the peculiarities of series even

though the ultimate use of most series information will be on mono--
graphic records.

Serials Department Management of Series Authority Control

The serials department at Southern Illinois University at Carbon--
dale took over series control from the monographic cataloging
department in late 1980, as part of an overall decision to institute
new authority procedures before the adoption of AACR2. Before
that time, series authority records had been created by individual
monographic catalogers as they happened to encounter the series.
There was no consistent system for determining whether an appa--
rently "new" series was in fact a title change from a previously
known one or for carrying over the decisions regarding the old title
to its new manifestation. There was no overall consistent tracing
policy in effect. There was insufficient information on the series
authority records to distinguish between similar or identical titles.
There was no information as to what kind of numbering the items
in the series had. There was no system of review to determine
whether the series as established on the authority records were
correctly established. There was inconsistent compliance with
the series authority records on the part of the catalogers.

The serials department (which includes serial cataloging as well
as serial processing) volunteered to take over the management
of series control for a number of reasons. Series form an important
part of the description and access for the works on which they ap--
pear, if not for the average student or patron, at least for bibliogra--
phers, professors, and librarians. The usefulness of series as access
points is diminished when there is inconsistency in the way that
the series are recorded on records for the individual pieces. One of
the ways to keep inconsistency to a minimum is to have the same
few people responsible for all series authority work, so that those
people become series experts. Serials department personnel, who are
already familiar with title changes, title inconsistencies, links be--
tween titles, numbering peculiarities, and the formulations of serial
and series titles according to cataloging rules and Library of Congress
rule interpretations are in the best position to undertake the task
with a minimum of difficulty. The decision--making processes which
enable us to decide whether a collective title should be handled
as a serial or not can be extended to include the decision--making
processes which enable us to decide whether and how a series should
be traced. Keeping up to date with the latest rule interpretations
concerning series can best be done by experts intimately concerned
with those aspects of cataloging.

The monographic catalogers, concerned with all the coming

effects of AACR2 and name authority work, were very willing to have this part of their work, always troublesome, handled by who--ever felt confident to do it. They understood that the series areas of descriptions and access form a subset of monographic cataloging that is in many ways akin to serial work.

Scope of the Serial/Series Control Task

Because our serials department has added series control to the previously existing task of identifying actual serial titles, it is now in the business of what might be termed collective title control. All collective titles except those traditional uniform titles which collecate the various manifestations of literary and musical works (the MARC 240 fields) are the province of this collective title con--trol. This encompasses the old task of deciding whether a collective title is going to be handled as a serial, set, or series, as well as the new task of series authority control per se.

In the widened scope of its task, the serials department now not only catalogs serials, it also controls the correct form of those serial titles when they occur as added entries on monographic records. It controls the correct form of added entry for supplements to serials or sets. It controls pseudo--series titles that used to be recorded in series fields but are now handled as report numbers or notes. And it controls series statements and series added entries. The scope of this task is broad, and includes a great deal of judge--mental decision--making and re--evaluation of those decisions as title change in the real world, and as methods of bibliographic handling change in the library world.

This job requires the participation of a number of people and a new design of the work flow. Formerly, the serials department saw only known serials and a few new items that were suspencted of being possible serials. Now it must see, in addition, all pieces, and records for those pieces, which have or will need added entries for serials or will need series statements. In order to enable the serials department to see all the items it needs to control, it is neces--sary to identify all those pieces that enter the library which bear a collective title of this kind and funnel those pieces to the serials department. This is done by the order and gifts departments at the time of receipt of new pieces. It is necessary to handle those titles already known to the library system by checking in pieces of serials or sets on standing order, and encoding series or serial added entry fields on the bibliographic records for pieces which are monographs. This is done by the serials department check--in personnel as an extension of the check--in process. And finally, it is necessary to create new records which direct the proper handling of serial and

series titles new to the system. This is done in the serials department, principally by one cataloger, working half-time.

Fundamental to the operation of such title authority control
are 1) the records which direct the handling of the titles (serial
records, series authority records, decision records), and 2) the work
flow which moves the titles through the system.

Serial Records, Series Authority Records, Decision Records

Although this library is part of the LCS automated circulation
system and has brief bibliographic records with volume--specific
holdings in an on--line system, it does not as yet use any automated
check--in system and has no on--line authority records of its own.
It uses OCLC for cataloging, but all records relevant to the title--
control system are in paper format.

The serials department maintains a file called the Central Serial
Record, which contains catalog and holdings cards for serials, decision cards, and, now, series authority records. The problem in
bringing the series control task into the department was partly
one of designing the format of the series authority card.

Series Authority Records

Before series authority control was managed by the serials
department, series authority records were interfiled into the (paper)
name authority file and looked like this:

```
Studies in business education



Extra card for series in public catalog
```

The authority card gave the series entry and the trace decision
(either "extra card for series in public catalog" or "Series not
traced"). Cross referencing was sporadic or non--existent and auxiliary information such as imprint and numbering was not given.
This type of record is insufficient for real series control.

Now, whether authority records are kept in paper or machine

format, there are two problems to solve: 1) you have to figure out how to record a lot of information about the series on the authority record; and 2) you have to see to it that the series, as recorded on the authority record, gets properly transferred to bibliographic records. In the case of paper authority records which will control the series field on MARC bibliographic records, that means recording the information about the series on a paper record, and seeing to it that the series show up, properly coded and sub-fielded, on a machine record. If series are recorded on an authority card as in the example above, field and subfield tags will have to be added somewhere along the line.

A similar problem occurs even if you have the authority records in machine format. You will have authority records with authority field tags in the authority file, and bibliographic records with bib-liographic field tags on the bibliographic records. How do you translate the information from the authority record into the precise, fielded string demanded by the bibliographic record? One way to handle that is to have the staff perfectly comfortable with trans-lation. The staff must be able to translate format A (the authority record) into format B (the tag structure of the bibliographic format). For instance, a MARC authority record would show the series title in a 130 field, and this would have to be translated into a 440 field, or a 490 field, or an 830 field in the bibliographic record, depending on the trace decision and various other factors.

Alternatively, the authority record can be set up in bibliographic format. Operating with a paper file, a library may do that without impinging on any national system. Needing a new and better authority format than we had before, and wanting to keep the translation problem to a minimum, we decided to create new authority records which included the bibliographic fielding. We did that because we wanted to handle series authority as a kind of check--in process. We wanted check--in personnel -- library technical assistants -- to be able to find the series authority record, and automatically, with relatively little mental work, properly encode that series either onto worksheets or onto printouts of bib-liographic records. When the LTA has found the series authority record, he has found out exactly how the series ought to appear on a MARC bibliographic record.

To facilitate the handling of series within the check--in process, it was also necessary to move the series authority records out of the name authority file (which happened to be located inconven-iently in the catalog department rather than the serials department) and into the Central Serial Record where they are interfiled with serials records.

Now, it makes a lot of intuitive sense to file series authority records in an entity called an authority file. That is how the OCLC on–line authority file is constructed, for instance. However, it also makes a lot of sense to interfile series authority records with serial records. For one thing, it keeps confusion of identity between the two at a minimum. For another, it completes the series author–ity file in the sense that the serial records act as the authority records for those series that are classed together as serials. A separate authority record for a serial title in addition to the bibliographic record for the serial is not needed.

The new series authority records, designed to interfile into a paper card file which also includes serial catalog records and decision cards, look like this:

```
Studies in business education, +x 1234-5678 ;
  +v no. 9-
  Bloomington, Ind. : Center for the Study of
  Business Education, Indiana University, 1976-


  SCATTER 440  bØ

  Continues: Research in business education.

  Library has:
    no. 9-16

  C123J23F - Pub. - no. 9              (over)
```

```
  pc xx  Research in business education.
  pc x   Indiana University.  Center for the Study
           of Business Education.
         Studies in business education.
     x   Studies on business education.
```

In this example, we have the same traced series as shown in the previous example, but with a great deal of information (from various sources) added. The card leads with the bibliographic string that would be used in the 440 field of a MARC bibliographic record: title, comma, delimiter x, ISSN, semicolon, delimiter v, no period, 9, hyphen. (The contents of subfield v show the number caption and start number followed by a hyphen. The LTA would, of course, replace the "9, hyphen" with the actual volume number of the piece in hand.)

The field tag itself has been removed from the front of the title string and dropped to the middle of the card where it follows the word "SCATTER." The word "scatter" is the local word used to identify a series which is not to be classed together as a serial, but which is "scattered" all over the library under the call numbers appropriate to each piece. It serves as the label for "series authority record." The field has been dropped to follow it because it was felt that leading numbers would interfere with filing into a paper alphabetical file.

Following the series string on another paragraph is imprint information, given in ISBD format, but not fielded because it is merely informational on an authority record.

The middle of the card is used for notes, such as continues/ continued by information. The bottom of the card (and extra cards if necessary) is used to record either holdings information if the series is received on standing order, or the number of the piece on which the series decision was made. The back of the card records cross references to be made either for the Central Serial Record alone (shown as x or xx) or for both the Central Serial Record and the public catalog as well (shown as pc x or pc xx).

Compare the rendering of this same imaginary title as it would appear in the MARC authority format (leaving aside fixed fields, etc.):

```
022 bb    1234--5678
130 b0    Studies in business education
410 20    Indiana University.   ≠b Center for the Study of
          Business Education.   ≠t  Studies in business educa--
          tion
430 b0    Studies on business education
530 b0    Research on business education  ≠w annn
640 0b    9 (1976)--
642 bb    no. 9
643 bb    Bloomington, Ind.  +b Center for the Study of Busi--
          ness Education, Indiana University
644 bb    f  ≠5 SOI (SOI is this library's OCLC symbol)
645 bb    t  ≠5 SOI
646 bb    s  ≠5 SOI
```

The paper format covers the same information which the MARC authority format includes:

1) the established form of the entry

2) number caption information (if it can be supplied)

3) start number (if it can be supplied)

4) ISSN

5) imprint information, including the start date (if it can be sup‐
   plied)

6) continues information (shown in the paper format in a note,
   in the MARC format by the 530 field with its associated w
   subfield)

7) see from and see also from references

8) tracing practice (shown in the paper format by the 440 tag
   and in the MARC format by the value "t" in the 645 field).

The paper record, however, also shows the precise form of the string
to be used on bibliographic records.

The MARC format separates out two aspects of series treatment
in the 644 and 646 fields which are reflected in the paper format
in a collapsed fashion.   The MARC 644 field indicates whether
the series is analyzed or not (that is, whether separate records are
or are not made for each piece of the series) and the 645 field
indicates whether the series is classed together or not. In this library,
only two of the four possibilities implied by those paired options
are in fact used at this time. The four options implied by the MARC
fields indicate that a series may be:

   analyzed and classed together
   analyzed and not classed together
   not analyzed and classed together
   not analyzed and not classed together.

The latter opposition is an empty option implying that neither
separate records nor a collective record is produced and is of little
interest.   The first option indicates the situation in which a serial
record is created and, in addition, monographic analytic records
are created for each piece of the serial.   This library, like many
others, has many analyzed serials created in the past.   However,
it no longer creates analyzed serials.   If the items in the series are
such that monographic records can be usefully created for each
piece, this library employs the second option, creating monographic
records for each piece, each separately classed.   It is this option
that is indicated by the local term SCATTER.   If the items in the
series are such that it is impossible or not useful to create separate
records for each piece, the third option, of creating a serial record
and not analyzing the individual pieces, is employed.   Thus, with

the exception of a number of analyzed serials from the past, which are maintained as such but which remain outside the operation of current title management, this library has only two types of records: serial records for which the pieces are classed together but not analyzed, and series authority records for which the pieces of the series are analyzed, but not classed together. (Partial analysis, provided for by the MARC format, is either not done, or is handled by separate records in the file.) The local term SCATTER on the paper records is thus equivalent to the paired values of f in the 644 field and s in the 645 field of the MARC record.

The MARC record is in many ways clearer than the paper record in the way that information is displayed and formatted. It is par-- ticularly useful in a national context where series treatment may differ from library to library. It is less desirable for the local pur-- poses of this library because it requires translation into bibliographic coding. Because we wish to handle the bulk of series control by a kind of check--in process, we do not wish the person who validates the bibliographic series fields to have to do this extensive translation into bibliographic fields. We want that person to be able to refer directly and quickly to a record which shows him/her how the series is to appear on bibliographic records in MARC format.

Other examples of the local series authority records follow.

Series not traced:

```
Collection littéraire
   Paris : Librairie lit,  19-- -

SCATTER   490  Øʙ

unnumbered   0583   SAM
```

This series is not traced, is not numbered, and we cannot supply a start date. With a 490 field, the check--in personnel have some leeway to allow slight variations from the authority record in record-- ing the series. For example, if the piece reads *Collection "litteraire",* or even merely *Litteraire,* the LTA may so encode it on bibliographic records as long as he/she is sure he/she is dealing with the same series that is on the authority record.

Series traced under uniform title:

```
Research report (Midwest Center for
   Bilingual Education) ; ⧧v no. 1-
   Chicago, Ill. : The Center, 1981-


SCATTER   830 ƀ∅
490 1ƀ   Research report / Midwest Center
for Bilingual Education, ⧧x 2345-6789 ;
⧧v no. 1-


no. 2   E34J26G         0783 SAM
```
```
   pc x  Midwest Center for Bilingual Education.
         Research report.
```

In the case of a uniform title, the uniform title itself leads the
card, and the field tag is given as 830 b0. In such cases, a suggested
form for the 490 field is included also, because that is the only
place in this card format where information like statements of
responsibility, parallel titles, or ISSN, which are stripped of the 830
field itself, can be recorded. Again, in the case of the 490 field,
the check-in personnel have some discretion -- they are to use
the 490 field to record the series as it appears on the piece (even
though that may differ somewhat from the suggested form on the
authority record), but to trace it exactly as it is shown in the lead
string.

   Because the catalog in this library is not closed, and we have
series running under both AACR2 and pre--AACR2 forms, we
often have to have two authority records for some series, one re--
cording the old invalid form (and marked as no longer valid) and
one recording the new valid form:

Series traced under pre-AACR2 rules, entry no longer valid:

```
Illinois. ⧧b University. +b Dept. of
   Astronomy. ⧧t Research publications in
   astronomy ; ⧧v v. 1-
   Urbana, Ill. : The Dept., 1967-
            NO LONGER VALID FOR CODING


SCATTER 810 1ƀ
490 1ƀ  Research publications in astronomy ;
⧧v v. 1-


v. 3  pt. of C47M22J      0482  SAM    (over)
```
```
   pc xx  Research publications in astronomy.
```

154

Same series traced under AACR2 rules, entry now valid:

```
┌─────────────────────────────────────────────────────────────┐
│ Research publications in astronomy ; ‡v v. __               │
│    Urbana, Ill. : Dept. of Astronomy, University            │
│    of Illinois, 19-- -                                 ┐     │
│                                                        │     │
│ SCATTER  440 ₿∅                                        │     │
│                                                        │     │
│ v. 16  pt. of C47M22J    0482  SAM    (over)           │     │
└────────────────────────────────────────────────────────     │
      ┌───────────────────────────────────────────────────────┤
      │    pc xx  Illinois.  University.  Dept. of            │
      │           Astronomy.                                  │
      │           Research publications in astronomy.        │
      └───────────────────────────────────────────────────────┘
```

See also from references link the two forms of entry in the public catalog and in the Central Serial Record. (The see also reference from the older form also does double duty as a name/title see refer-- ence to the title entry.) The authority record for the invalid form of entry is marked (in red) as NO LONGER VALID FOR CODING.

In cases such as the above, the series will appear in two different ways in the public catalog, and the different forms of the tracing will be uncorrelated with the numbers of the pieces. If volume 1 is received, it will be the AACR2 form of tracing, even though volumes 2 and 3 might be traced under the old form.

In cases where it is possible to split the file cleanly between the two forms of entry, the "not valid for coding" statement is worded somewhat differently. If it can be clearly established that we have all or virtually all of a run of a series up to the current volume in hand running under the old pre–AACR2 form of entry, we attempt to control the runs of different added entries more closely to benefit the patron:

Series traced under pre-AACR2 rules up to volume 19
   (one or two pieces possible missing):

```
Wisconsin. ǂb University. ǂb Center for Adult
   Education. ǂt Studies in adult education ; ǂv 1-
   Madison, Wis. : The Center, 1974-
                  NOT VALID FOR CODING AFTER 19


   SCATTER 810 1ƀ
   490 1ƀ   Studies in adult education ; ǂv 1-

   Library has:
     1-16
     18-19

C148D12E - Pub. - 1                  (over)
```
```
   pc xx Studies in adult education.
```

Series traced under AACR2 rules after volume 19:

```
Studies in adult education ; ǂv 20-
   Madison, Wis. : Center for Adult Education,
   University of Wisconsin, 1983-
             NOT VALID FOR CODING BEFORE 20


   SCATTER   440 ƀ0

   Library has:
     20-21

C148D12E - Pub. - 1
```
```
   pc xx   Wisconsin. University.   Center for
                Adult Education.
             Studies in adult education.
```

In this latter case, if volume 17 is later received by the library, the series on the record for volume 17 will be coded in the pre--AACR2 form of entry (unless an original record will have to be created, in which case conformance to national standards will require the use of the AACR2 form and the library will lose the neat split in the card file between the run up to volume 19 and the run after 19). The ability to specify the precise point of a split between forms of entry in this way is not always possible, but we try to do this for the sake of the patrons where it is possible.

Serial Records

The Central Serial Record contains catalog cards and holdings cards for serials in addition to the newly added series authority records. In the majority of cases, the use of these serials records is limited to the serial check--in and serials cataloging functions. However, the serials catalog cards also serve as the authority record for serial titles when it is necessary to use such titles as added entries on records for monographs and other serials. The use of such records as authority records is more difficult for the check--in personnel because, unlike the series authority records, they provide no direct information as to how to code such added entries. The check--in personnel must simply have some knowledge of the coding of 630 and 730 fields and a basic understanding of their function and of the need for the library to have the added entry for serials match our own main entry for those serials, not some other library's for--mulation of the entry.

Occasionally it is necessary to encode or validate a serial title which this library does not own for an added entry field. In such cases, a kind of authority record is created for such titles so that there is a record in the serials department so that the title, although not owned by the library, exists as an added entry in the public catalog. Such a card looks like this:

```
Zeitschrift für Balkanologie
  Wiesbaden : Harrassowitz,  19-- -

Traced in public catalog in 730 field.
```

Imprint information or other relevant information will have been taken from OCLC, Ulrich's, or some other source. If the library later acquires and catalogs the title as a serial, this card is compared with the actual serial entry used in our cataloging. If the entry is different, the added entry is pulled from the public catalog and changed at that time. The information card is then pulled from the Central Serial Record and the card for the serial itself replaces it.

Decision Cards

Most serial departments probably have the kind of decision cards which record that a particular serial is not to be cataloged but is to be discarded, kept in a sample file, or otherwise disposed of. In addition, many may keep records of titles which have been identified as requiring monographic rather than serial treatment but which keep being referred over and over again to the serials department as each piece is received. Set titles and proceedings series are frequent in this category.

These records are traditionally important in the serials depart-- ment and become even more important when *all* possible serial and series titles are routed to the department routinely. Cards recording the decision that a title is not to be cataloged as a serial are created in this library as part of the title control procedure. They conform to the basic catalog card structure of the new series authority records, leading with the entry followed by the imprint, but with different instructional wording replacing the word SCATTER. Some examples follow:

Proceedings series not cataloged as a serial:

```
International Electronics Research Association.
  [Proceedings of the conference]
  S.l.  : The Association,  19-- -

NOT CATALOGED AS A SERIAL

4th (1979)  SC46D12E    0683 SAM
```

```
      x  Association international pour la recherche
            électronique.
         Comptes rendus.
```

158

The title "Proceedings of the conference" in brackets is understood to cover a multitude of variant ways in which the proceedings volumes may actually be titled, including renderings in different languages and also such English variants as "Papers presented," and "Annual conference papers." If there is any suspicion that a title on a new piece represents a series genuinely different from the proceedings run, the item in question is referred to a serials librarian for confirmation, or for another decision card, or for additional cross references that will cover the variant titles.

Sets not cataloged and checked in by the serials department:

```
NMSA handbook of oceanographic science
   Washington, D.C. : National Marine Science
   Association, 1978-

SET: SERIALS WILL NOT RECORD

v. 2   SC49J15GG     0783 SAM
```

The decision that an item is part of a set rather than a series or serial is based on OCLC information, publisher's information, searches of sources such as NUC, NST, Ulrich's.

Although serial records, series authority records, and decision records differ in various fundamental ways, they all function to tell someone how to handle a piece bearing a certain title. For instance, if you have a piece that matches a serial record, you check it in in the way shown on the holdings record; if you have a piece of a series, you check it in if it is on standing order, and then you encode the series on the catalog record for the piece in the way shown on the series authority record and send it on to monographic cataloging; if you have a piece which matches a decision card indi-cating that the item is part of a serial--like entity which is not cata-loged as a serial, you insert a slip indicating that fact and send it on to monographic cataloging. It is possible to make use of the similarity of function of these records to bring series authority work into the check--in procedure. If serial records and series authority records and decision records are interfiled into the same file, check--in personnel can match a collective title on a new piece against the titles in the file and properly handle the majority of items received. If no title match is found in the file the new piece is referred to a serials cataloger who will create an appropriate record for the new title so that the next time another piece bearing the same title is received, it can be properly handled.

The entire process for this title control involves a number of steps. Each of the steps, except for serial cataloging itself, is described in the following pages. In summary the steps are as follows:

1) Initial identification of possible serial and series titles and the routing of items which bear them to the serials department.

2) Matching of the titles against the Central Serial Record, and the check–in, series coding, and/or routing of pieces for which a match is found.

3) Creation of new records directing the handling of titles new to the system.

4) Typing of the new records.

5) Revision and management.

Initial Identification of Possible Serial and Series Titles

The catalogers in this library, both monographic and serials catalogers, operate from OCLC printouts or workforms. Failing to obtain a printout after about three OCLC searches original cataloging on a workform will be done.

Initial searching for OCLC records is done by the order and gifts department upon receipt of an item, so that in the majority of cases a printout accompanies a piece by the time it gets to the serials department. (The monographic cataloging and serials depart–ments themselves have built into them re–searching procedures for items for which no printout was originally found, or for trying to find a better record.) In order for the serials department to see every item that bears a series or serial title, it is necessary to identify those items and funnel them through the serials department. This is done at the time of searching.

The order and gifts personnel who do the original searching identify all items that have a serial record in the data base, or that bear a series title on the piece and/or on the printout of the OCLC record, and/or on the dealer packet which accompanies the piece. Any item that has an indication of a series or serial on any or all of these sources is funneled to the serials department for handling. The bulk of items bearing series are identified at the time of this initial searching.

During the later stages of the actual cataloging of an item, additional information may turn up that makes it necessary to refer a piece to the serials department that was not referred initially. The series authority procedure includes not only the control of series fields but also the control of any title added entry field that represents a serial (730 and 630 fields). At the point of actually cataloging a piece, a record which contains or will contain a 730 or 630 field representing a serial title is also funnelled to the serials department for verification.

The serials department thus ultimately receives:

1) Any item perceived as a possible serial (this includes a number of sets)

2) Any item which has an indication of a series on the piece

3) Any item which has an indication of a series on the dealer packet

4) Any item which has an OCLC printout containing a 4xx, 800, 810, 811 or 830 field

5) Any item which has an OCLC printout containing a 630 or 730 field representing a serial title

6) Any item that is being cataloged originally and will need any of the above fields on its MARC record.

Check--in/Series Coding

The initial match of a serial or series title with the cards in the Central Serial Record is done by library technical assistants in the serials department. Originally the job of these LTA's was simply to check in serials and route pieces covered by decision cards. The job was extended to include verification and encoding of series on monographic records. The check--in personnel now receive not only all pieces of serials or possible serials which enter the library, but also all monographs which have been identified by the order, gifts, or cataloging departments as bearing a series title. The routine handling of series for which authority records already exist has been made into an extension of the check--in process. Very basic--ally, the task consists of these processes:

1) Match collective titles against the Central Serial Record.

2) If the item is part of a serial or is received on standing order,

check it in.

3) If the item matches a decision card reading NOT CATALOGED AS A SERIAL or SET: SERIALS WILL NOT RECORD, insert a slip in the piece indicating that decision and route it to mono-graphic cataloging.

4) If the title matches a series authority record, ensure that the proper coding of the series is transferred from the authority record to the printout of the piece (or, lacking a printout, to a cataloging worksheet).

5) If the item has a collective title that does not match any record in the Central Serial Record, pass the item to the serial cataloger who will decide how to handle the new title and create a new record for it.

This relatively simple process is, of course, complicated by various factors. Not all items come with a printout and a re--search--ing loop is built into the check--in procedure for such items. Not all of the series authority records in the Central Serial Record are in the new authority format -- some are left over from the bad old days. In such cases, although a match has been found, the old card must be pulled and given to the serials cataloger along with the piece so a new card can be prepared. It is not always easy to be absolutely sure that a match exists between the piece and an authority record -- titles change and layouts vary. If the check--in people have any doubt about a match, the card and piece must be given to the serials cataloger for a decision and possibly for the creation of new cards.

The basic procedures of the check--in personnel can be summed up by the following work flow chart:

Creation of Records for Titles New to the System

The check--in personnel send any item for which no title match is found in the Central Serial Record to a serials cataloger for a decision as to how to handle the new title. Theoretically, any of the serials catalogers can make these decisions, and all do so occa--sionally. However, one cataloger is assigned half--time to this deci--sion--making process and handles the majority of decisions. This librarian is thus presented with all items which enter or re--enter the library processing system which bear a serial, series, or series--like title which does not precisely match a title in the Central Serial Record. The job consists of two distinct but overlapping functions.

162

WORK FLOW OF THE CHECK-IN PERSONNEL

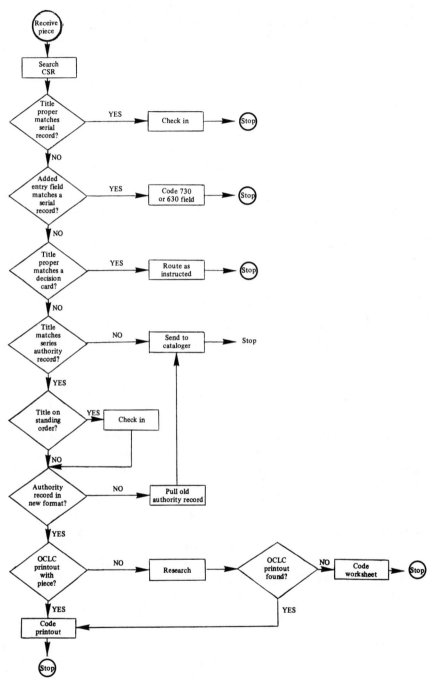

The first consists of identifying those titles which are the title proper of serials and sets, and those which, in spite of series--like appearance, are best handled as the title proper of the piece in hand (proceedings, for instance). The second consists of examining the remainder as possible series titles and deciding how they should be handled. While the former is not part of a series authority work per se, it is part of the overall function of controlling collective titles of a serial nature.

In making decisions about whether an item should be treated as a serial, set, or monograph, the librarian is not working in isola--tion. Cooperative cataloging records and various tools of the trade are available to aid in deciding how to handle a piece. OCLC print--outs accompany most pieces, indicating a bibliographic level of monograph or serial. Order information also accompanies the pieces. Items coming as part of standing orders, subscriptions, or documents depository often hint at the possible serial nature of some items.
Library of Congress practice, especially the recent summary of monograph versus serial treatment published in the *Cataloging Service Bulletin*[1] is helpful. Other sources such as the *National Union Catalog, New Serial Titles,* and Ulrich's may also provide help.

The librarian, in making the initial cut between items in which the collective title will become the cataloging title and those in which the collective title will appear as a series, is not expected to be infallible. Items for which no information is available except the piece in hand will receive a tentative judgement and further searching will be done at the time of cataloging. If an item judged to be a serial later turns out to be a set or a single monograph on the basis of information that turns up later, the item will be appro--priately rerouted. Likewise, a serial record may turn up for an item thought at first to be a one--time occurrence of a monograph. The initial cut is not a decision carved in stone.

In regard to whether a monographic series should receive a serial record or individual monographic records instead, this library uses what we understand to be Library of Congress practice in deciding whether to create a serial or not. If the individual pieces bear their own titles or authors and titles and are monographic in nature, the pieces are "scattered" (in Library of Congress terms, analyzed and not classed together). The title in question gets a series authority record, not a serial catalog record. If the individual pieces bear no title except the collective title, or bear individual titles but remain essentially periodical--like in nature, the pieces are cataloged as a serial (in Library of Congress terms, classed to--gether but not analyzed). A serial record only is created.

Given this background, and without going into great detail,

the librarian takes the steps outlined on the workflow chart below to separate out and properly handle those collective titles in which the collective title will become the cataloging title of a serial, set, or monograph.

Having separated out those titles which will become serial, set, or monograph titles, the remainder of the titles the librarian has to deal with fall into the province of series authority work. A worksheet exists to help in the decision--making process and to serve as the typist's worksheet when the authority cards are typed up. The worksheet is actually used to create decision records of various kinds as well, but the focus here will be on its use for series.

Before beginning a worksheet, the librarian must ask herself whether the title she is being asked to examine is a valid series title. Either the piece or the printout or both may bear a report number or statement of the publisher's name or some other "title" which the Library of Congress in recent rule interpretations has declared to be no longer valid to record as a series. The librarian first examines the printout to see if such an entity is recorded in a series field. She then checks the piece to see if the entity ac-- tually appears on the piece. If the entity is not actually on the piece, she merely lines out the series fields on the printout that contain the "title." If the report number or publisher's statement appears on the piece, she sees to it that the fields on the printout are modified to show the information in non--series fields such as 500 notes or report number fields. If the "title" is sufficiently series--like to cause future pieces bearing the same information to continue to come to the serials department as possible series, she makes an information card for the Central Serial Record as follows:

```
"An American Chemical Society publication."


CODE AS 500 ₿₿
```

If the collective title is indeed a valid series, the librarian uses the series authority worksheet to create an authority record.

FLOWCHART OF DECISION PROCESS TO HANDLE ITEMS INCOMING FROM CHECK-IN (UP TO THE SERIES AUTHORITY PROCESS ITSELF)

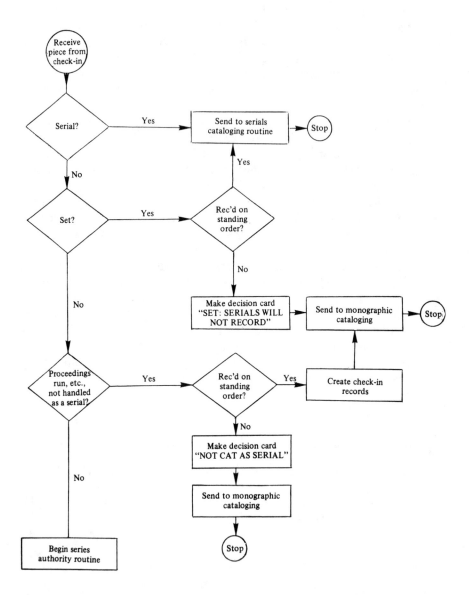

The series decision worksheet, an example of which is shown on the following page, is designed to help the librarian ask herself questions about the series that will lead to a correct handling of the series in description and access fields. The worksheet, when filled out, is given to a typist who transfers the information on the worksheet into the required card format, using a typing manual specific to that purpose.

The worksheet is designed to be worked through from top down, although in practice the librarian may skip around on it. It consists of several areas of information.

Area 1

The worksheet leads with a box called Area 1 in which the librarian records the series as it appears on the piece she has in hand. It is designed to ensure that the series is described according to the AACR2 rules for description of series (title, followed by statement of responsibility if any, ISSN, and numbering, separated by the prescribed ISBD marks of punctuation.) MARC subfield coding is not shown on the worksheet, but is included automatically by the librarian as the information is being filled in. Parallel titles and other information that may be appropriate to the description are now shown on the worksheet but would be included as well. The number caption is shown, but not the numbering itself unless the starting number is known.

In order to supply the required information, the librarian may consult sources other than the piece in hand, although no great efforts are made to establish starting number, ISSN, and the like, if the information is not readily available.

Having recorded the description of the series, the librarian may double check at this point to see whether the title represents a title change, or double check to make sure this library does not have the series already in a slightly variant form.

Having thus described the series and having established its ante--cedents, the librarian is then free to contemplate the series and decide whether or not it should be traced. Judgements about whe--ther to trace a series or not are made on the basis of AACR2, LCRI, and local practice. A section in the local *Series Decision Manual* details the bases on which series are or are not traced.

If at this point the decision is *not* to trace the series, the librarian goes on to record the imprint information on the worksheet and circles 490 0 in Area 4. If the decision is to trace the series, she goes on to Area 2.

SERIES DECISION WORKSHEET

Area 1 490	Title / Statement of responsibility ; numbering of series as it appears on piece:
Area 2 440 830 800 810	Series as it will appear as an access point (title, uniform title, or author/title), including all subfield coding:
Area 3	Place : Publisher, date:

___NO LONGER VALID FOR CODING
___NOT VALID FOR CODING BEFORE/AFTER_____

Area 4	SCATTER Do not trace 490 ∅
	               Trace same 440 ∅
	               Trace diff 830 ∅∅ 800 ∅ 810 ∅
	                                  490 1 490 1 490 1

Area 5	Notes:

Card also in _____DA (type as last note)

Area 6	Holdings ___Piece no./order no./initials/date ___Lib. has/Stamp/_____contin ___Rider 490 1 ___Neither of above: record as below
Area 7	Cross references

Area 2 of the worksheet is used to record the form of the series as it will appear in an access point.

In many cases it will be clear at a glance that the series will be traced in the same form in which it appears on the piece. In this case the librarian would theoretically repeat the information appearing in Area 1 of the worksheet in Area 2. In practice, she simply runs an arrow up from Area 2 to Area 1.

In other cases, the entry may have to be structured as a name/ title entry (in the case of personally authored items, or in the case of creating an authority record for a pre--AACR2 form of the series), or as a uniform title. That structured entry is recorded in Area 2.

Judgements about the form of a series added entry are made on the basis of AACR2, LCRI, and MARC coding and, in the case of authority records for old forms of entry, on the basis of past local practice. It is at this point that an expert in handling series and serials is useful. The current form of entry for series is largely defined by the evolving Library of Congress Rule Interpretations (LCRI) published in the *Cataloging Service Bulletin.* Coding series successfully requires a person who is thoroughly up to date with those rule interpretations.

In addition to establishing the form of the series entry according to AACR2 and LCRI, the librarian may have to strip off certain kinds of information that may have appeared in the description of the series in Area 1 in order to correctly formulate the series added entry. Statements of responsibility and parallel titles will be stripped, and in the case of uniform titles or name/title entries, the ISSN will be stripped, since MARC coding does not allow for that information to appear in 8xx fields.

If a name is involved in the required form of entry for the series, either as a main entry or as the qualifier of a uniform title, the librarian must do the necessary name authority work to establish that the name is in AACR2 form. Her tools in this case will be the local name authority file and the OCLC online authority file. Authority worksheets may have to be filled out.

Having correctly formulated the series added entry and done the necessary name authority work, the librarian proceeds to Area 3. (In many cases she will in fact record the imprint information in Area 3 before establishing the series added entry).

Area 3

Area 3 of the worksheet is designed to record imprint informa-- tion. This information helps to uniquely identify a series, especially in the absence of any formal qualifier, and helps to keep series with identical or nearly identical titles from being confused with each other, and to trigger the formulation of uniform titles for series received later whose titles are identical to titles already in the file.

The imprint information is given in ISBD form but does not include MARC coding, since it is merely informational. Imprint information is taken from any available source -- the piece in hand, old authority records, or if necessary a search of bibliographic tools. No effort is made to make it reflect the earliest or latest piece or to search out a start date if that information is not readily available. It is chiefly useful to identify gross difference in source -- British or American place; Publisher A or Publisher B, and so on.

No Longer Valid Area

Below Area 3 on the worksheet is a place where the librarian can check that the series recorded above is no longer valid at all or is not valid before or after a particular number or date of the series run. It is necessary for us to provide for this kind of informa-- tion because our catalog is not closed and we often have both invalid pre--AACR2 forms of entry and valid AACR2 forms of entry for the same series in the same catalog, with see also references connect-- ing them.

Area 4

Area 4 contains the word SCATTER. This is the local word that signals that the title in question is a series and has been retained as the local label for a series authority record.

The librarian, having already made the decision about how the title is to be handled as she worked out the tracing decision and the form of entry, now circles the relevant field tag or tag--pair following the word SCATTER to specify what field or fields the series is to appear in on bibliographic records.

Area 5

Area 5 is a free--text note area and is used to record a variety of information about the series that is not accommodated elsewhere. Some kinds of notes are:

Continues/continued by:
Issued as a second series with:
Also code main series separately as: (used on cards for subseries)

Code as above only if no subseries occur. If subseries occur, consult card for subseries, e.g.:

Numbering appears only on spine/dust jacket/list in back/etc.

1--49 classed together and analyzed; now unnumbered and scattered.

Line out subseries on printouts.

Insert flag: Class for Education Library.

Refer next piece to cataloger.

Use whole number Hefts for numbering, not the Band/Heft designation.

Area 6

Our series authority records double as holdings records when the library receives the series on some kind of standing order. Be-- cause the recording of holdings is not directly related to series authority work, it is not explained in detail here. In the case of a series for which holdings are not kept, the piece on which the decision was made is recorded, together with the order number or other indication of the source of the piece, the librarian's initials, and the date.

Area 7

Area 7 is used to record cross references. If a cross reference is to be made only for the Central Serial Record, it is merely desig-- nated x or xx. If a copy of the cross reference card is to be made for the public catalog as well, these designations are preceded by the letters "pc."

Cleanup: Old Runs of Series in Pre--AACR2 Form

Those series that cause the most work are those which the library formerly traced in pre--AACR2 entry form. Because the catalog is not closed, both the old and new forms of entry will exist in the same catalog and see also from references must be created between the forms. To minimize the difficulties with this situation we do two things. First, if the number of series tracings in the old form is few (up to 4 or so), we pull the old added entry cards and change them to the new form. Second, if the number of series tracings in the old form is large, we try to minimize the searching back and forth between the old and new forms by speci-- fying where in the run the change to the new form occurs, running the series in the old form up to that point, and then running the series in the new form after that point. Examples and further dis--

cussion of this are given earlier in this paper. The librarian's task is to establish how many series added entries are in the public catalog under the old form of entry and split the file as best she can. Clean-up of the library's archive tape to match the split files in the paper public catalog was abandoned a while ago. Series were not con-trolled by the serials department for the half–million records which went on to the archive tape during the library's retrospective conver-sion of monographs. Entering the current series authority file on–line and passing it against the archive tape records will have to be the way the archive tape gets cleaned up, should the library ever actually use its tape to create a full on--line catalog of its own.

Added Entries for Serials and Supplements to Serials

Sometimes the collective title which the librarian is asked to evaluate is a serial title used as an added entry. In most cases the serial title will appear in a 630 or 730 field. The check--in personnel will have validated any of these fields which match a serial title in the Central Serial Record. The librarian will be presented with those pieces whose records have added entries for serials or periodi--cals which this library does not have. She will search standard sources for verification that the added entry field contains the correct formulation of the serial entry and validate the field on the printout by initialling it. She will then make an information card recording that the serial exists in the library only in an added entry field. An example of this kind of card is shown on p. 17 above.

Supplements to serials and periodicals are treated within the framework of the series authority worksheet, but are handled ac--cording the Library of Congress rule interpretations relating to rule 21.30G, most recently revised in *Cataloging Service Bulletin* 20.[2] The statement relating to the supplement in the description area of the record is recorded in a 500 note field rather than in a series field, and the added entry for the supplement is recorded in a 730, or title added entry field, rather than in the 830, or series added entry field. The librarian writes in the field tags on the worksheet since they are not provided for. The authority record that results looks like a series authority record but has field tags which are not series fields:

```
Annals of photography. ‡n Vol. ___ (Supplement _)
   New York : American Council of Photography,  19-- -

SCATTER  730 Ø1
500 ƀƀ  "Supplement _ to Annals of photography,
volume __."

Library has:
   v.44, sup 1-2
   v.45, sup 1

pt. of sub.
```

Typing

Because the Central Serial Record is a card file, the series deci--
sions and disposition decisions must be recorded on cards. The series
decision worksheets are passed to a typist who types all the cards,
including cross references according to a manual for the transfer
of this information to cards.   The typist spends about half time
typing the cards, supervising a student typist who also types cards.
After the cards are typed, they are returned, with the worksheets,
to the decision--making librarian who revises the typing. The cards
are filed into the Central Serial Records (and cross references associ--
ated with them are filed into the public catalog) within regular
filing routines.

Very briefly, the typing rules are as follows:

Use hanging idention throughout
Type the information from Area 2 at the top of the card
Start a new line and type the information from Area 3
Skip two lines
Type the information from Area 4
   If an 8xx field is circled in Area 4, start a new line and
   type the information from Area 1, preceeded by 490 1b
Skip two lines
Type the information from Area 5
Skip two lines
Type the information from Area 6
If there is any information in Area 7, type the word "(over)"

at the bottom right of the card
Turn the card over, hole up
Type the information in Area 7.

Type a white cross reference card for any cross reference starting with x or xx.

Type a white *and a buff* cross reference card for any cross reference starting with pcx or pcxx.

Revision and Management

Any technical service activity that requires both judgements and a high degree of detailed accuracy in the resulting products of those judgements is usually backed up by a revising process. The revisor is a double check that judgements made were sound and that most errors of detail are caught. Such activities also require someone who acts as the overall manager of the process and who keeps the overall picture in mind. The manager keeps up to date with the latest changes in bibliographic handling, creates manuals of procedures for the various aspects of the activity and modifies those manuals in the light of bibliographic changes, trains staff, organizes and oversees the workflow, acts as a problem solver for the staff and provides liaison with other library activities. At this point in the serials department's control of series titles, the manager devotes some 10 to 15% of her time to overseeing the procedure and revising series authority work.

At the present time, there are two large in–house manuals and two small instruction manuals which govern the activities of series control. The local *Series Handbook* is a compilation of all sections of AACR2 and all Library of Congress rule interpretations relating to series, supplements, and the like. It is updated with each issue of new rule interpretations in *Cataloging Service Bulletin.* The local *Series Decision Manual* is a large compendium of instructions and examples which explains how this library handles series situa-tions.

The *Series Decision Manual* includes detailed sections on the following topics:

General instructions
Decision theory
Author/title entry
Conferences
Cross references
"His" series
Holdings statements

Imprint
Made--up series
Non--series
Notes
Numbering
Parallel titles
Previously classed together series
SCATTER area of the worksheet
Second series
Sets
730 and 630 situations
Split files pre-- and post--AACR2
Statements of responsibility
Subseries
Subtitle, other title information
Supplements
Title
Title changes
Uniform title

In addition to these manuals which essentially cover the theory of series management, there is a typing manual and a manual of procedure for the check--in personnel.

Training has been done both on an individual basis and in work--shops which covered the nature of series, the MARC coding for series and serial added entries, searching techniques for accessing items in a series, and various other matters.

Undertaking Series Authority Control

In undertaking series authority control, the serials department had to work out several logistical questions, and these can now be discussed in the light of over two years of experience.

1) How much work are we talking about? How many monographs are coming into the library and how many have series associated with the work?

We did a brief initial test on several trucks of monographs chosen at random before we began series control. We found at that time that 50% of the items on those trucks were part of some kind of series. Of that 50%, half had series which were not in our authority file. We have just recently run another informal test, monitoring all items received through the gifts and order departments over a six--week period. In this latter test we found that only about 25%

of the items were part of a series. The percentage of titles not in our authority file, or in our authority file but needing new records in the new format remained the same at about half. The reason that the statistics on the number of items that have series varies so widely is probably due to the haphazard nature of the test procedures. In any case, it seems to be true that the serials department is seeing at least a quarter of the monographs that enter the library because a series is involved.

2) Can the serials department handle that workload?

For purposes of comparison with other libraries, it should be stated that this library has some 18,000 standing orders and subscriptions and receives some 30,000 monographs a year through order and gifts. (The total collection size is some 1.6 million volumes and another 1.7 million microform items.) Approximately the following time is spent by library workers on series control: The gifts and order departments which do the initial searching routinely search for records anyway, whether series are involved or not. The equivalent of about 15% of one person's time is involved in spotting collective titles and routing them to serials. The serials department check--in personnel spend about the equivalent of 40% of one person's time processing series as opposed to the ordinary check--in of serials. The serials cataloger in charge of decisions spends about 50% of her time in hadling series/serial decisions. The serials department typist spends about 50% of her time typing series authority records and related records. The supervisor spends perhaps 15% of her time revising the work, keeping the manuals up to date and overseeing the entire process.

3) What degree of control will be maintained by the serials department?

Because our previous authority system was gravely inadequate and because compliance with that system had fallen to a woeful level, we decided to keep total control of the series in the serials department, at least initially. That meant that the monographic catalogers would not even be able to consult the series authority records and code their series fields from it. Every series occurring on an OCLC printout or needing to be added to a printout would be coded or added by serials department personnel who then initialled the relevant fields. The OCLC monographic inputters were instructed not to input a record that included a series field that was not initialled by someone from the serials department.

This degree of control may sound appalling, and, in fact, at this point in time seems excessive to me, but it was a product of various aspects of the local situation and is still in place. The system is working well and is not so far placing an intolerable burden on the serials department. A side effect that should have ben foreseen, but was not, is that the monographic catalogers have become so used to having the series coded for them that they have often not kept up with the changes caused by AACR2 and LCRI and many no longer know how to formulate and code series at all. This is unfortunate, and I would take the opportunity to warn others that this degree of control may not ultimately be wise.

4) Where should the series authority file be physically kept?

In order for the serials department to manage series, the series authority records need to be kept near the serials personnel. Moving the authority records out of the name authority file and into the Central Serial Record was a logical move for this library. However, the physical location of the series authority records in the serials department makes it as difficult for the monographic catalogers to easily access the records as it was difficult for the serials depart-- ment to access the records when they were located in the name authority file in the monographic cataloging department. Libraries which have less physical separation between the departments might find other solutions viable. We would reemphasize the value, how-- ever, of interfiling the series authority records with serials records.

5) What local peculiarities exist that will affect the conventions and usages of the series authority records?

The chief local factor that affected the construction of the series authority structure in this library was the decision not to close our catalog and start a new AACR2 catalog. This decision meant that old forms of entry would exist in our catalog alongside the new form, with extensive cross referencing between the two, with interfiling in some cases, and with informational cards explain- ing the interfiling.

In the case of series this meant that many series would be al- lowed to exist in split files. The old form of the series entry (for instance, a corporate body/title entry) would be allowed to remain in the catalog for the pieces of the series already cataloged, and the new form of entry (for instance, a uniform title), would enter the catalog as new pieces of the series were cataloged.

The only different between this situation and the situation of a library that has closed its old catalog is that for us it is often necessary to create two authority records for the same series and to generate references linking the old and the new forms *both* ways. In a library that has closed its old catalog, it is possible to create links going only one way – from the old catalog to the new, or from the new catalog to the old, but not necessarily both ways. The fact that we consistently provide links both to and from the old form of entry pleases us. Our public catalog is akin to the OCLC online union catalog which contains records with series tracings in both old and new forms depending on when the cataloging was done (and who did it). However, our system also includes see also from references for the catalog generated by the series authority system.

6) Who will do the work?

Bringing series validation into the check–in process enabled us to fit the process into an existing set of procedures with a minimum of difficulty. The identification of items with series at the time of searching, the check–in/validation process, and the decision-making on new titles were all treated as simple extensions of procedures that already existed. The flow of items through the system was the principle area that had to be altered. The design of the authority records was the other major change.

7) What effects does the availability or future availability of MARC series authority records on–line in the OCLC system have on this procedure?

At the present time, when series are still not directly searchable in OCLC, the chief use of MARC records is as an occasional informational source. It will probably remain merely an informational source for some time to come, even when the records are routinely available. Having our own authority records on–line is a very distant future possibility. Someday it would be wonderful to encode our series authority data into machine readable form and pass the authority file against our own active record catalog. At such time, we could stop the process of splitting files by old and new forms of entry, convert all series to AACR2 form, and then rethink the entire procedure for getting new items properly coded. Until that time, we are, and must continue to be, bound by our own local split--file policies which govern our forms of entry. The MARC OCLC file will become a greater and greater source of information for the construction of AACR2 series entries and a source of information about national practice. We are, and will remain, committed to conforming to national practice in the construction of AACR2 entries but we also have a commitment to our local practice.

Conclusion

In sum, the present system of series authority control works for us with a minimum of difficulty, is not an intolerable burden on the serials department, saves monographic catalogers a lot of time, and does a better job of controlling series than we ever man-- aged to do before.

FOOTNOTES

1. "Library of Congress Rule Interpretations." *Cataloging Service Bulletin* 20:8--10 (Spring 1983).

2, "Library of Congress Rule Interpretations." *Cataloging Service Bulletin* 20:11 (Spring 1983).

Analytical Access:
Old Problems, New Frontiers

Karen Roughton
Head, Catalog Management
and
John K. Duke
OCLC Systems Specialist
Iowa State University

Traditional library processing methods die hard. Technological changes in the publishing world, such as on–line indexing systems, are beginning to obviate the need for much of the detailed catalog-ing that takes place in many libraries. Few of us can envision the changes that may occur over the rest of this century, and most of us only attempt to respond piecemeal to automation rather than overhauling technical services each time technology leaps forward. One of the most convoluted library functions that will gradually disappear is local processing and cataloging of analytics.

The flexibility of a catalog derives from its ability to treat one item in many ways. For example, a catalog entry may be made for any of several authors or for a variety of subjects. The user is not restricted to one way of approaching the record. Librarians have devised a similar method to provide access to materials that have been grouped together in a single classification number as sets or serials, but for which it is also desirable to treat one or more of the units as individual bibliographical records in their own right. These individual units are called "analytics," and the process of creating them is called "analysis."

Iowa State University (ISU) librarians have developed a set of policies and procedures to accommodate analytical cataloging. The routines have been shaped by a variety of conditions peculiar to ISU, including separate Serials and Monographs departments with their own cataloging sections within the Technical Services Division an Order Department that processes only monographic orders and receipts, a separate computer–produced book catalog of serial holdings,[1] and dependence upon the Online Computer Library Center (OCLC) for cataloging. The procedures also have been defined by constraints that affect all libraries: the time, money, and staff available for analysis, the nature of the collection and its patrons, and the existence of other analytical tools.

Organization and Staffing

Because serial analytics cross the boundaries of both the Mono-graphs and Serials Departments at ISU, close coordination, open communication, and detailed, written procedures are vital to the success of efficient processing.

Lynn Smith maintains that the responsibility for cataloging serial analytics should rest squarely with the serials department.[2] She feels that bibliographic control is better, that decisions can be made more quickly and records updated faster, and that cata-loging can be done by people who are experienced in the problems of serials when total responsibility is vested in the serials department.

ISU is aware of the problems in splitting bibliographic control between two departments, and has taken steps to minimize the difficulties. The most important organizational principle has been to assign monographic staff specific duties for cataloging analytics, rather than scattering the cataloging among all members of the department. This has the advantage of concentrating the attention of a few people on the problems of analytics, yet allowing those who are experts in monographic cataloging to catalog what is essen-tially a monograph according to the appropriate rules. One librarian, the Analytic Cataloger, is responsible for original cataloging of analytics. She also defines and writes procedures and resolves problems. She is assisted by a paraprofessional (Library Assistant III), who does the analytics with cataloging copy from the Library of Congress and other OCLC contributing libraries.

The clerical and paraprofessional staff in the Serials Department comes into contact with analytics during the check-in process. The staff at the visible check-in file is trained to spot the occasional issue that needs analysis but for which no formal decision about the series has been made. They are, therefore, a crucial link in the processing chain. The head of the Serials Acquisitions Section, a librarian who is responsible for the check-in records, takes an active role in identifying serials for analysis.

The cataloging staff in the Serials Department does not perform the analytical cataloging. A serials cataloger, however, can decide that a serial should be fully or partially analyzed when a serial is cataloged. Ambiguous cases are resolved by the head of the Serials Cataloging Section. If the question cannot be satisfactorily settled within the Serials Department, it is referred to the Analytic Cataloger within the Monographs Department or to the Cataloging Decisions Committee, a Technical Services Division committee.

Identifying and Controlling Analytics

ISU has developed some general guidelines to follow for identi-fying titles for analysis. The most important concern is that each

Figure 1

DS485 H6 F684	\multicolumn{8}{l}{Forschungsunternehmen Nepal Himalaya.}

DS485 H6 F684   Forschungsunternehmen Nepal Himalaya.

ANALYZED SET

VOL. OR NO	PERIOD COVERED	IMPRINT DATE	DATE OF RECEIPT	VOL. OR NO.	PERIOD COVERED	IMPRINT DATE	DATE OF RECEIPT	CLAIMS
v.8,t.1	Geschichte und beitragen sozialordnung der...	1968	7-12-72					
v.9,t.2	Religioses leben der Sherpa	1969	7-12172					
v.10	Materielle kultur und kunst der Sherpa	1975	3-15-76					
v.11	Anthropologie der Sherpa	1977	4-26-78					

SOURCE Harrassowitz

PUBLISHER Univ. Verl. Wagner München

Figure 2

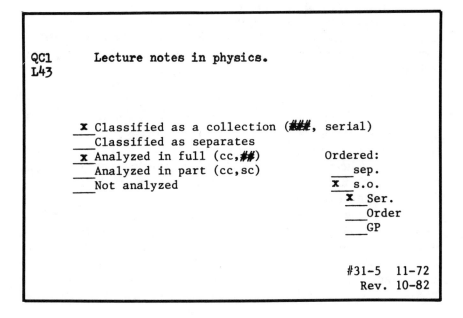

QC1
L43

Lecture notes in physics.

x Classified as a collection (###, serial)
___ Classified as separates
x Analyzed in full (cc,##)   Ordered:
___ Analyzed in part (cc,sc)   ___ sep.
___ Not analyzed   x s.o.
                                 x Ser.
                                 ___ Order
                                 ___ GP

#31-5   11-72
Rev. 10-82

issue have a title distinct from the series or serial title. Usually this means that the issue focuses on a particular subject. Serial issues that touch on subjects crucial to the academic programs at ISU, as well as the proceedings of conferences, congresses, and symposia, are good candidates for analysis. International conferences are always analyzed, while Festschriften are often analyzed. If the Monographs Department receives a monographic order for an issue of a serial, the serial will always be analyzed. The requests of a subject bibliographer carry a large weight in the decision to analyze a serial. Although catalogers attempt to follow the treatment given a serial by the Library of Congress, they are not bound by any hard and fast rule. ISU does not generally analyze an item that does not have its own title page or title cover, or that cannot be cited as a complete monographic work -- e.g., articles, plays, -- within an issue.

Although the scope of what to analyze is fairly easy to define in theory, making certain that appropriate material is actually analyzed is a different matter. Analytical processing is complicated by the fact that analytics are handled by every library department involved with technical processing, each with its own bibliographic control files.

The Order Department is responsible for monographic sets, some of which are analyzed. Analytic decisions are recorded in a visible check-in file. The names of the individual titles in the set are also noted in the file (see figure 1). Order cards for sets that have not yet been received may have analytical information if this can be determined in advance.

The primary file for analytics in the Monographs Department is the series authority file (SAF). This file contains a record of every series held by ISU, its tracing decision, analytical treatment, call number if classed together, and other information (figure 2). Every serial or set that is fully or partially analyzed is recorded in this file, as well as those serials that ISU has decided not to analyze. Every monograph with a series is checked against the SAF before it is cataloged. The analytic catalogers maintain a second file of all the analyzed sets and serials that are currently received. This file duplicates much of the information on the SAF cards but may include some information the catalogers find useful when dealing with a particular title.

The Monographs Department maintains the shelf list, which includes a serial or set card only for all analyzed sets and serials. A reference card filed in front of the serial shelf list card for an analyzed set or serial refers the user to the "supplementary shelf list," which is a separate shelf list that contains only the individually analyzed titles. A reference card in the supplementary shelf list

Figure 3

QC1 L43 CAT.A	LECTURE NOTES IN PHYSICS/							
VOL. OR NO. / PERIOD COVERED		IMPRINT DATE	DATE OF RECEIPT	VOL. OR NO.	PERIOD COVERED	IMPRINT DATE	DATE OF RECEIPT	CLAIMS
180	Group theoretical methods in physics	1983	6-14-83					
181	Gauge theories in the eighties	1983	7-12183					
182	Laser physics	1983	7-12-83					
183	Intro. to the theory of metastable and...	1983	7-12-83					

SOURCE Direct PUBLISHER Springer Verlag
175 Fifth Ave.
New York, NY 10010

Figure 4

Q334 A8 Part. CAT.A	SIGART NEWSLETTER/ Any issue called: SYMPOSIUM, WORKSHOP, CONFERENCE, INT'L. CONF., PROCEEDINGS OF..., etc. is PART. CAT.A															
Year	Vol.	JAN.	FEB.	MAR.	APR.	MAY	JUNE	JULY	AUG.	SEPT.	OCT.	NOV.	DEC.	Date of Bill	Period covered	COST	CLAIMS
1982		79 2-15			80 5-21			81 9-3			82 10-2						
1983		83 2-18			84 5-27			85 8-12									

SOURCE Direct PUBLISHER Association for Computing Machinery
Special Interest Group for Artificial
Intelligence
1133 Ave. of the Americas
New York, NY 10036

185

Figure 5

QA76
L4

MATHEMATICAL FOUNDATIONS OF COMPUTER SCIENCE/

Also checks in on card for LECTURE NOTES IN COMPUTER SCIENCE/

CAT. to ADD

VOL. OR NO.	PERIOD COVERED	IMPRINT DATE	DATE OF RECEIPT	VOL. OR NO.	PERIOD COVERED	IMPRINT DATE	DATE OF RECEIPT	CLAIMS
53	1977	1977	9-7-77					
64	1978	1978						
74	1979							
88	1980							
118	1981							

SOURCE Direct

LECTURE NOTES IN COMPUTER SCIENCE/

MATHEMATICAL FOUNDATIONS OF COMPUTER SCIENCE/ has own card and is CAT. to ADD

CAT.A

QA76
L4

VOL. OR NO.	PERIOD COVERED	IMPRINT DATE	DATE OF RECEIPT	VOL. OR NO.	PERIOD COVERED	IMPRINT DATE	DATE OF RECEIPT	CLAIMS
149	Cryptography	1983	4-7-83					
150	Enduser Systems and their human factors	1983	4-15-83					
151	CONLAN Report	1983	5-4-83					
152	Specification and design of software	1983	5-25-83					
153	Graph-grammars and their application...	1983	7-27-83					

SOURCE Direct

PUBLISHER Springer Verlag
175 Fifth Ave.
New York, NY 10010

186

refers the user back to the primary shelf list for the set or serial cataloging. Every issue that is analyzed receives a series added entry in the card catalog.

The most important file in the Serials Department is the serial check–in file, which contains information on each of the more than 17,000 serial titles ISU currently receives. Library staff work-- ing at the check--in file record each issue of a title as it is received by the Serials Department. The person processing the issue also looks at the check--in card as a source of information about the title, including whether or not it is analyzed. Government publica-- tion serials received in the Government Publications Department are checked in by clerks and processed following similar procedures. The Serials Department also records analytical decisions in the serials catalog and on a main entry card known as the "official."

As with many aspects of technical services, routines that have a significant effect on how successful a user will be in retrieving the material are concentrated at rather low levels of the library hierarchy. If a decision has been made by a librarian to analyze a serial completely, the check--in card is marked "CAT. A." and annotated with the appropriate call number (figure 3). It is the responsibility of the check--in staff to notice this at the point of receipt. If each issue of a title should be analyzed, the staff member sends the issue to a paraprofessional (Library Assistant III) who does the initial processing, including making certain that there is the required link in the serials book catalog referring users to the card catalog for the analyzed issues. If no analytic note exists, or if the analytic note is incorrect, the library assistant forwards the correct information to Serials Cataloging so that analytic notes are added or changed. The library assistant also checks the issue for other important details, such as the presence of a subseries that must be noted on the check--in card and in the serials catalog, before sending the issue on to be analyzed.

Serials that are only partially analyzed are noted "Partial CAT. A." (i.e., partially cataloged as an analytic) on the check--in card (figure 4). The staff member who checks these issues in forwards them to the Serials Acquisitions Librarian, who decides if an issue should be analyzed. For some questionable cases she may consult another librarian, such as a subject bibliographer, regarding the desirability of analyzing a particular issue. If a decision is made to analyze the issue, it is sent to the LA III, who processes it as described earlier.

Some serials require more complicated processing than simply full or partial analysis. The check--in card may be marked "CAT. To ADD" or "Partial CAT. A/CAT to Add" or "CAT. A/CAT To ADD" (figure 5). These are serials for which there is a subseries.

The subseries is an analytical part of the main series, which may have its own cataloging. The parts that make up the subseries may or may not also need analysis. The check–in staff member must be alert to note both the main series and the subseries, and determine from the notation if they need analysis. They are then processed as usual.

When a librarian decides that a serial should be analyzed, links between the serials book catalog and the monographs card catalog must be established. The co--existence of the two catalogs at ISU makes for sometimes awkward conventions to preserve complete bibliographic control. It is important not only for patrons who are checking one catalog to know of additional records in the other, but also for staff who are performing maintenance on the catalogs, such as withdrawing or reclassifying a serial. Therefore the two catalogs are linked with standard phrases. For items in the card catalog that are analyzed, a card at the beginning of the series reads:

> This serial completely [partially] analyzed. For numerical listing see the following cards and/or shelf list.

At the same time, a note on the serials record reads:

> This title completely [partially] analyzed. For authors/ title of individual issues, see serial title in card catalog and/or call number in supplementary shelf list.

Monographic sets, some of which are analyzed, are received in the Order Department. Clerks who check in the monographic sets forward all volumes to the Monographs Department's Added Volume Cataloger, who adds the volume to the cataloging record for the set. If she discovers a title is an analytic, she forwards it to the Analytic Copy Cataloger, who completes the cataloging.

What we have described up to now are those titles that have been flagged at some point and a decision made regarding their treatment. Arriving at this stage is much more problematical. Ideal--ly, a new serial is identified at the point of acquisition or cataloging as one needing analysis. The same is true of monographic sets that are cataloged by the Monographs Department.

It is often difficult to predict the analytical treatment that will be appropriate over the course of a serial or set's existence. Typi--cally, these titles give no indication when they are ordered, received, or cataloged that there may be issues that need to be analyzed. The first few issues of a serial may not carry distinct titles, or the publisher may later devote an entire issue to the proceedings of a named conference, or include a special supplemental issue with the

serial. Backsets of serials that are ordered may contain issues re--
quiring analytic treatment. Library personnel who check--in the
serials are trained to spot these issues but inevitably there are some
that are not detected. There is a trade--off in many library opera--
tions between processing material efficiently and maintaining an
acceptable level of quality. Taylor calls this the "first great prin--
ciple" of serials work:

> libraries deal with serials by creating a routine for handling
> them that minimizes decisions . . . When a serial falls outside
> of the channels of the routine it is *routed to someone who*
> *is capable of making a decision about it.*[3]

The objective is to allow the majority of materials to be handled
at the lowest level of staff at which they can be processed compe--
tently, and to train the check--in staff to recognize the conditions
that require more qualified staff. The expense would be too great
if each issue of a serial had to be examined by a librarian to deter--
mine if it needed analysis. The check--in process is admittedly
the weakest link in the chain, since the clerk who is good at spotting
analyzed serials is certain to be promoted out of the position.

Checking in the serial is only the first line of defense against
errant analytics. Some issues are received and shelved before it
is determined that analysis is appropriate. A bibliographer, reading
room supervisor, or patron may recognize that greater access is
needed, and request analytic treatment. The issue is then sent to
the Monographs Department. At this point, other issues in the
series may be examined by an Analytic Cataloger to determine
if retrospective analytic cataloging is required. The check--in card
will then be annotated ("Partial CAT. A." or even "CAT. A.")
to alert the check–in staff to future analytical treatment.

Problem Analytics

It is difficult for any one person to retain all of the knowledge
associated with processing analytics. Our guidelines for identifying
analytics are straightforward, but publishers do not always take
pains to accommodate them. We find it is prudent in establishing
procedures for analytics that there be a mechanism to resolve the
difficult cases that inevitably arise. The Analytic Cataloger, based
in the Monographs Department, serves as liaison between all staff
members who handle analytics. Her experience with both mono--
graphs and serials enables her to identify and resolve analytic pro--
cessing problems.

One of the most important parts of her work is maintaining

```
┌─────────────────────────────────────────────────────┐
│            CATALOGING DECISIONS STREAMER             │
│  Tech Serv Rep:                    Date:             │
│  Bibliographer:                                      │
│  Serial/Set/Series Title:                            │
│                                                      │
│                                                      │
│  Background Data:                                    │
│  1.  Acquisitions:  Serials/Order/Gov Pubs           │
│         Purchase____  Gift____  Exch____  Deposit____ │
│         Standing order:  Serial/Set/Series           │
│         Separate order:  Serial/Set/Mono sep(s)       │
│  2.  Cataloging:                                     │
│        LC:                                           │
│                                                      │
│        NSDP:                                         │
│                                                      │
│        OCLC member:                                  │
│                                                      │
│        ISU:                                          │
│                                                      │
│                                                      │
│  3.  Cat treatment of Similar Serials/Sets/Series:   │
│                                                      │
│  4.  Comments:                                       │
│                                                      │
│                                                      │
│                                          Biblio-     │
│  Recommended Cataloging:   (initial)                 │
│                          Tech Serv Reps    grapher   │
│  CAT AS SERIAL          _____    ____      │
│  CAT AS MONO. SET       _____    ____      │
│  Analytic treatment for serial or set:               │
│    Part anal in cc      _____    ____      │
│    Full anal in cc      _____    ____      │
│    Part anal in sc      _____    ____      │
│    Full anal in sc      _____    ____      │
│    If anal in sc, list subseries wanted:             │
│                                                      │
│  CAT AS MONO SEP(S) _____        ____      │
│  DO NOT CATALOG                            ____      │
│  If a standing order is wanted, the Bibliographer    │
│  should submit either a Serials Request Order form   │
│  or an Order Card.                                   │
│  Comments:   (initial)                               │
└─────────────────────────────────────────────────────┘
```

Figure 6

the section of the monographs procedural manual that concerns analytics. She must define and document new procedures, and be alert for any snags or inefficiencies that should be rectified in the procedures. Currently, this section of the manual is a formidable 75 pages. Although the size is cumbersome, staff members who do not handle analytics on a regular basis welcome the opportunity to consult documented procedures. The guidelines also serve as an authoritative source to help resolve disagreements or ambiguities in processing. Because analytics are only one part of a complicated and interdependent library organization, it is often the case that a change in one part of technical services, or even the library at large, will disrupt the procedures for analytics. On the other hand, the Analytic Cataloger must also be aware of how analytic decisions might affect other parts of the library, thus drafts of proposed new procedures are routinely circulated by the Analytic Cataloger to all who might have an interest. Finally, documentation ensures continuity in the library.

Part of the Analytic Cataloger's responsibilities is to determine what should or should not be analyzed. In many instances she can make this determination on her own, using the established guidelines and her own knowledge. Sometimes, however, it is not clear what the treatment for a particular title should be. There might be doubt, for example, that the series should be classed together. Although the decision that the Library of Congress makes regarding a title carries significant weight for ISU catalogers, there might be important local reasons for varying from LC practice. It is also true, of course, that LC does not catalog every title that ISU receives, so local decisions must be made.

The Analytic Cataloger has two aids to assist her in determining the analytical treatment of a title. One is the Cataloging Decisions Committee (CDC). This committee was set up as a forum to decide on the manner in which materials should be cataloged when alternatives exist. The committee is composed of the heads of the Serials and Monographs Cataloging Sections, along with the heads of the Serials and Monographs Departments. In addition, the bibliographer into whose province the title falls will sit in on the committee's sessions. After a decision is made, it is recorded on the check-in card and the SAF (series authority file) card. The decision is noted on a form and returned with the issue in question (figure 6).

The existence of the CDC might be considered overkill given the level and number of staff involved. In fact, the CDC was set up before there was a professional Analytic Cataloger. There has been less need for the committee to consider analytics as the workflow around the Analytic Cataloger has matured. Difficult problems are usually handled by the Analytic Cataloger in conjunction with the heads of the Serials and Monographs Cataloging Sections. Quarterly meetings between the Analytic Catalogers and the head of the Serials Cataloging Section are held to discuss problems and to draft proposals to present to higher levels. This informal network has in many cases supplanted the need for the CDC in analytic work. The Assistant Director for Technical Services arbitrates the rare problem that cannot be resolved at the lower level.

Cataloging Analytics

OCLC has simplified cataloging analytics at ISU. One change has been the greater number of items that are analyzed, following the realization of the extent of LC analytical cataloging. The ready availability of contributed copy by members of OCLC has also fostered analytical cataloging at ISU, as it is generally easier to adjust member copy than it is to create an original cataloging record.

Cataloging analytics is a straightforward application of the principles for cataloging monographs, with a few important variations. This is the main reason why ISU has decided to locate analytical cataloging within the Monographs Department.

All analytic issues or volumes are sent to the Analytic Copy Cataloger, who searches OCLC for copy. If copy is found, the issue is cataloged at the terminal with the item in hand. If copy is not found, the item is held for three months and periodically searched. Some items are cataloged by the paraprofessional even though they do not have copy, such as volumes for which LC cataloged a different edition.

Certain fixed and variable fields in an LC record are examined, but others are ignored. It is assumed that most information on LC copy is correct, and it is not efficient to check for every possible error.

The call number field in particular is scrutinized. In recent years, ISU has accepted in almost all instances LC classification and shelflisting, but older sets and serials may have a locally assigned number. The classification number is recorded on the SAF card, and it is verified on the copy. In particular the call number "parsing," or OCLC rule for how call numbers are coded, is examined to make certain that it will print correctly on the cards. The length and complexity of analytical call numbers require that this be done with care.

If the analysis is for a multi-volume set within a larger set or series, the card for the whole set will be printed with the first volume number that is analyzed, followed by "etc." (Osborn frowns upon such an expedient, preferring to list all of the volume numbers in the call number.[4] ISU relies upon the series statement to inform the reader of the individual volume numbers, since we do not put the complete information there. If the set within the series is itself analyzed, each individual record in the set contains the entire call number, complete with its volume number.

The series is an important access point, and is rigorously checked. The authoritative form is found in the series authority file (SAF). For multi--volume sets within a numbered series, ISU makes one series added entry, with the range of numbers following, such as:

Space science series ; v. 23, no. 2–3.

However, ISU makes it a policy to create a separate series entry for each volume if the set has noncontinuous numbering; for example:

Proceedings of the Steklov Institute of Mathematics ; no. 74.
Proceedings of the Steklov Institute of Mathematics ; no. 77.
Proceedings of the Steklov Institute of Mathematics ; no. 89.

This is not standard LC practice, which is to give the first volume number followed by "etc."[5] ISU feels that the patron is better served by listing each volume number separately so that an entry may be found for each numbered volume. Nor do we agree with Osborn that users should have to consult an outside source, such as LC's *Monographic Series,* in order to find the titles under the series.[6] The flexibility of OCLC easily permits us to change the series statement and create a new card set with the additional series tracing.

If copy is not found for an item after the three month holding period, it is sent to the Aanlytic Cataloger. Original cataloging is performed according to OCLC and LC guidelines.

AACR2 and Analytics

The second edition to the *Anglo–American Cataloguing Rules* (AACR2) has had a significant impact on the procedures at Iowa State. ISU changes all headings in its card catalog to the AACR2 form as new entries are added in order to maintain the integrity of the catalog. To date, some 4400 names and 1200 serial or series titles have been modernized in the card catalog.

Changing or establishing the form of the series requires coordination between the Monographs and Serials Departments. Many serial analytics have been established in a pre–AACR2 form and the correct form of the entry is not discovered until it reaches the Monographs Department. If the Analytic Cataloger does not think that the series is in its proper AACR2 form, the item is re--turned to Serials Cataloging for evaluation. A serials cataloger will establish the new form of the heading, and ensure that all related serial records, such as the serial catalog and the check–in file, are updated. The issue with the new heading and a revised series author--ity file card is then returned to the Analytic Copy Cataloger, who is responsible for seeing that the old analytics in the card catalog are updated to the new form, and that the authority files in the Monographs Department reflect the new information.

Work that originates in the Serials Department may also cause a title to be upgraded to AACR2 form. If a librarian is revising the cataloging for a serial, the title will be examined for conformity with AACR2. If the title is changed and analytics are in the card catalog, the Analytic Cataloger is notified so that all files and cata--logs reflect the new heading.

Prognosis and Prescription

The success of any technical services operation depends on its ability to process efficiently the varied materials that pass through its doors. The goal in processing analytics at ISU is to create an efficient workflow, yet to try to ensure that all the material that requires attention receives high quality cataloging. The accretion of time and tradition have encumbered the process with redundant files and wasteful procedures, but it is part of the challenge of library work to discover and eradicate these inefficiencies. A com--plex organization with separate processing departments and separate catalogs compounds the difficulties; nevertheless, we are reasonably satisfied that we are accomplishing our goal.

We are disturbed, however, by the thought that our goal is too limited. We do provide a service to our patrons by describing and making accessible materials at the level of the individual volume. However, real analysis of a library's holdings requires indexing that goes beyond the title page to the actual contents -- the articles and essays that make up the volume. It is true that a reference librarian can point a patron to the various indexes and abstracts, each with its own idiosyncratic organization and conventions, or even perform a computerized search (for a fee) of one of the innumerable data bases now available. This is at best a tedious or expensive process.

A number of user studies suggest that naive library patrons often assume that the catalog contains citations to all of the material in a library, and those who know better wish it were so. The time and expense of checking external sources is considerable. Moreover, the proliferation of office and home microcomputers equipped with telephone modems and appropriate software threatens the library's pre--eminence as the primary source for bibliographic information. We possess, in effect, "the fund of analytics in some central information pool" that Daily envisioned 15 years ago.[7] It is no longer good enough. The problem has become one less of applying cataloging rules than of providing the operational frame--work into which outside records may be satisfactorily integrated.

Given the unlikelihood of libraries hiring armies of indexers, what is the future of detailed analytical cataloging? The answer must come from improved technology and innovative librarians. One direction might be that taken by Pauline Atherton Cochrane in her experimental Books Project,[8] in which the tables of contents and indexes to books were used to perform subject analysis, at a competitive cost to conventional cataloging. A similar structure might be used for descriptive analysis, and the results shared among libraries. Hyman has suggested adding detailed contents and sum--mary information to machine--readable records, and providing access to them for computer searching.[9] Assuming some such plan were implemented, the problem would then be to provide economical mass storage and efficient access. Although such a scheme would be feasible for limited monographic sets, it would not be possible for continuing serials.

Another alternative would be to have the current indexing services provide the citations, but allow libraries to subscribe to the machine--readable records on a selective basis according to their journal holdings. *Chemical Abstracts* has given a hint of how such a service might operate. *CA* is currently allowing institutions to copy ("download") up to 50,000 citations to a local system for in--house manipulation.[10] Journals that are not indexed by the vendors could be cooperatively indexed by libraries.[11] A library would probably want to keep this file logically separated from its monograph and serial files, and perhaps linked for call number and holdings information. Vendors would still be able to sell search services to libraries for items not in a particular collection. Again, mass storage and retrieval mechanisms would have to advance to accommodate such an ambitious project. Another hurdle would be to resolve problems in authority control, perhaps through a computerized switching mechanism to normalize names and terms.

The outline for this plan is not as futuristic as it may sound. At least one library has implemented such a catalog for 258 journals based on National Library of Medicine computer tapes.[12] The small number of indexed journals should not blind us to the possi- bilities of what tomorrow's computers may be able to accomplish. Although libraries would not have complete control over the des--

cription and indexing of analytics, they would be no further behind than they are at present.

Analytical cataloging is an exciting frontier for libraries to explore. We need to carve out a place for ourselves before our users defect to the emerging alternatives that cannot provide the same service or low cost that libraries have traditionally offered. Accelerating technology holds out the best promise for libraries, given that we possess the vision, the will -- and the finances -- to master it.

REFERENCES

1. Helen H. Spalding, "A Computer–Produced Serials Book Catalog with Automatically Generated Indexes," *Library Resources & Technical Services,* 24 (1980): 352–360.

2. Lynn S. Smith, *A Practical Approach to Serials Cataloging* (Greenwich, Conn.: Jai Press, c1978), p. 209.

3. David C. Taylor, *Managing the Serials Explosion: The Issues for Publishers and Libraries* (White Plains, N.Y.: Knowledge Industry Publications, c1982), p. 38.

4. Andrew D. Osborn, *Serial Publications: Their Place and Treatment in Libraires.* 3rd ed. (Chicago: American Library Association, 1980), p. 246.

5. Library of Congress. Processing Services, *Cataloging Service Bulletin,* 18 (1982): 48--49.

6. Osborn, p. 264.

7. Jay E. Daily, "Analytics," *Encyclopedia of Library and Information Science,* 1 (1968): 394.

8. *BOOKS Are for Use: Final Report of the Subject Access Project to the Council on Library Resources,* Pauline Atherton [Coch--rane], director (Syracuse, N.Y.: Syracuse University, School of Information Studies, 1978) (ERIC ED 156 131) For a summary article, see Barbara Settel and Pauline A Cochrane, "Augmenting Subject Descriptions for Books in Online Catalogs," *Database,* 5 (Dec. 1982): 29--37.

9. Richard J. Hyman, *Analytical Access: History, Resources, Needs* (Flushing, N.Y.: Queens College of the City University

of New York, 1978), pp. 29–31.

10. *"Chemical Abstracts* Pioneers Fee–Based Downloading from Its Database," *Library Journal,* 108 (1983): 1307.

11. Herbert H. Hoffman, "The Analytic Catalog," *Technicalities,* 1 (Feb. 1981): 12.

12. Pauline A. Cochrane, " 'Friendly' Catalog Forgives User Errors," *American Libraries,* 13 (1982): 304.

Standing--Order Series:
Serials or Monographs?

Betty Landesman
Serials Librarian
Wellesley College Library

There has been a great deal of discussion in recent years about the value or disservice of maintaining separate serials departments, "form vs. function," and the like. One of the topics in question is the handling of monographic series on standing order, straddling as they do both the monographic and serial worlds. Individual volumes must be checked in, or claimed if not received, as for any serial; individual volumes must also be fully analyzed to make their contents accessible, as for any monograph. In January 1982, the Wellesley College Library adopted a procedure that crosses the boundary lines and allows Catalog and Serials Department staff to each do what they do best.

Background

The technical services function at Wellesley is divided into three departments: Acquisitions, Catalog, and Serials. Monographic cataloging is done by Catalog Department personnel; serials catalog-- ing is done by the Serials Department. The Serials Librarian also serves as a resource person if there is a question on a form of series tracing, while the Senior Catalog Librarian is the authority on name headings. All departments are housed in one large open room, making such cross--fertilization easy. All volumes on standing order, including monographic series for main or department libraries, are routed directly to the Serials Department for checking in. All records in the Serials Department, including the check--in card, match the form of cataloging entry exactly. Series on standing order are distinguished in the card catalog by the addition of a full set of catalog cards for the series as a serial publication; the main entry card precedes the individual series added entry cards (figure 1).

Traditionally, Serials cataloged everything that came into the department, including items in monographic series. This formed an exception to the division of monographic and serials cataloging.

Figure 1

```
|‾‾‾‾‾‾‾‾‾‾‾‾‾‾‾‾‾‾‾‾‾‾‾‾‾‾‾‾‾‾‾‾‾‾‾‾‾‾‾‾‾‾‾‾‾‾‾|
|          Smithsonian folklife studies ; no. 1.|
| NK                                            |
| 4210      Rinzler, Ralph.                      |
| M35R56      The Meaders family, north Georgia  |
|           potters / Ralph Rinzler and Robert   |
```
```
|‾‾‾‾‾‾‾‾‾‾‾‾‾‾‾‾‾‾‾‾‾‾‾‾‾‾‾‾‾‾‾‾‾‾‾‾‾‾‾‾‾‾‾‾‾‾| .           |
|                                             | 1)          |
|    Smithsonian folklife studies. -- No. 1-  |             |
|    date       . -- Washington, D.C. :       |             |
|    Smithsonian Institution Press, 1980-     |             |
|    date                                     |             |
|      v. : ill. ; 23 cm.                     |             |
|    FOR INDIVIDUAL WORKS IN THIS SERIES      |             |
|  SEE CARDS FOLLOWING.                       |             |
|                                             | itle        |
|                                             |             |
|                                             |             |
|                                             |             |
|    1. Ethnology--Collected works.           | 7995        |
|  2. United States--Social life and          |             |
|  customs--Collected works.                  |             |
|                                             |             |
|                                             |             |
| MWelC   14 DEC 81   s            WELLat      |             |
|_____|             |
```

200

We had a standing order with LC for all analytics cards for series received on subscription. The Serials Librarian received the cards, checked all headings, made notes for a typist, and revised the cards before filing. If LC didn't analyze something that we did, the Serials Librarian did the cataloging. Around 1967, we started getting depository cards which had to be duplicated; otherwise the process remained the same.

In 1973, Wellesley went on OCLC; this necessitated changes in all cataloging procedures. Serials now typed multi–part slips for the monographs it received. The slips contained descriptive cataloging for the book, an indication of whether it was to be classified separately or together, and the form of series tracing to be used; the classification and series information was taken from the check–in record. At this point, a distinction was made between series classed separately and series classed together. If the item was to be classed separately, the slip and book were turned over to the Catalog Department to be searched and integrated into their workflow. If it was part of a series we classed together, Serials continued to deal with it. The slips were filed to be searched on OCLC, printouts were made and edited from the slips, and the Serials Librarian or Serials Assistant produced the cards.

By 1981, a number of factors had contributed to a reexamination of how we were handling these monographs. High on the list, as for so many other things, was the implementation of AACR2. As a new volume of each series is received, the Serials Librarian checks the form of series tracing for AACR2 compatibility and indicates any changes necessary. Internal Serials and Acquisitions records are fairly simple to adjust, but retyping catalog cards and generating appropriate cross references encompass a much larger field of operations, especially if it also involves a second catalog in a department library. On the other hand, this is just the sort of thing at which the Catalog Department has become quite skilled, as they are handling all the AACR2–mandated name heading changes.

A number of other internal procedures were gradually coming under scrutiny as well. Once upon a time, as every library did, Wellesley had the time, money, and staff to follow more non–standard and/or idiosyncratic practices than we can now afford to do. We were doing analytics for titles like *Essays by Divers Hands* and adding the contents of anthologies of plays to catalog cards. At the time these titles were set up, the quality of indexing was not as good as it is today; but since these things are now accessible through various indexes, we felt it was no longer justifiable to spend the time and money to provide that depth of analysis through the card catalog. We were also not analyzing each series to the same degree. Most series had full sets of cataloging cards produced for each volume in the usual way, but some had only author and title cards generated, or only a title card, or no separate cards but the author and title were typed on the series card. These different treatments obviously could not be processed in the usual way. When all cards were being typed anyway we could handle this sort of thing easily; but since we are now doing everything on OCLC and no longer have an army of typists available, it was clearly to our advantage to try to standardize our handling of ana--lytics.

Not least among the considerations leading to change were organizational and in a sense "political" ones. Any library that has a separate serials department finds that occasionally items that should have come to serialists are being handled by monograph people, and vice versa. Monographs in series not on standing order come to Serials because they *look* like something we handle. Other monographs that should be checked in bypass Serials and wind up on a cataloger's desk. A volume of an annual is cataloged in the "regular" way and not referred to Serials for cataloging, because after all, we only have the one. At the risk of supplying ammunition to those who would abolish separate serials departments, I will admit that a certain amount of time is occasionally spent defending one's turf. At any rate, when Serials complained about non--serialists cataloging items we felt should have come to us, Cataloging could justifiably point out that after all, we were doing monographs, so why shouldn't they do serials?

It was therefore agreed that in the interests of consistency and efficiency we should take a good look at how we were handling our standing--order monographic series which are analyzed ("anals," for short). Serials and Catalog Departments, together with the Associate Librarian for Technical Services, met over a period of time and worked out new procedures that we find are working very well.

Current Procedures

The Clerical Assistant in Serials checks in the volume as usual and counts it for our monthly statistics. She writes the call number (if the series is classed together) and fund (if any) on the verso of the title page; if the volume is soft cover, she also stamps "Welles--ley College Library" on the verso. This matches exactly our proce--dures for checking in materials that are not analyzed. The classifica--tion and fund information, together with the way the series is to be traced, whether or not it is in AACR2 form, and any special notes on handling are all contained in one place on the check--in

202

card (figure 2). If the series is not indicated as being in AACR2 form, the volume is referred to the Serials Librarian to verify the heading. She indicates the correct form and whether a cross–reference is to be made.

The Clerical Assistant in Serials then types a six–part slip for each book. This slip corresponds to slips that are generated in pre–order searching for all monographs that are *not* on standing order. The slip contains bibliographic information through the imprint area (author, title, place of publication, publisher, date) and the series statement in the form in which the series is to be traced. If the series is classed together, the call number is typed on the slip (figure 3); if it is classed separately, the call number area is left blank (figure 4). The series statement is in AACR2 form, as verified by the Serials Librarian, indicated by "=cn" appearing after the parentheses. This designation is one that catalogers are accustomed to seeing, indicating an AACR2 form of name heading appearing in converted OCLC records. If this is the first volume where the series is traced in a changed form from pre–AACR2 practice, the slip also indicates a cross–reference to be made from the old form (figure 5). This alerts Catalog Department staff that cards under the old form of series tracing in the card catalog need to be changed.

The six–part slip, together with any special instructions, is then inserted in the book to be sent on to the Catalog Department. Cataloging assistants search OCLC for copy. If LC copy is available the book is processed according to the regular routing except that a flat clip is placed on the slip to indicate that the title will not be counted when cards are received from OCLC. (The volume was already counted when it was checked in.) If LC copy is not yet available, the book is held for regular follow–up searching. In other words, these monographs are now integrated into the regular monographic cataloging workflow. Serials never sees the book again. If changes in choice or form of entry or in descriptive cataloging need to be made to the slips, Cataloging can proceed without consulting us because we acknowledge their expertise in monographic cataloging; they in turn are expected to follow our indications as to classification and series form.

Conclusion

These new procedures went into effect in January 1982. Since that time, the operation has been running very smoothly, with remarkably few bugs needing to be worked out of the system. We have added some modifications upon request. For example, after trying it out for a while Cataloging asked us to add the date

Figure 2

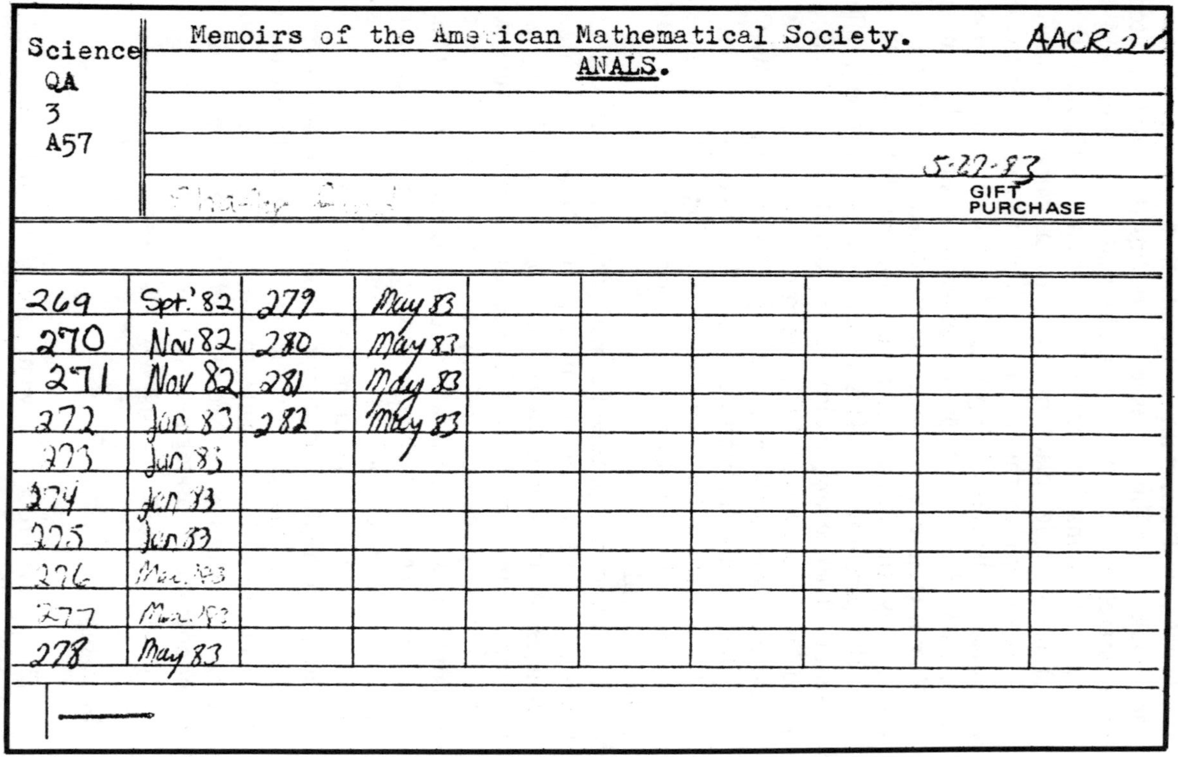

Science
QA
3
A57

Memoirs of the American Mathematical Society.   AACR2

ANALS.

5-22-83

GIFT
PURCHASE

269	Sept'82	279	May 83
270	Nov 82	280	May 83
271	Nov 82	281	May 83
272	Jun 83	282	May 83
273	Jun 83		
274	Jun 83		
275	Jun 83		
276	Mar 83		
277	Mar 83		
278	May 83		

Figure 3

```
Science
QA        Akin, Ethan, 1946-
3           Hopf bifurcation in the two locus genetic
A57       model / Ethan Akin. Providence, R.I. :
no.284    American Mathematical Society, 1983. (Memoirs
          of the American Mathematical Society ; no.
          284)=cn
ANAL.




                                              8-1-83
```

Figure 4

```
          Grossberg, Kenneth Alan.
            Japan's renaissance : the politics of the
          Muromachi Bakufu / Kenneth Alan Grossberg.
          Cambridge, Mass. : Council on East Asian
          Studies, Harvard University, 1981. (Harvard
          East Asian monographs ; 99)=cn
ANAL.




                                          8-1-83
```

Figure 5

```
JA        SALT handbook : key documents and issues
28          1972-1979 / edited by Roger P. Labrie.
A314      Washington, D.C. : American Enterprise
214       Institute for Public Policy Research, 1979.
          (AEI studies ; 214)=cn

ANAL.


x American Enterprise Institute for Public Policy
    Research. Studies.
                                          8-1-83
```

to the six–part slip so that if the book is not processed immediately they have some idea how long it has been around. The Acquisitions Department asked us to pull one of the six parts of the slip before sending it on for filing in their "in–process" drawer, as is done regularly for all monographs not on standing order. This has pro-- vided an added safeguard against accidentally ordering a book we already receive. Serials has been happy to comply with these requests, but in fact alterations to the originally planned procedure have been minimal.

We find that the Catalog Department has been able to absorb the extra books and the extra card catalog adjustments with little or no difficulty. In fact, I am sure that materials are being processed more quickly than when they were waiting in Serials for time to be found for them to be inserted into an already overfull, otherwise all--serial workload. We have basically separated the monographic and serial aspects of these standing–order analyzed monographic series, and allowed each department to handle those aspects which are most appropriate to it. Some people may think that we are carry the "form vs. function" division to extremes. However, here at Wellesley all the participants are happy with the present system and, more to the point, it works.

Series Control and Procedures

Jean Decker
Head, Serials Cataloging
State University of New York at Buffalo Library

Background

In the beginning, some editor/publisher/vendor said, "Eureka! I shall create a thing of beauty that will serve to identify, relate, and sell our titles." On the heels of that thought came the idea of a "supertitle" with a scholarly, subject–oriented tone and a uniform binding to lend esthetic neatness. From that day to this the monographic series has held fast in all its homogeneous and monochromatic glory. Actually series today are not quite monochromatic in color nor homogeneous in content. Their only constant aspect is a "supertitle" which may not sound scholarly at all.

The series is an element of description that librarians once upon a time could choose to take or leave. The choice is no longer available. In the automated present the series is a full–blown access point which has to be controlled with the best procedures we can devise. In order to assure a complete searchable series file, the entry for every part of a series has to be entered in exactly the same form and that form has to be tagged consistently to permit retrieval of the total file. The traditional means of controlling consistency is the authority file. That brings up the questions of how one keeps the authority file consistent. Years of experience have shown that control needs to be centralized. "Centralized" can mean one section, one group, or one person has the decision–making responsibility. To determine what will work best in your processing operation, consider your own organization and personnel.

Administration

Series control and how it can best be accomplished is at least a three–faced administrative problem. 1) What degree of automation exists? None, some, or complete? (2) How's the organization arranged? What are the working relationships and responsibilities of sections and departments? 3) What are the skills, experience, and numbers of the staff?

Fact 1, automation, may be an administrative "given." Let's assume that most libraries have access to a bibliographic utility and are cataloging online. They also have the capability of searching whatever name and series authority records the Library of Congress has made available. Perhaps a library is building and maintaining its own authority files online. Whatever the degree of automation, terminal time needs to be arranged for the individual(s) checking for correct AACR2 forms of series, tracing decisions, title proper conflicts, i.e., two different series with identical titles proper, and correct AACR2 forms of names used as qualifiers of series and/or in references.

Fact 2, the organization, can come in as many varieties as there are technical services operations in existence. Monographic series control will in most instances fall into the cataloging or serials department. A workflow that was already in place when AACR2 was implemented may have determined where or when monographic series decisions would be made. Take a look. Is efficiency and con--sistency being best served by your present arrangements?

Fact 3, the people, are the most crucial and non--standard variables in the equation. Monographic series are hard to search. The guidelines are somewhat vague. There are series within series, serials within series, series with no titles, series qualified by place, series qualified by body, series with or without designators, series reprinted in other series, and more. Since series authority decisions affect access, those decisions should be made or reviewed by a professional librarian. On the surface, consistent rule interpretation and application appear simple and possible; however, certain series and conditions can make the whole process complex and impossible. Much of the series work can be handled well by an experienced searcher, an accurate typist, and an alert filer. Should you be fortu--nate enough to have these skills in one person, that person working with a knowledgeable professional would maximize the chances for good series control.

Procedures

Any procedure reflects a stage of development and a philosophy of the moment. Procedures are always subject to refinement and/or replacement. This is especially true of procedures in technical processing. The bugaboo to beware is the belief that anything in writing is holy writ. In analyzing what we currently do to estab--lish a new series, I'm amazed at the complexity of what seemed like a simple task. Now may be the time for the above--mentioned "refinement." At any rate, the procedures currently in use in

Central Technical Services, SUNY at Buffalo, follow.

Decision Making

In order to build a consistent Series Authority File, decisions must be based upon standards and guidelines. The standards used in our library are a combination of Library of Congress AACR2 records, Library of Congress online series authority records, Library of Congress rule interpretations found in the *Cataloging Service Bulletins,* and local series history found in our pre--1981 Series Authority File. Since guidelines and interpretations have to be generalized to a degree, their application requires a case by case judgement. Consistency in the Series Authority File obviously will depend upon consistent judgements and careful review. In our operation, a professional cataloger is responsible for making the final decisions. Many people make decisions as a series travels through processing; however, a final arbiter provides the best guarantee of uniformity.

All series are not created equal. Some are clearly evident on the cover, on the title page, on the verso of the title page, or somewhere in the preliminaries. Others are on the back cover, in a list at the back, in introductory paragraphs, only in the CIP (Cataloging in Publication), on dust jackets, or buried in fine print describing other printings. Lone numbers on spines or in the middle of a white page are like blinking lights to a series person. What is being numbered? It may be a series.

The standard series questions and recommended sources of information are listed below.

1) What makes a series a series and how does one decide?

The best guidance relevant to this questions is found in *Cataloging Service Bulletin (CSB)* no. 21, pp. 9--12.

2) What is the correct form of the series, its designator(s), and its numbering?

Information re question 2 is scattered. One must distinguish between what is included in a series statement in the description and what is included in a series heading or series tracing. *CSB* no. 21, p. 9 provides useful examples. The same bulletin on p. 10 treats corporate body names followed by numbers. *CSB* no. 13, p. 11 deals with variant forms of a series title and sets, whose parts have appeared in more than one series. *CSB* no. 18, p. 14 gives help on numbering within series titles and series with more than one system of designation. *CSB* no. 14, p. 11 deals with main series and subseries. *CSB* no. 18, pp. 48--49 considers the form of the series tracing and non–consecutive numbering.

3) Should the series be an access point, i.e., should it be traced?

This question has proved to be a difficult area to handle consis-- tently. The latest interpretation and guidelines appeared in *CSB* no. 18, pp. 47–48. Three statements from this bulletin have allowed libraries and individuals to chart separate and diverse courses. "Do not trace . . . series published by a commercial publisher in which the title conveys little or no information about the content, genre, audience, or purpose of the works in the series." "Trace . . . series in special cases in which the cataloger feels that a useful collocation would be served by creating added entries for the series despite the lack of informative words . . . " "Trace . . . series in any case of doubt." To gain some sense of how the Library of Congress was applying these guidelines, we have watched their decisions. The patterns have been somewhat erratic. "Pocket poets" is traced; "Pocket poets series" is not traced; "Poetique" is traced; "Poesie der Welt" is not traced. We have been forced to do exactly what the Library of Congress intended – make our own decisions. Ob-- viously the role of the final reviewer is particularly important in this area.

4) How should the series be classified?

If we are establishing a series for the first time we generally follow the decision in the Library of Congress record. Most series are separately classified. The exceptions fall into three categories: 1) the series is old and has been kept under a common call number for years, 2) the scope of the subject content is extremely narrow and limited, and 3) the titles are the work of one author. In all of these cases, keeping the titles together best serves the users and adds to the expediency of the cataloging process. Since a common call number has to have a unique designator, only numbered series are candidates for this treatment.

5) Is the series title proper identical to the title proper of another serial in the catalog?

This can be a difficult question to answer. Within the Series Authority File a conflict is easily spotted. Conflicts with the titles of other serials, even those entered under a corporate body, are very well hidden. In case we are tempted to guess, in *CSB* no. 20, p. 25 we are cautioned, "Do *not* predict a conflict."

6) In case of a conflict in titles proper, what qualifier should be used and what is the correct form of that qualifier?

How to create a uniform title for a series has been a controversial subject. Proponents of the corporate body as the preferred qualifier appear to be losing to the proponents of place of publication as the preferred qualifier. The latest word on uniform titles, choice of qualifying term, and form of qualifying term can be found in *CSB* no. 20, pp. 26–31. Beyond the usual, series decision--making can include some very unusual problems. The following appeared as a series in a group of publications.

Social Work Education and Practice:
A Saul Horowitz, Jr. Memorial Series
of the Hunter College School of Social Work

In various records, the series appeared in three forms: Social work education and practice, Social work education & practice, and Saul Horowitz Jr. memorial series. Publishers contribute to the confusion by rearranging word order, throwing in abbreviations and symbols, and fooling around with prepositions. A series in the CIP can cause everyone in the processing chain to search for a series that was *not* printed in the volume or the series in the CIP is totally different from the one on the title page. Occasionally a uniform title is used for a series in order to keep related series together rather than to keep identical titles separate. In the examples below the series in French and in English will file next to each other.

SEP	Canadian historic sites. French ; no. -	A/T
		LML
		UGL
	x Lieux historiques canadiens.	SEL
CALL NO.		Mth
	x₁ Parks Canada. National Historic Parks and Sites Branch.	Poet
		AED
	Lieux historiques canadiens.	Art
		Map

(second card)

IS	SEP	Canadian historic sites ; no. -	A/T
			LML
		x Parks Canada. National Historic Parks and Sites Branch.	UGL
In	ALL NO.		SEL
		Canadian historic sites.	Mth
			Poet
			AED
			Art
			Map
			Doc
	SSN/LCCN		Chem
			Asia

A corporate body used as a qualifier can appear in variant forms from one volume to the next. A recent example is the British Institute of Archaeology *at* Ankara and the British Institute of Archaeology *in* Ankara. One series from Duke University has been established three ways in three L.C. AACR2 records:

1. Duke University. Center for Commonwealth and Comparative Studies (Series)

2. Publication (Duke University. Center for Commonwealth and Comparative Studies)

3. Duke University Commonwealth–Studies Center publications.

The three forms may have been valid at different times but someone must search and make that determination.

Recording Decisions

An authority file may consist of cards or automated records. The elements in the authority records may be arranged in many ways. The arrangement should be clear, logical and, above all, con–sistent. If possible, the Series Authority File should be located near those who use the decisions recorded therein. Figure 1 is an example of a series authority card and the information it includes. Figure 2 is the same card with information about a specific series.

Figure 1

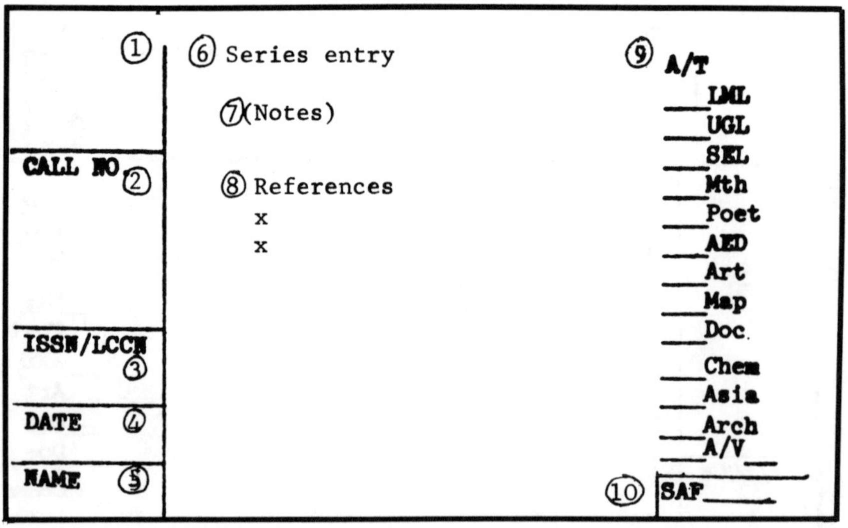

1) Treatment or tracing decision

    a) SEP = trace the series and assign a *sep*arate call number to each title.

    b) ANAL = trace the series and assign the same call number with a unique designator to each *analy*tic.

    c) SRNK = *s*eries *r*record *n*ot *k*ept, i.e., do not trace the series.

    d) No series = do *not* trace it as a series, although it looks like a series.

2) Call number
This block is left blank except for ANAL decisions which require a call number and the type of designator to be used, such as Bd.--, v.--, t.--, no.--.

3) ISSN/LCCN
*I*nternational *S*tandard *S*erial *N*umber and *L*ibrary of *C*ongress *C*ard *N*umber if the record is AACR2.

4) Date the decision is typed.

5) Initials of the person who made the decision.

6) Established form of the series entry.

7) Notes can include publisher, numbering irregularities, or any information that will help to promote consistency and eliminate questions.

8) Cross references
The most common cross references are those made up of a cor-- porate body and title which would have been the correct form under earlier cataloging rules.

9) Record of those Author/Title catalogs for which references have been typed and filed.

10) Record of references made for the Series Authority File.

Figure 2

SEP	Publication (Northeast Regional Names Institute) ; -	**A/T** X **LML** ___**UGL**
CALL NO.	x Northeast Regional Names Institute. Publication.	___**SEL** ___**Mth** ___**Poet** ___**AED** ___**Art** ___**Map** ___**Doc**
ISSN/LCCN 82-142710		___**Chem** ___**Asia** ___**Arch**
DATE 9/82		___**A/V**
NAME JD		**SAF** x

The above series is traced and separately classified. It is pat-terned after the record bearing Library of Congress card number 82–142710. The form of the series entry is a uniform title made up of "Publication", a generic term, qualified by a corporate body, "Northeast Regional Names Institute." It is a numbered series which has no designator with the number. The cross reference is to assist those who may know this series as a corporate body plus title. References have been typed for the Lockwood Memorial Library (LML) and for the Series Authority File (SAF). In this case, no notes were required.

Workflow

Our present workflow has evolved out of a personnel crunch and not out of longterm planning and careful evaluation. I'm re-porting on a material flow that is keeping us abreast of the mono-graphic series workload by using staff in Monograph Cataloging, Serials Cataloging, Serials Records, and Catalog Maintenance. The flowchart below may make it easier for the visually-minded to follow the stream.

Explanation of Flowchart

1.) Each volume appearing to be a part of a monographic series arrives in the Serials Cataloging Section with a printout of an OCLC record, unless the material is coming from an original cataloger. If the title has arrived in the library as a result of a new continuing order, the searching has been done by a Kardex Assistant from Serials Records. If the volume is coming from Mnograph Cataloging,

FLOWCHART

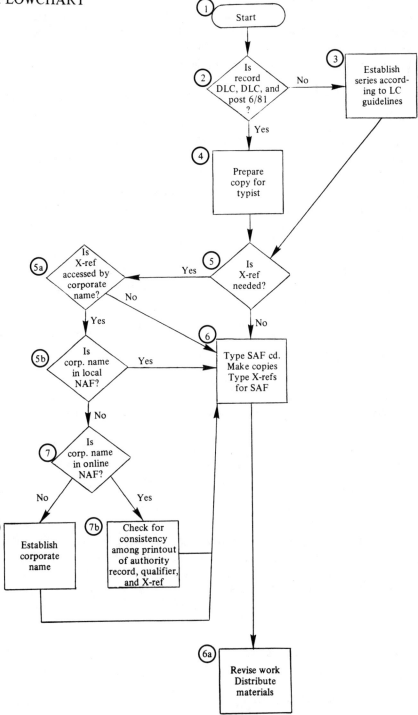

215

the searching has been done by a clerk from Catalog Maintenance or by a Systems Copy Cataloger. A photocopy of any record found in the pre–1981 Series Authority File is also placed in the volume and is the main means of discovering that an old series was kept together under a common call number.

2.)   A check by a clerk determines if the series in the book matches the one on the printout; if the copy is from, and was input by, the Library of Congress; and if the record was entered into the database after 6/81. We used mid–1981 because early in 1981 interpretations and guidelines were still being formulated.

3.)   If the decision at step 2 is negative, a series/serials cataloger establishes the series according to L.C. guidelines. Additional searching by a clerical searcher may be required in order to uncover any identical title(s) proper.

4.)   If the decision at step 2 is positive, a series/serials cataloger prepares the printout for the typist by adding any required notes, cross reference, and so forth.

5.)   If cross references are not needed, the material goes to the typist. (Step 6).

5a.)   If the decision is negative, the material goes to the typist. (Step 6). If the decision is positive, i.e., a cross reference is accessed by means of a corporate name, the material goes to a searcher. (Step 5b).

5b.)   If the decision is negative, i.e., the name has not been established in the local Name Authority File, the material goes to an online searcher. (Step 7). If the decision is positive, the material goes to the typist (Step 6).

7.)   If the decision is negative, the material goes to a series/serials cataloger who establishes the corporate name. (Step 7a).
    If the decision is positive, i.e., the corporate name has been established by L.C., the searcher makes a printout of the record and inserts it in the volume. The material then goes to the series/ serials cataloger. (Step 7b).

7a.)   Series/serials cataloger establishes the corporate name and gives the material to the typist (Step 6).

7b.)   Series/serials cataloger checks the Name Authority printout to insure consistency among the form of the qualifier, the form of the cross reference and the form found in the LC Name Authority File. The material is next given to the typist. (Step 6)

6.)   The typist types the Series Authority File card, makes photocopies for each volume, types the cross references for the Series Authority File, and gives the material to the series/serials cataloger.

6a.)   Series/serials cataloger makes a thorough final review and distributes the materials.

  a. Series Authority File cards to filer for filing.

  b. Materials needing Name Authority File (NAF) cards go to the typist in Catalog Maintenance who does NAF typing.

  c. Materials that originally came from Serials Records are returned to that section along with new kardexes.

  d. Materials from original or copy catalogers are returned to the individuals working on the titles.

  e. The remaining materials are shelved in Monograph Cataloging.

One category of materials not included in the flowchart is personal author series. They are established by catalogers in Original Cataloging and given to the series/serials cataloger for final revision.

Conclusion

Series may be mysterious, complex, and frustrating, but they are never predictable and routine. As I stated earlier, procedures are fluid things. I have recorded what we are doing with series this week. The review of our procedures will benefit us and possibly you too.

Distributed Check-in of Serials:
A Case Study of the University of Illinois-Urbana Library

Karen A. Schmidt
Acquisitions Librarian
University of Illinois--Urbana

Introduction

Serials have always posed problems in a number of areas: selec--tion, binding, budgeting, storage decisions, cataloguing, and process--ing are some of the major administrative issues which are frequently addressed. The processing of serials – check--in, marking, claiming, and noting -- has always been a factor in the debates over the proper role and function of serials administration in academic libraries. Since the beginning of this century, discussion on the place of processing and the centralized serial record generally has led to a single conclusion: that no matter where the serials function lies in an organization, centralized processing is an important factor in the successful management of serials. Attendant to this conclu--sion is the centralized record which allows not only the recording of precise cataloguing information, but also the complete check--in, claiming, and financial records of any serial in question. This cen--tralized form of control over serially issued titles in a collection, it is generally believed, provides a complete set of data which can be administered and manipulated by a group of individuals who are especially trained to handle the unique problems which serials can pose.

As anyone who has dealt with serials can attest, however, not all serials are created equal, and not all elements which occur in the central serial record can claim equal importance. In fact, many of the items maintained in serials records may not be central to the successful management of serials and the recording of many items in a central location may only serve to impede the rapid process--ing of serials. In an large academic library, particularly one in which a substantial number of departmental libraries exist, any impediment to the quick delivery of serials and information about the status of serials can seriously hinder the library's ability to aid its clientele.

The Centralized Serial Record as an Information Source

A detailed look at what normally constitutes a centralized serial record shows that not all of what is recorded is necessarily important to the successful management of serials. In the pre--machine age, there is a generally accepted need to establish information on exactly what titles are held and how these titles relate to the rest of the collection. Such information is important not only to the primary user of a collection and to the personnel administering that collection, but also is important in shared cooperative ventures in which most libraries are engaged. Additionally, a centralized serials record may contain fiscal data which provides important information for the payment, budgetary control, and auditing of a library's materials budget. These two points of control are fundamental to a general scheme of good administration of library materials. Other points commonly included in a centralized serial record are less convincingly important to the proper maintenance of any library material. These points are generally associated with inventory control, including the noting of received issues, missing issues, action taken, and correspondence noting. While it is important that this information be maintained somewhere, it does not perform the same functions in a centralized record as do cataloguing control and fiscal control records and is, in a sense, supporting data which can be maintained elsewhere.[1] There is little argument over the necessity for a serials record, be it integrated with other records or not, as a tool enabling libraries to add or delete titles, claim missing issues, respond to requests for information, and perform myriad other functions.[2] The arguments which exist revolve around how much of importance can and should be recorded, and if all elements must be recorded centrally, if manual files are maintained. In the larger academic libraries which serve many departmental libraries and handle thousands of serial titles, such work is highly labor--intensive, most of it clerical in nature, and because of extensive recording of receipt, claiming, and correspondence, can be debilitating to the very goal the library wishes to achieve, that of getting material to the user in the most efficient way possible.

Centralized Check--in

The question, then, is how to circumvent unnecessary delays in the recording process without undermining the integrity and usefulness of a centralized record. An answer can be found in distributed processing, that is, in identifying the elements of serials control which can be handled most efficiently at the point of receipt in the various departmental libraries, while maintaining centralized control over those portions of serials processing which necessitate this level of management. With this concept in mind, the Acquisitions Department of the University of Illinois–Urbana Libraries began a project of distributing serials processing to its departmental libraries.

In the situation described below, a centralized serials record existed for a number of years, but was replaced with a combination of an automated system which notes where a serial title is housed, its classification number, what issues are bound, and where current issues are received, and with the serials processing file in the Acquisitions Department, which records information on specific issues, as well as claiming, noting, and fiscal information. For all the various serials they receive, departmental libraries maintain a file duplicating, to a certain extent, the information found in the Acquisitions' files: issues received, claims made, and any other special notes concerning the titles. The centralized serial record exists, then, but in a less traditional manner, and with elements of inventory control and fiscal control separated from the more formal centralized record available through the automated system. Through this configuration of files, which realistically addresses the various levels of importance of data maintained for serials, distributed processing is a possibility because the centralized file is also a "distributed" file, "distributed" in the sense that it is available to anyone with a computer attached to the central automated system, regardless of that person's location.[3]

The University of Illinois–Urbana Acquisitions Department, which orders and receives both monographic and serial publications for the central collections and the 38 separate libraries serving the Urbana campus, receives and checks–in an enormous number of periodical issues each year. In 1982, the number of issues handled was estimated to be over 600 each day.

Staffing for handling this level of check–in activity included six full time lower level non–professional staff, one senior clerical staff member, and one professional. Besides handling the regular routines of noting receipts of issues in the Acquisitions Department's check–in files, this unit was also responsible for noting and sending claims on gaps in receipts found during the check–in process, and for filing claims initiated by the receiving libraries. In addition, all noting of title changes, publication pattern changes, correspondence inquiries and replies, and other pertinent title information was handled by the six check–in clerks. Training of new personnel (a constant process because of the high turnover of staff in the check–in unit), review and establishment of procedures, contact with departmental libraries, and resolution of the complex and varied check–in problems attendant on the high volume of complicated serials titles was handled by the senior staff member and the serials librarian.

To maintain control over this daily flow of periodicals, the periodicals receipt unit worked within a set of priorities established to insure that each library received its periodicals as quickly as possible. Of primary importance was the routine noting and processing (including date and property stamping and writing the call number) of titles easily found in the 224–drawer check–in file. Entries which could not be located after two or three attempts were set aside for later searching, or for attention by the senior staff member and the librarian. At the same time, claiming notices for gaps evident in the check–in records were filled out. The next priority was that of verifying and completing claims for missing issues submitted by the receiving libraries. Finally, correspondence information was noted. Each checker was responsible for specific letters of the alphabet for the titles of the periodicals (with some accompanying division by language as talent and need arose), and so this unit also sorted all incoming issues in preparation for handling the check–in operations. When optimum conditions existed -- that is, when no vacancies occurred, no holidays intruded, and no extraordinary title problems amassed – this group was able to keep a steady flow of current issues through the Acquisitions Department, with an average turnaround time per issue of one day within Acquisitions. Such ideal conditions rarely exist, however, and backlogs of difficult entries and claims were frequent sources of frustration for the unit.

Together with the check–in records maintained centrally within the Acquisitions Department, the libraries receiving the periodicals also maintained a local record of receipt, which allowed them quick and easy access to information on holdings for patron queries, binding status, and claiming needs. While plans were being developed to convert the centralized check–in records to machine–readable format, allowing automated access to these records from any library within the Urbana system, such automated control was not yet a reality. In these libraries, a duplicate record on–site was believed to serve an important function in providing adequate service to each library's users, particularly during those hours of public service when Acquisitions was closed.

In criticizing the effectiveness of this duplicative system for receiving, noting, and dispersing periodical issues, Acquisitions librarians at the University of Illinois–Urbana recognized not only the duplication of effort in maintaining centralized and local records of receipts, but also potential and real frustrations for both the Acquisitions Department and the libraries in not being able to identify consistently those periodical titles of greatest importance to each library, titles which were most in demand by library patrons in various disciplines and which needed to be checked–in and processed most promptly. An obvious solution was to suggest that libraries identify titles of greatest priority, and then establish a mechanism for sending as many of these titles as possible directly from the vendor to the receiving library, where local records could be noted as usual. With a small number of libraries agreeing to try such an experiment, the project of direct receipt of periodicals was begun.

Distributed Check–in: Problems Encountered

An important factor in beginning this project was the prior consolidation of the bulk of the libraries' domestic subscriptions with one major vendor. The consolidation effort, accomplished a short time before the direct receipt project was initiated, enabled the Acquisitions Department to set new procedures with a minimum of effort. Some stipulations had to be established: the Acquisitions Department would continue to maintain fiscal control over all periodicals, with invoices coming to and payment approval coming from the Acquisitions Department; any gifts, foreign titles, ex–changes, international documents, and domestic titles not handled by the vendor would continue to be received centrally; additionally, some irregular, analyzed, or problem titles identified by Acquisitions would need centralized receipt. The library wishing to participate would need to agree to mark ownership, date of receipt, and the call number on each piece, as it was deemed necessary by each library. In exchange for this activity, the library was assured of getting each issue as quickly as possible, and of being able to initiate claims directly to the vendor without delay.

To begin the operation, the vendor provided a listing of all titles sent, arranged by the fund number (i.e., by receiving library). The fund number printouts were sent to each library to choose the titles to be sent directly. After checking these selected titles against the Acquisitions check–in files for possible problems, the Acquisi–tions Department sent the list to the vendor, who began the neces–sary notification of the publishers. Much of the initial work in converting shipping information fell to the vendor, and to the Acquisitions Department in correcting records; additionally, each library was given a list of suggestions to enable their staff to handle this new procedure. It was suggested that the receiving library's Kardex check--in cards be clearly marked with a highlighter pen and stamped with the name of the vendor to aid in identification for both check--in and claiming. To help in claiming, each Kardex card needed to have the unique ship number, the established mailing address, and the date of first receipt added. Sample claim forms, which would be completed on–site and sent directly to Faxon, were provided, and an invitation was extended to each library to discuss the new procedures. Additionally, information was given on how to identify title or bibliographic changes needing possible cataloguing attention. In this latter discussion, it was agreed that photocopies of the title page(s) and verso(s) be sent to the Acquisitions Department, where verification of title changes could be accomplished in tandem with the Cataloguing Department. Finally, potential problems which could arise in the early part of the mailing transfer were enumerated: duplicate copies received, one directly and one from Acquisitions; multiple copies sent to one address instead of being dispersed among several libraries; no issues received; and "final notice" invoices received were foreseen as the major problems.

The initial shipping transfer included some 29 libraries, with approximately 1700 titles to be transferred. The internal procedures established to handle this project created few problems for Acquisi--tions or the departmental libraries involved: titles were easily identified, and necessary noting of the transfers was done with a minimum of work. Problems did arise, however, between the vendor and the publishers in communicating all of the necessary ship--to changes to be initiated. Very early in the project, and on a scale far greater than anticipated, all of the potential problems noted above occurred, with one library receiving every copy for the entire system for one particular issue. In an interesting twist, one library began receiving all issues of all titles published by a learned society. Other problems included the transfer of some titles not handled by the major vendor (perhaps the result of having both a foreign and domestic title published by the same publisher), and confusion over which address should be used for claiming when issues were lost. Communicating the address changes to the pub--lishers was indeed the most aggravating problem experienced, and a good deal of energy was spent both on the part of the Acquisitions Department in straightening out where each copy should have gone, and on the part of the vendor in establishing clear instructions to the publishers. With a good deal of initial work, however, all of the appropriate procedures were finally established, so that problems of this type and magnitude did not arise in the future.

Within the libraries receiving serials directly from the vendors, most of the transfer process was handled smoothly, although initial confusion was caused by the strange mailing patterns of some of the serial titles. In some cases, libraries did not mark their check--in records accurately and so continued to claim missing issues through the Acquisitions Department. Occasional panic occurred when invoices were inadvertently sent to the shipping address rather than the billing address or when final notices arrived. The benefits outweighed the problems, however, so that more libraries joined the group who worked with the initial project.

Advantages of Distributed Check--in

In contrast to the problems have been some clear advantages to the library system as a whole. Most importantly, the libraries joining in this venture do receive the most needed journals more quickly. In addition, they are able to forecast the next arrival date of issues more accurately, have greater control over the claiming process of heavily used items, and, and a by--product, have come to know Acquisitions personnel better and to understand the acquisitions process more fully. The libraries also benefit tangentially from a shift in Acquisitions check--in personnel and routines made possible, in part, by this direct receipt. There is a strong correlation between the titles transferred to direct receipt, and the ease with which the issues of these titles can be checked--in.

With some of the more easily--handled journals by--passing the Acquisitions Department, there has been a resultant lessening of material coming into the department, allowing more time for processing the more difficult titles, and for preparing and sending claims for these titles. The direct receipt project has been responsible in part for a departmental reorganization which now has four full--time lower level staff members handling periodical check--in and claiming of issues, with one senior staff member handling trouble--shooting in connection with problem titles. Journal issue claims initiated by departmental libraries for titles not received directly are now handled in a separate unit, which also handles monographic claims. In theory, the "gap claiming" done by the Acquisitions serial processors, in tandem with the claiming for direct titles handled by the departmental libraries, should substantially lower the number of departmental claims which the Acquisitions Department needs to process. In addition, automated serials check--in projects currently being developed at the University of Illinois--Urbana Library will continue to modify this personnel structure, and simplify the claiming process.

Conclusion

Currently, 30 libraries are participating in direct receipt of periodicals, accounting for some 3500 titles. The percentage of total titles received directly in any one library ranges from 3% to 100% of all vendor--ordered titles, with an average of 50% of any one library's titles being received directly in the library. Of all titles ordered through this vendor, 41% are sent directly to the departmental libraries, with more being added monthly. As a method of periodical check--in management which makes recognition of the various levels of the serials check--in record which must be handled centrally, this program of distributed processing has proven to be a successful, fast, and effective method of supplying heavily--used titles and important information to library users.

NOTES

1. William Gray Potter, "Form or Function? An Analysis of the Serials Department in the Modern Academic Library," *The Serials Librarian* 6 (Fall 1981): 85--94.

2. Samuel Lazerow, "Serial Records: A Mechanism for Control," in *Serial Publications in Large Libraries,* ed. by Walter C. Allen, (Urbana, Illinois: University of Illinois Graduate School of Library Science, 1970), p. 109.

3. On--line interactive computerized record obviates much of this discussion.

Kardex to Keyboard: Creating a Serials Check–in File in Faxon's LINX System

Bonnie Postlethwaite
Assistant Manager LINX Services
Faxon Co.

One of the major problems that a library faces in the automating of any aspect of library services is the conversion of the data into machine–readable form. The expense and time involved cannot be overlooked as a library prepares any automation process, and the automating of serials processing functions is no exception. Even the conversion of basic check–in records into machine–readable form without the information stored in auxiliary serials files, e.g. invoicing, binding, requires a great deal of time and evaluation on the part of the serials staff. In 1980, Faxon created SCIS (Serials Check–in System -- also referred to as SC–10), a component of LINX, Faxon's serials management system. This service was de–signed to streamline and simplify serials processing from the creation of the online file to the full utilization of the system.

The conversion process for a Faxon customer's data base creation begins with the 'downloading' of all titles which Faxon supplies to a library. This is the process whereby the system retrieves all of the titles for which Faxon has invoiced a customer and automati–cally creates a basic, or skeletal, serials check–in record for each copy of those titles. Depending on a library's previous use of other Faxon serials management services a large volume of local informa–tion may be downloaded with the skeletal records.

Faxon's Contribution to the Conversion

The basic check--in record provided by the Faxon system consists of the title, the copy number, the total number of copies the library receives, the frequency, the number of issues per year, the check--in matrix and claiming interval (arrival number) based on the fre--quency, ISSN, the Library of Congress code, the indexing and abstracting codes and the title page indicator. Figure 1 depicts a sample skeletal record created by Faxon. The various pieces of information are taken from Faxon's computer files, which contain the invoicing information for that customer's titles. The LINX

227

Figure 1

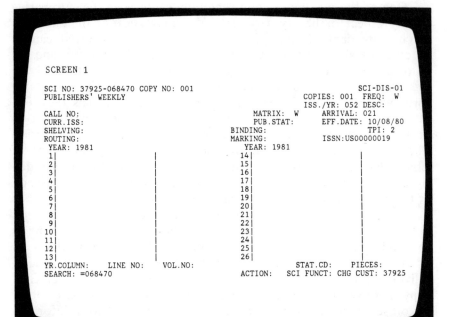

```
SCREEN 1

SCI NO: 37925-068470 COPY NO: 001                        SCI-DIS-01
PUBLISHERS' WEEKLY                          COPIES: 001  FREQ:  W
                                            ISS./YR: 052 DESC:
CALL NO:                        MATRIX:  W     ARRIVAL: 021
CURR.ISS:                       PUB.STAT:      EFF.DATE: 10/08/80
SHELVING:                       BINDING:                 TPI: 2
ROUTING:                        MARKING:       ISSN:US00000019
  YEAR: 1981              |       YEAR: 1981                  |
  1|                      |      14|                          |
  2|                      |      15|                          |
  3|                      |      16|                          |
  4|                      |      17|                          |
  5|                      |      18|                          |
  6|                      |      19|                          |
  7|                      |      20|                          |
  8|                      |      21|                          |
  9|                      |      22|                          |
 10|                      |      23|                          |
 11|                      |      24|                          |
 12|                      |      25|                          |
 13|                      |      26|                          |
YR.COLUMN:   LINE NO:   VOL.NO:              STAT.CD:   PIECES:
SEARCH: =068470                 ACTION:   SCI FUNCT: CHG CUST: 37925
```

Figure 1 (cont.)

```
   SCREEN 2

SCI NO: 37925-068470 COPY NO: 001                              SCI-DIS-02
PUBLISHERS' WEEKLY                                COPIES: 001  FREQ:  W
                                                  ISS./YR: 052 LCC:  Z
CALL NO:                            ALTERNATE ACCESS:
  AISL:                             ORDERED:           SOURCE: O
  FISL:                             I&A: BP RG LL
  SISL:                             ID#:
  PISL:                             USE TALLY:      ISSN: US00000019
HOLDINGS:
TYPE:    MISSING ISSUES:     DATE: |  TYPE:    COMMENTS:
                                   |
                                   |
                                   |
                                   |
                                   |
                                   |
                                   |
                                   |
  SEARCH: =068470                  |  ACTION:   SCI FUNCT: CHG CUST: 37925
```

staff initiates the download by requesting that all except cancelled titles from a library's recent invoices on the Faxon system be loaded into the library's recent invoices on the Faxon system be loaded into the library's private database. The download process occurs the same night the request is submitted. Check–in activities may commence the following day.

With the request for the download, the LINX staff indicates whether or not the customer wants any Information Service Lines (ISLs) transferred from their invoicing records to the serials check--in file and, if so, if any of those ISLs should also be targeted for other fields within the check--in record. Faxon provides three ISLs for customer use and one ISL for publisher use.

> AISL (Address Information Service Line) -- Used as a variable line of a mailing address. For example, libraries may chose to use an individual's name, or a department or branch library name.

> FISL (Financial Information Service Line) – Used to identify the fund or account to which the serial is assigned or the title's purchase order number.

> SISL (Serials Information Service Line) – Used for subjects, curriculum codes, or call numbers.

> PISL (Publisher Information Service Line) – Used to record a publisher's identification code at the request of the publisher. (Not for use by the library.)

The library may choose to include or exclude the information from an Information Service Line in SCIS. However, once the download is completed there is no further connection between the SCIS records and their corresponding invoicing history (HIST) record for the purposes of information transfer. Before the conver--sion, the librarian should consider whether any ISLs should be added or changed and then submit the ISL updates to Faxon for input. In both HIST and SCIS, the ISLs provide the means of producing print--outs sorted first by the specified ISL and then alphabetically by title. Once a title has been created in SCIS, the library may choose to have the ISLs differ in the two separate files.

Understanding the structure and use of the ISL fields in SCIS is critical to the conversion process. Each of the ISL fields are 30 positions in length and can contain alpha/numeric characters. Printout sorts can be produced off of any position within the ISL making consistency paramount. Some libraries have devised short codes of consistent length for subjects so that multiple codes could be input in the SISL. Sorts from the various positions in the SISL allow for comprehensive subject lists. During the download, an ISL or a portion of an ISL may be targeted for another field; for example, if the SISL contains the call number, the SISL information can also be targeted for the call number field. Although the ISL fields can be updated at any time after the creation of the records, accurate information and targeting insures a simplified conversion process.

In addition to providing the basic subscription and claiming services for Faxon supplied titles, Faxon can also provide serials management reports for libraries by creating invoicing records for non--Faxon supplied titles from data supplied by the library to Faxon. At a present cost of $2.00 per record per year, the Faxon system stores the prices and subscription periods for all titles a library receives through other sources. If a library utilizes this service in addition to SCIS, Faxon will also create serials check--in records for all the non--Faxon titles a library receives by means of the same process described above for Faxon titles. Prior use of the non--Faxon service by a library virtually enables Faxon to establish a library's SCIS file overnight at no additional cost to the library. If a library opts for both the non--Faxon service and SCIS at the same time, Faxon will create the non--Faxon in--voicing records prior to the download.

The library also needs to decide if all Faxon charge--to and ship--to accounts are included in the serials check--in database. If a library has numerous account numbers, the librarian may want to specify which number will be used for the SCIS database. This SCIS customer number serves as the umbrella account number for all serials check--in titles regardless of its invoicing account number. If a library decides to begin using SCIS for the central library only and to later add branch libraries which are invoiced under different charge--to or ship--to numbers, Faxon will download only the titles associated with the central library account number and at a later date, at the request of the library, will download other charge--to or ship--to numbers.

Finally, prior to the conversion, the library must decide if check--in will begin with the current issue or if retrospective check--in data will be input for the entire current year. The computer assigns the current year when setting up the matrices for each check--in record. Unless otherwise instructed, the computer will also assign the current quarter of the year for matrices that consist of more than 13 lines. Thus, if the file is created in April, the computer will set up the weekly matrix beginning with the four--

teenth week of the year. If the library desires to record all check--in data from the first of the year, LINX staff need to request first quarter matrices.

After the download, LINX staff request a print--out of the titles coded in the DESC (Description) field for membership/combi-nation subscriptions. Description codes indicate a publication's type: cassette, newspaper, microfilm, microcard, microfiche, com-bination subscription, or membership. LINX staff, using the mem-bership/combination print--out, add records for all the titles received on a membership or a combination subscription since only the records on which payment were made are automatically loaded into the database. After adding these titles to the customer's serials check--in database, the LINX staff add comments in all of these records which serve as cross--references between the subscription record and the check--in records.

The Library's Role in the Conversion

After training by Faxon staff on the use of the system, the library begins inputting any non--Faxon titles not already in the SCIS database. Adding a new record requires the six--digit Faxon title number which is found by searching either ATTL (Alpha Title file) or TKEY (Title Keyword file). ATTL is an alphabetical listing of all titles in Faxon's title file. To search ATTL, the searcher inputs the ISSN or the exact title name. TKEY searching provides the most accurate results because keywords are input in any order so the exact title is not required. If the searcher fails to locate the title in ATTL or TKEY, s/he simply fills out a special screen in Faxon's electronic mail system, Courier, to notify Faxon that the title needs to be added to the title file. Faxon will add the title to the customer's check--in file at the same time. When the title number is located, the library transfers back to the serials check--in file and inputs the title number and changes the SCIS function to "ADD". As soon as the "ENTER" key is depressed, the skeletal record appears on the screen. The SCIS function changes to "CHG" assuming that the person at the terminal will have local data to enter in the record. By moving the cursor to the appropriate fields, the inputter simply types the local information in the fields and presses the "ENTER" key. The record is now ready for check--in activities. Depending upon the processing requirements of the library, the amount of local information to be added to a record can range from very minimal to complete utilization of every field.

Field Uses

Figure 2

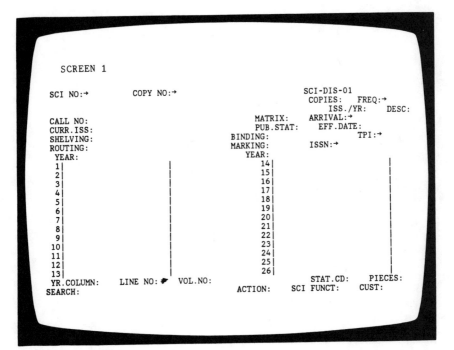

Figure 2 (cont.)

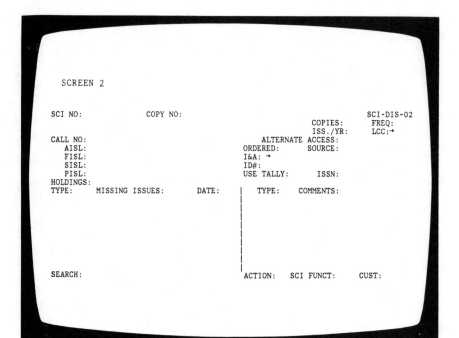

```
  SCREEN 2


SCI NO:              COPY NO:                                      SCI-DIS-02
                                                  COPIES:         FREQ:
                                                  ISS./YR:        LCC:→
CALL NO:                                  ALTERNATE ACCESS:
  AISL:                                   ORDERED:      SOURCE:
  FISL:                                   I&A: →
  SISL:                                   ID#:
  PISL:                                   USE TALLY:     ISSN:
HOLDINGS:
TYPE:    MISSING ISSUES:      DATE:   |   TYPE:    COMMENTS:
                                      |
                                      |
                                      |
                                      |
                                      |
                                      |
SEARCH:                               |  ACTION:   SCI FUNCT:    CUST:
```

Figure 3

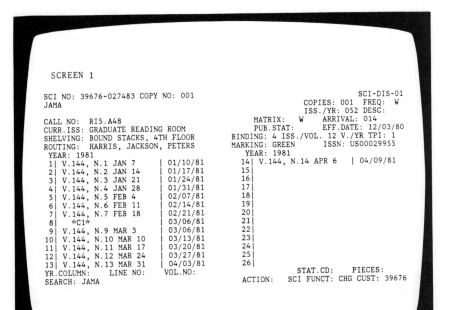

```
  SCREEN 1

  SCI NO: 39676-027483 COPY NO: 001              SCI-DIS-01
  JAMA                               COPIES: 001  FREQ:  W
                                     ISS./YR: 052 DESC:
  CALL NO:  RI5.A48                MATRIX:  W    ARRIVAL: 014
  CURR.ISS: GRADUATE READING ROOM    PUB.STAT:     EFF.DATE: 12/03/80
  SHELVING: BOUND STACKS, 4TH FLOOR  BINDING: 4 ISS./VOL. 12 V./YR TPI: 1
  ROUTING:  HARRIS, JACKSON, PETERS  MARKING: GREEN    ISSN: US00029955
   YEAR: 1981                         YEAR: 1981
   1| V.144, N.1 JAN 7    | 01/10/81  14| V.144, N.14 APR 6  | 04/09/81
   2| V.144, N.2 JAN 14   | 01/17/81  15|
   3| V.144, N.3 JAN 21   | 01/24/81  16|
   4| V.144, N.4 JAN 28   | 01/31/81  17|
   5| V.144, N.5 FEB 4    | 02/07/81  18|
   6| V.144, N.6 FEB 11   | 02/14/81  19|
   7| V.144, N.7 FEB 18   | 02/21/81  20|
   8|    *C1*              | 03/06/81  21|
   9| V.144, N.9 MAR 3    | 03/06/81  22|
  10| V.144, N.10 MAR 10  | 03/13/81  23|
  11| V.144, N.11 MAR 17  | 03/20/81  24|
  12| V.144, N.12 MAR 24  | 03/27/81  25|
  13| V.144, N.13 MAR 31  | 04/03/81  26|
  YR.COLUMN:    LINE NO:    VOL.NO:          STAT.CD:   PIECES:
  SEARCH: JAMA                       ACTION:   SCI FUNCT: CHG CUST: 39676
```

235

Figure 3 (cont.)

```
    SCREEN 2

    SCI NO: 39676-027483 COPY NO: 001                              SCI-DIS-02
    JAMA                                              COPIES: 001  FREQ:  W
                                                      ISS./YR: 052 LCC:  R
    CALL NO: R15.A48                        ALTERNATE ACCESS: AMERICA MEDI AS
       AISL: MORRISON BRANCH                ORDERED:            SOURCE: 1
       FISL: YM79-67548                     I&A: BA IM PS SC DL PH SA CL
       SISL: MEDICINE                       ID#: 56784343 (WLN)
       PISL: 67884                          USE TALLY:         ISSN: US00029955
    HOLDINGS: V.121-  ,1971-

    TYPE:    MISSING ISSUES:         DATE:  |  TYPE:   COMMENTS:

    C1   81   V.144, N.8 FEB 25   03/06/81  |  FT JOURNAL OF THE AMERICAN
                                            |  FT MEDICAL ASSOCIATION
                                            |  CA JAMA
                                            |  RC INDEXED IN DECEMBER
                                            |
                                            |
                                            |
                                            |

    SEARCH: JAMA                     ACTION:   SCI FUNCT: CHG CUST: 39676
```

236

Most of the fields in the SCIS record are self--explanatory. However, some of the fields have specialized uses and functions and are, therefore, worthy of note. As seen in Figure 2, which contains examples of blank screens, each record consists of at least two screens. Screen 1 contains the current check--in matrix, a group of numbered lines where the actual check--in data is recorded and displayed. Screen 2 contains processing and claiming information as well as general information about this particular copy of a title. Figure 3 demonstrates what an actual record with filled--in check--in data would look like. The arrowed fields in Figure 2 are system--supplied input fields. The remaining fields are library input fields.

Several of the fields in the SCIS records are searchable online. Because there are the access points to any record, the accuracy and utilization of these fields demand the library's thorough under--standing. SCIS has seven online search fields:

1. Faxon form of title (system supplied)

2. Library form of title (library supplied as a CA, Catalogued As, comment in the Comment area on Screen 2.)

3. ALTERNATE ACCESS (library--supplied)

4. CALL NO. (library supplied)

5. ISSN (system supplied)

6. ID NO. (library supplied)

7. Faxon title no. (system supplied).

The first three fields are all forms of the title and are searched in the same manner by keying in the first seven characters in the first important word of the title, the first four letters of the second important word of the title, and the first two letters of the third important word (7--4--2 formula) or, alternatively, the full words may be input. The Faxon form of title is automatically supplied and appears at the top of each screen unless the library's own form of title is used in the CA (Cataloged As) Comment in the Comments area on screen 2. When a CA comment is input, the computer immediately switches the Faxon form of the title with the Cataloged As title. The Faxon title now appears in the Comments area on screen 2 as a FT comment. Both forms of the title can be searched. The Alternate Access form of title provides the library with yet another form of entry. It is input using the 7--4--2 formula and appears on screen 2. Usually the Alternate Access field is used for titles that are popularly known by abbreviations or initials, such as *AJR* for the *American Journal of Roentgenology*.

*The numeric searches co*nsist of two system supplied fields and two library supplied fields. The Faxon title number and the ISSN may not be changed by the library. The CALL No. and ID No. are used by the library as needed. The ID No. may be used for library control numbers such as network I.D. numbers (e.g., OCLC, WLN, RLIN), local automated system ID numbers, and CODEN.

Another area of concern to serials staff is the summary holdings statement. This appears on screen 2 and consists of two full lines of input. This field may include details about volumes, issues, dates input according to the standard favored by the library. A phrase like "Latest year only" may also be input in this field if the library does not keep a full serial run.

The system provides the appropriate check--in matrix for a title based on the frequency code found in the FREQUENCY field. For irregular or variable frequencies the system automatically supplies a monthly matrix. The library may need to adjust the matrix to a more appropriate matrix configuration based on the pattern of receipt. The matrix code does not need to be the same as the frequency code so the library may adjust it at any time to accommodate frequency changes. Whenever the matrix code is changed, the ARRIVAL number should also be changed. ARRIVAL is the number of days allowed to elapse between receiving one issue of a title and the next. If no check--in activity has occurred in the number of days found in the ARRIVAL field the system reports this title on a lapse report indicating the need to claim the title. The system adds this number based on a title's frequency. In order to produce the new matrix, the library will change the matrix code and then type "FREQUENCY CHANGE" on the last line of old matrix. This action will automatically move the old matrix over to the left side of the screen and create the new matrix on the right side.

The library will probably want to input outstanding claims into SCIS to begin using the system to its best advantage. To claim missing issues, the appropriate missing issues code is used on screen 1 after keying in the issue information as if one were checking in the issue. This procedure causes the missing issues code to appear on the matrix on the appropriate line and the claim comment will appear in the Missing Issues area on screen 2. If the library prefers not to input the missing issues code on screen 1 because the issue is older than the current year, the claim may be entered directly on screen 2. Some available codes for the Missing Issues area are:

BI issues at bindery
C1 first claim
C2 second claim
C3 third claim
CG claim gap
DY issue has been delayed and therefore not claimed
NP issue not published for this time period
OP out--of--print
RE replacement issue ordered
WL want--listed issue

The library may request lists of titles with any of these codes indicating issues at the bindery, want lists to send to dealers, and so
forth. The system automatically generates claims reports for the
CG, C1, C2, C3 codes. These reports are arranged by the SOURCE
code. SOURCE indicates how a library ordered the subscription
for a title. The SOURCE field contains two subfields. The first
consists of a one digit code.

1 Faxon agency--placed title
2 order direct -- free
3 order direct -- priced
4 exchange
5 gift
6 non--Faxon agency--placed title

The system automatically provides a 1 for Faxon--placed titles
and a 0 for Non--Faxon titles. Before check--in can be performed
the 0 must be changed to one of the valid codes. The second subfield is five characters in length and can be used to sort claim reports
by a specific supplier (i.e., ALA).

Finally, the COMMENTS area on Screen 2 provides the library
with input space for an unlimited amount of information about
a title. The valid COMMENT codes are:

BD Bound volumes comment

CA The library's form of entry for the title name. Use of this
comment code replaces the Faxon title at the top of the screen
with the title is input next to the CA comment code. Both the
library's form of entry and Faxon's form of entry are searchable
on--line.

239

CL Claim comment (time span, special conditions)

DU Duplicates received; indicates the action to be taken regarding duplicates.

DY Delayed publication note; date when next issue should be expected.

FT Faxon's form of entry for the title. This is created when a CA comment is entered.

LE Linking entry information – Continues.

LL Linking entry information – Continued by.

MB Membership or combination subscription note. Lists the titles received through a membership or a subscription.

MS Miscellaneous comment.

PI Publishing irregularities; used for normalized irregulars to specify when a publication is or is not published.

RC Receipt of special one–time titles coming with subscription (index, special issue).

SH Shelving comment.

X-, Y-, Z- Codes defined by the library as needed.

The library may create up to 84 comments with library specific meanings. These comments should be standardized to facilitate locating specific types of information online and in on–request print–outs. Libraries have used these comments for a variety of information such as:

a. Claiming addresses for non–Faxon titles

b. Payment history

c. Binding instructions

d. Labelling instructions

e. Retention schedules

The library should give careful consideration to what kind of printed reports may be needed concerning the serials collection and standardize input accordingly. Many of the fields in SCIS can be used for sorting purposes on a print–out:

AISL
BINDING
CALL NUMBER
COMMENT CODES
CURRENT ISSUES
DESCRIPTION CODE
FISL
FREQUENCY
ID NUMBER
ISSN
LCC
MARKING
MARKING WITHIN SHELVING
MISSING ISSUES CODES
PISL
PUBLICATION STATUS
ROUTING
SHELVING
SISL
SOURCE

Approaches to Local Data Entry

The method a library chooses to input the local data about each record will depend upon the size of the collection, the number of files where the data is currently located, the number of terminals and staff available for data entry, whether check--in data back to the first of the year will be input, and whether the library will start check--in immediately or wait until all processing information is in the data base. The first option is to go through the former check--in system alphabetically. This method insures that every record in the former system has been converted into LINX. A second option is to transfer the data as issues are checked–in. This method requires a final pass through the former system, otherwise irregular and infrequent titles will be missed. If a title which is not supplied by Faxon has stopped coming, the library will never find it. Some libraries have done a combination of the two methods. In this situation, the library completes the record whenever an issue is checked--in and at the same time the library systematically goes through the old files until all the records are completed. Other

241

libraries postpone check–in until that part of the alphabet has been completed. Many libraries prefer to input the basic information needed for check--in for all titles and later to go back through each record to input additional information about a title. The monthly master list of serials in SCIS can be used to identify any titles that lack specific fields of information.

Other options for data conversion exist. If the library has information on machine--readable tape, Faxon staff will examine the tapes to see if the data can be loaded from tape. To make this at all possible, the absolute minimum is some sort of unique numeric match--up such as the Faxon title number, the ISSN, an ID number or purchase order number that has been keyed into one of the ISLs. Faxon does charge for the tape examination and the loading of records from machine--readable tape. The second option is to contract Faxon to load the non–Faxon titles and basic local information into the serials check–in records for the library. Faxon charges $1.00 per record loaded.

Finally, changes are continually needed. There are always new subscriptions to add, title changes, frequency changes, transfers of business. At the time that an order for a new title is placed, whether through Faxon or by any other means, the library adds it to the serials check–in database. If the title number is not in the Faxon title file, the library sends an electronic message to the LINX staff to add the title to the title file. LINX staff will then add the title to the library's SCIS database as well. Frequency changes require the changing of the matrix code and the arrival number and inputting the message "FREQUENCY CHANGE" on the last line of the old matrix in order to create the new matrix. Other changes simply require the typing of the new information over the old.

If a library chooses to use additional services available through Faxon, such as Route or Union List, conversion efforts for these modules affect the SCIS records as well due to the link between modules. For Route, the characters "AUTO" must appear in the first four digits of the ROUTING field in order for the route slips to automatically print when an issue is checked–in. For Union List, two comment codes must exist for the data to be automatically transferred from SCIS to Union List. These comment codes are the UL (Union List) comment for the Union List group code and the AD comment for the library's union list profile information.

No conversion project is simple. However, Faxon has developed a process of generating the basic information for a customer's titles to reduce a great deal of the work involved. The library still needs to carefully consider the potential use of every field and how to standardize the data for the production of reports and listings to obtain the maximum benefits of the system. The fact that check--in and claiming activities can begin immediately after the download means that the library staff can transfer the local data at their own pace and still take advantage of the basic services provided by the LINX SCIS online check--in system.

The Effects of Automation on Serial Record Staffing

Frank D'Andraia
Head Technical Services
University of Southwestern Louisiana Dupree Library

Introduction

The operation and organization of serial records activities are more and more being affected by automation. Subscription agencies and various national bibliographic networks are offering an increasingly attractive array of on--line services to order, claim, and process periodicals. While the use of these new services is not as prevalent as it is in such areas as cataloging and acquisitions, the pressure is mounting on library administrators to begin making use of the new technology. As these on--line services become more reliable and cost--efficient, and as library expenditures and labor costs increase, the new technology will be hard to resist.

In the ensuing effort to incorporate the latest technology in serial operations, library managers will need to become more cognizant of how automation affects the management and supervision of clerical employees. To appreciate the impact automation has had on personnel, let us look at a library activity that has actively made use of the new technology for more than a decade: Cataloging.

Effect of Automation on Cataloging Staff

During the 1970's many academic libraries re--organized their cataloging operations. The new procedures evolved as a result of library affiliations with various national bibliographic networks. The procedures called for increased dependence upon computers and clerical staff to locate and accept the most appropriate cataloging available for materials being processed.

The University of Southwestern Louisiana (USL) Libraries adopted a similar concept in 1979. The automated cataloging unit, or Receipt Team, as it is called at USL, is staffed and supervised by non--professional or clerical workers. The team operates as a semi--independent unit and reports to the Head of Acquisitions.

Interaction with the activities of the Original Cataloging Department is limited.

The principal duties and responsibilities of the Receipt Team are, of course, to locate acceptable catalog copy. To do this a series of set procedures must be followed. The operation is geared to realize fully the efficiencies offered by USL's affiliation with the Southeastern Library Network (SOLINET). To locate an acceptable OCLC record, a team member is required to look at specified fields, review the data in these fields, and follow the prescribed action outlined in the acceptance procedures. When an appropriate record is located, it is accepted without substantial change. Those fields in which in–putting is allowed have instructions explaining and limiting the action to be taken.

The concept of shared cataloging not only changed how material is processed and how tasks are organized, but also how personnel are selected and supervised to carry out the new routines.

The duties of the Receipt Team, for example, require personnel to have an understanding of general cataloging procedures in order to perform their work efficiently and correctly. As a consequence, the duties of clerical workers have become significantly more complex and demanding. Because assignments have become more specialized, such clerical skills as typing, filing, and knowledge of general office procedures are no longer key criteria for employment. "Optimal use of computer technology," wrote Craig Brod, "necessitates a high level match between people and machines."[1] The qualities sought to make the optimal match include the ability to demonstrate good problem--solving skills, to show attention to detail, to be able to concentrate for long periods of time, to work well in an unsupervised setting, and to be unintimidated by machine technology.

In addition to selecting competent and compatible people, it is also important that staff turnovers be kept to a minimum. Efficiency levels of highly automated activities, such as the Receipt Team, are very vulnerable when staff shortages occur. Temporary workers do not easily replace a missing team member. Terminal literacy and appreciation of cataloging concepts are not readily transferable skills. Re–assignment of workers from other sections also does not work well unless these employees frequently practice Receipt Team procedure.

The inability to quickly fill personnel vacancies only further accentuates the problems caused by staff shortages. Not only does the workflow slow, but the backlog becomes very noticeable due to the high volume of material that can be processed in an automated operation. Because it is counterproductive to fill a vacancy temporarily, operations usually remain unstaffed until a new employee can be fully trained. Periods in which vacancies occur can thus be very stressful for the remaining staff turnover, the employment pattern for clerical workers can be highly cyclical.[2] An unstable work force therefore can seriously challenge the efficiencies obtained by establishing sophisticated and highly automated procedures.

To counter this problem, it would seem logical that libraries would offer a salary and a job classification that would encourage good workers to apply and existing workers to remain. Yet, as Martin has pointed out,

> "There is frequently very little latitude in setting salaries for the support staff, since these are often determined by government scales (civil service) or by institutional–wide decisions. Nowadays, however, most libraries employ numbers of people with special qualifications or duties, such as computer programmers or paraprofessionals, sometimes called library assistants. The first group is the most likely to command market place premiums. The second is usually regarded as an anomaly in personnel classifications, and job analysts are frequently at a loss to determine an appropriate grade and therefore appropriate salary."[3]

Due to restrictions on pay and classification, the type of applicant who applies for a position on the Receipt Team has very little prior work experience. Consequently, the training period for new personnel is longer and more involved than it would be for more traditional clerical positions. The extra time is needed to train personnel not only in terminal procedures but also in the basic concepts of cataloging. It is also important to note that the activities of the Receipt Team are performed in a manner and frequency which does not allow errors to quickly be detected. Consequently, a slower and more intensive training period is encouraged.

An extended training period is also advantageous for other reasons, chief among which is the phychological factor. Learning to use computers remains a stressful activity for many individuals. Treating computer anxiety by a pre–training period, as suggested by Galagan and Schrami, is one way to counter the fear and hostility common to new users.[4]

Organization of Clerical Staff for Serials Processing

Clerical workers who are assigned duties in a serials unit which is highly automated may experience some, but certainly not all, of the same problems which have affected personnel involved in

247

assisted cataloging operations. Those who oversee serial operations will, of course, wish to employ competent individuals and individuals who feel comfortable working with machines. Unlike cataloging operations, automated serial activities such as check--in, claiming, ordering, and bindery, will not require clerical personnel to develop semi--professional skills. For example, many of the automated services being promoted by the major subscription agencies, such as EBSCO and Faxon, are designed to be operational without extensive staff training. Consequently, newly hired personnel are more likely to learn routines quickly and thus operations may run smoothly and with little disruption. Automated serial activities are not as dependent on staff skills as cataloging operations. The work, while at times complex, is not as sophisticated.

Role of the Supervisor

What may prove to be a more vexing problem is the change automated routines cause in the relationship between workers and non--professional supervisors. This should be of acute interest to those who oversee serial records operations, since these units are usually made up of mostly non–professional workers. For example, once personnel are trained in automated activities, co--workers tend to interact more with the computer than with fellow employees. Moreover, the use of the computer makes close super--vision somewhat redundant. As a consequence, Peter Druker be--lieves that the role of the supervisor in an automated process is changing. It is his opinion that first line supervisors should act "to bring out the strengths of the work force: competence and knowledge and capacity to take responsibility."[5]

The change in the role of the supervisor could be a particularly troublesome problem for Serial Records operations. Unlike the activities involved with copy cataloging, the automation of serial routines will most likely be grafted on to existing operations. As Stine pointed out in her survey, with the exception of Serial Cataloging, most Serial Records activities are staffed and supervised by clerical workers.[6] It will be difficult and at times painful to simultaneously change both the routine and the power structure. This may indeed be a particularly nettlesome problem if clerical supervisors view automation as a threat.

As previously mentioned, the increased application of automation to serial activities should not provoke the same degree of controversy afflicting Cataloging. Because many serial operations are already highly clericalized, the fine line between professional and non--professional is not as apparent. Nevertheless, the automation of Serials Record operations will draw further attention to

what Ellard and others feel is a blurring of what distinguishes between professional and non–professional duties.[7] The increased
use of automated routines will further enhance the position of the
clerical worker and encourage administrators to use fewer professionals and para–professionals in line positions. The ability of
workers to work more independently also further blurs the fine
line between departments that Hurowitz and McDonald mention.[8]
The ability of highly automated routines to need little interaction
or supervision further supports the concept of a unified technical
operation in which many clerks and few professionals are present.

While the controversy goes on about the changing role of clerical
workers, it is clear that automation has expanded their overall duties
and responsibilities. As a consequence, employees involved in
highly automated tasks must possess different skills and abilities
than those required of their co–workers of the past. The work
force must also remain stable in order for operations to be effective.
At the same time, the new procedures demand a new look at the
traditional relationship between supervisor and worker. The new
technology has affected both procedures and people.

Serial Records personnel will not be immune from the effects
caused by the accelerated use of automation in daily work routines.
However, the effect of automation on serial personnel is neither
as profound nor as controversial as it has been with workers involved
in cataloging. In serials, the clerical staff will need to develop new
skills, and supervisors will need to adjust to the change in their
status. More importantly, library managers must remain aware
that automation affects personnel, as well as procedures.

NOTES

1. Craig Brod, "Managing Technostress: Optimizing the Use of
   Computer Technology," *Personnel Journal,* 61 (1982): 754.

2. James G. Neal, "Staff Turnover and the Academic Library,"
   Foundation in Library and Information Science, 17 (Part A)
   (Greenwich, Connecticut: JAI Press, Inc., 1982): 104.

3. Murray S. Martin, "Issues in Personnel Management in Academic
   Libraries," *Foundations in Library and Information Science,*
   14 (Greenwich, Connecticut: JAI Press, Inc., 1981), p. 165.

4. Patricia Galagan, "Treating Computer Anxiety with Training,"
   Training and Development Journal, July 1983: 57–60.

   Mary L. Shrami, "The Psychological Impact of Automation

on Library and Office Workers," *Special Libraries,* 72 (1981): 149–155.

5. Peter F. Drucker, "Twilight of the First–Line Supervisor," *Wall Street Journal,* June 7, 1983, Sec. 1, p. 28.

6. Diane Stine "Serial Department Staffing Patterns in Medium–Sized Research Libraries," *Serials Review,* 7, No. 3 (1981): 84–85.

7. Kevin Ellard, "An Overview of Developments in Technical Services," *Studies in Library Management,* Vol. 6 (New York: Clive Bingley, 1980), p. 149.

8. Robert Hurowitz and David R. McDonald, "Library Automation and Library Organization: An Analysis of Future Trends," *Foundations In Library and Information Science,* Vol. 17 (Part B), (Greenwich, Connecticut: JAI Press, Inc., 1982) p. 618.

Checking It in the OCLC Way

Susan, Davis, Head of Serials
Illinois Institute of Technology
Chicago, IL

This paper discusses the OCLC Serials Control Subsystem's Check--in component. It will cover the basics of the system as well as the implementation of the subsystem and current practice at the Illinois Institute of Technology Libraries. Some knowledge of basic serial terminology and prior OCLC experience are assumed. Those desiring a more detailed discussion of the OCLC Serials Control Subsystem itself should consult OCLC's *Serials Control: User Manual.*

Background

The Institute is a medium--sized university with slightly over 3,000 serials titles in two libraries. The Serials Department handles ordering, payment, check--in, binding, and cataloging of all serials received by both libraries. Serial publications are defined in the broadest sense, including newspapers, conference proceedings, con--tinuations, periodicals, and monographic series. Staff consists of two check--in clerks, one bindery clerk, and one professional librarian.

The Institute decided to implement the Serials Control Sub--system in the fall of 1980. The Serials Department began the neces--sary preparation and training in early 1981. This led to the start of the actual online check--in in April.

In the discussion which follows, a general overview of the OCLC Serials Control Subsystem will be presented, followed by a discussion of IIT's local system application.

What is the OCLC Serials Control Subsystem?

The OCLC Serials Control Subsystem is an online inventory of serial publications for an institution or a library. It allows the maintenance of holdings, both current and retrospective, and the prediction of the arrival of future issues. The serials control process

Figure 1
Examples of completed LDRs.

Serials review.
ISSN: 0093-7913 CODEN: OCLC no: 1562672 Frequn: q Regulr: x

Hld lib: IAHP Copy: 1   Repr: Subsc Stat: a Loan: PHOTO COPY AT COST

```
 1 CINO   Periodicals
 2 LOCN   Kemper
 3 FUND   81072 FAXON 2-41903-442
 4 RMKS   Pierian Press, 5000 Washetenaw Ave., Ann Arbor, MI 43104
 5 RMKS   ROUTE/MB/SD/Return for shelving.
 6 EEFN   ‡v vol. ‡p no.
 7 NEXT   ‡v 2‡p 3‡a 331115
 8 DTRD   820613 820728 830103 830421 830620 830815
 9 CRHD   ‡v 2‡p 1-2‡y 1933
10 RTHD   ‡v 3‡y 1982
11 SCHD   ‡1 3301‡g 0‡e 4‡v 3-‡y 1932-
12 SIHD   IAH‡1 3301‡g 0‡e 4‡v 3-‡y 1982-
13 BNDG   Do not use
```

Figure 1 (cont.)

The Serials librarian.
ISSN: 0361-526X   CODEN: SELID4   OCLC no: 2705034   Frequn: q   Regulr: r

Hld lib: IAHP   Copy: 1   Repr: Subsc Stat: a   Loan: PHOTO COPY AT COST

```
 1 CLNO    Periodicals
 2 LOCN    Kemper
 3 FUND    31072 FAXON 2-41903-442
 4 RMKS    Haworth Press, 149 Fifth Ave., New York, NY  10010
 5 RMKS    ROUTE/MB/SD/Return for shelving
 6 DEFN    #v vol. #p no.
 7 NEXT    #v 3#p 1#d 330917
 8 DTRD    820723 821004 821123 830329 830519 830620
 9 CRHD    #v 7#p 1-4#y 1982/83
10 RTHD    #v 1-6#y 1976-1982
11 SCHD    #d 8211#g 0#e 4#v 1-#y 1976-
12 SIHD    IAH#d 8211#g 0#e 4#v 1-#y 1976-
13 BNDG    Not in use
```

253

involves creation and maintenance of local data records that contain local information as well as system--supplied data, specific to a particular title or copy of that title. The local data record, or LDR, is associated with the bibliographic record in the online union catalog for that particular title. Creating an LDR adds an institution's symbol to the list of holding libraries (without having cataloged the title), but does not affect the archival tape. A number of com-- ponents are planned for the subsystem: check--in, claiming, binding, union listing, and fund accounting. At this time, only check--in and union listing are fully operational. Claiming is due with the first enhancement package (due late 1983), fund accounting may be done through the use of the Acquisitions Subsystem, while bind-- ing is still under refinement.

The elements of an LDR may be seen in Figure 1. The heading information is pulled directly from the bibliographic record and includes name heading (1XX) if present; title (245); key title (222) if the first indicator of the 222 field is 1, 2, or 3; ISSN (022); CODEN (030); OCLC control number; frequency code; and regu-- larity code. Information may not be supplied directly by the user for these fields. Chnge requests may be submitted to OCLC if data is incorrect or lacking in these fields. This is important for the ISSN, frequency, and regularity codes which may affect search strategy success and proper updating during the check--in process.

The fixed field contains coded information describing the hold-- ing library (four letter OCLC code), copy number, form of repro-- duction, subscription status, and loan period. The data for these elements is locally determined, based on codes established by OCLC.

There are 12 main variable fields present in an LDR, however, use of all 12 is not required. Local needs determine the complexity of the LDRs at each institution. Following is a chart describing each variable field.

TAG	MEANING	DESCRIPTION
CLNO	call number	library call number for item
LOCN	location	≠a location or branch ≠b shelf designation
FUND	fund	payment information
RMKS	remarks	instructions, notes, routing information, free text area
DEFN	definition	indicates the numbering scheme of title
NEXT	next issue	number of next expected issue and predicted date of arrival
DTRD	date received	latest six receipt dates
CRHD	current holdings	numbering of current holdings, eg. ≠v 10 ≠p 1-5
RTHD	retrospective holdings	numbering of retrospective holdings, eg. ≠v 1-9 ≠y 1974-1982
SCHD	summary copy holdings	union list data — ANSI format holdings for this copy
SIHD	summary institution holdings	union list data — ANSI format holdings for entire institution
BNDG	binding	any binding information deemed necessary (new instructions will accompany the promised binding component)

Once an LDR is built, issues may be checked in automatically or manually. "R" is the automatic check--in function indicating an issue is received. The system adds one to the lowest subfield in NEXT, changes the expected date as indicated by the frequency code, places today's date in DTRD, and adds one to the lowest subfield in CRHD. The following example will illustrate this func-- tion.

DEFN   ≠v vol. ≠p no.   (freq:m)

NEXT   ≠v 13 ≠p 8 ≠d 830809

DTRD   830709

CRHD   ƒv 13 ƒp 1–7 ≠y 1983

We are expecting Vol. 13, no. 8 of a monthly publication on August 9, 1983. It is received on that date and checked in using the "r" function. The system will update the fields as described above.

NEXT   ≠v 13 ≠p 9 ≠d 830909   (adds one month to date and
                                      increments expected issue no.)
DTRD   830709 830809   (supplies today's date)

CRHD   ≠v 13 ≠p 1-8 ≠y 1983   (adds issue 8 to holdings)

The majority of titles can be checked in by use of the "r" function.

The "M" function is used to inform the system that the expected issue did not arrive. Generally, it indicates a missing, hence the use of "m", issue. Using the situation presented earlier, we receive Vol. 13, no. 9 instead of no. 8. After depressing "m", display record, send, the terminal responds:

NEXT   ≠v 13 ≠p 9 ≠d 830909

DTRD   830709 ??????

CRHD   ≠v 13 ≠p 1–7, ≠y 1983

Question marks are supplied in place of today's date and a comma indicates a gap. If we now check in issue 9, the following results:

NEXT   ≠v 10 ≠p 10 ≠d 831009

DTRD   830709 ?????? 830809

CRHD   ≠v 13 ≠p 1–7,9 ≠y 1983

The "r" and "m" functions are the only automatic system commands. All variable fields may be updated manually as needed, even after using "r" or "m."

Local Application

Preparation

Once the decision is made to go ahead with OCLC Serials Control, additional decisions are needed regarding local application. Is the available terminal time adequate? IIT ordered one additional OCLC terminal for the department work area to be used primarily for check–in purposes. Our experience has indicated that approximately eight hours per week are needed to check in 1,000 items per month.

What specific information is to be input into each field, and how complete should the LDR be? We made the decision to input complete LDRs, that is, 12 or 13 fields of data. This results in an initially slow input rate, but saves updating at a later date with more costly personnel. We also wanted data present in all the fields in anticipation of use in future enhancements. The specifics of each field were determined by the Serials Librarian, some based on information normally found in the kardex, others based mainly on system requirements. The *User Manual* provided the specific system requirements and examples of proper usage. Information in the NEXT, DTRD, and CRHD fields had to be properly formatted to accept the automatic check–in function. Non–numeric data had to be translated into numerics and defined. For example, if issues were designated spring, summer, fall, and winter, this was translated into number 1=spring, 2=summer, 3=fall, and 4=winter. Location notes such as "archives," "basement," "index tables," had to be uniformly applied. The contents of the RMKS field also had to be defined. This field is probably the most flexible, and therefore most locally specific, of all the fields present. Many options are available to the user. Our RMKS basically include publisher name and address, linking notes, routing information, and irregularities in publication pattern. We also made the determination that CRHD would contain the current year's holdings, with prior years in RTHD. Continuations were to be checked directly into the RTHD field as we were unable to make a logical distinction between current and retrospective holdings of this type of material.

256

(Some libraries record unbound issues in CRHD, bound in RTHD.) We made limited use of the BNDG field. At this time, it simply indicates our binding decision for paperback continuation volumes. Others may input out--to--bindery information, missing issues notes, replaced by microfilm, or other notes based on the local need. SCHD and SIHD were filled in according to the ANSI format as interpreted by OCLC and in accordance with our participation in the Serial of Illinois Libraries Online Union List of Serials.

How would information be input into the LDRs? What sources would provide this information? Who would select the proper bibliographic records to use? IIT was extremely fortunate to have just completed a retrospective serials cataloging project prior to entrance into Serials Control. OCLC bibliographic records had already been selected by professional cataloging staff, following the guidelines established by CONSER. Catalog cards were generated for all serials and contained the OCLC control numbers. It is important to select only successive entry records (especially important for union list participants) and LC/NSDP authenticated records (when available). Careful record selection will save rebuilding LDRs in the future. We also had a very thorough in--house serials holdings list to provide clear retrospective holdings data. (Shelf list records were not always interpretable by our student staff.) These two sources, along with our kardex records, provided data for the LDRs and allowed us to proceed quickly toward online check--in.

These decisions and instructions for implementation were for--malized for application. Written standards were particularly helpful for training personnel and resulted in uniform, coherent LDRs. In addition, future staff can benefit from an established set of guidelines.

Early Stages

Workforms were developed based mainly on the examples given in the *Serials Control Training Manual.* Some fields were automati--cally supplied on the form (our OCLC code for example). These were (and still are) reproduced as required. Our initial decision was to input only current subscriptions in order to begin checking in as soon as possible. Using a list of current subscriptions generated from our in--house list, we began filling out workforms with the A's in January 1981. One student assisted in this project, another was hired to input workforms to the system during evening hours. All workforms were reviewed by the Serials Librarian prior to input. We chose not to go through the kardex file one by one for our initial set of LDRs. This would have resulted in a major housekeeping operation, which was not an objective of the project. We would attend to the problem titles later. During this early phase we added approximately 2,000 LDRs to the data base over a four month period. One student worked 15–20 hours per week, averaging six to eight LDRs input per hour. (Less complete LDRs can be input at a faster rate.)

A few test titles were selected at the outset to facilitate training. These helped us gain familiarity with the system without the pres-sure of a full day's workload. To these initial test titles were gradu-ally added sections of the alphabet as they were input to the system. By the end of the summer of 1981 we were attempting to check in all material.

Dual check–in was temporarily retained with a goal of full online check–in set for December 1982. This goal has been met for 75% of the titles. Our time table was set back a year for the rest of our titles. A final clean–up project is set to begin in 1984 to complete the transfer from paper to online check–in. While dual check–in is more time consuming, we did not want to abandon our kardex records without verifying the accuracy and completeness of the online records. Sections of the alphabet were designated over time to undergo a review process. Upon receipt, the item was searched in the kardex. If a record was found, the kardex and payment card were pulled, placed in the piece and set aside for review by the Serials Librarian. The Serials Librarian called up the record on OCLC, verified the data, added notes or made other revisions if needed, and checked in the piece. Thereafter this title was checked in only online. Payment cards were retained in a separate file to facilitate invoice processing. Check–in cards were retired.

Training

Training began with a brief OCLC demonstration at a LITA meeting. The appropriate manuals, *Serials Control: Training Manual* and *Serials Control: User Manual,* were purchased from OCLC and carefully read. Proper OCLC authorization for the Serials Librarian was obtained prior to the official go–ahead decision, so there were no delays in getting underway online. The practice exercises in the manual are very useful, but a thorough online demonstration, by either network personnel or a current SCS user is probably the most instructive. We had neither luxury, as we were one of the first SCS users in Illinois. However, we did obtain valuable planning assistance from Knox College, one of the test libraries.

Using the test titles mentioned earlier was an excellent beginning.

As with any new online system, there is always the fear of ruining or losing records, or even crashing the system altogether! Our clerical staff had no prior experience with OCLC, an additional obstacle to overcome. Once these fears are alleviated, real learning can occur. Starting slowly with a few titles was very helpful. The clerks were allowed to "make mistakes" so they could learn how to manipulate the system without difficulty. This is a very important aspect of hands--on training which allows the staff to develop sufficient confidence to work independently. At the outset partial authorization was obtained for our check--in clerks. It was thought that this somewhat limited authorization would make them feel more secure, as the system would prevent them from performing certain tasks, such as deleting fields. Later, the authorization was upgraded to full so they could do more than just check in issues. They assumed responsibility for adding helpful notes, inputting new LDRs, and updating certain fields; all processes which were not allowed under their initial authorization. All Serials Department staff did attend a network training session on the Serials Control Subsystem. However, this was after we began online check–in.

A series of departmental orientations provided an ideal opportunity to demonstrate the use of the system to the rest of the library staff. Acquisitions staff now check the data base instead of the kardex for monographic series standing orders. Public services can verify latest issue received in response to a patron query. More library--wide use of the system is expected as improvements are made both to the system and our serials departmental procedures.

The Check--in Process

This section describes the events over a "normal" day's operation. Special problems will be addressed in a separate section.

After opening the day's mail, the clerk takes the material directly to the terminal. No alphabetization or other preparation is done. We decided not to use any form of a look--up index prior to check--in. We felt that the existence of such an index defeated the purpose of an online system and should not be necessary. The ISSN is our primary search key. Clerks have been trained to locate the ISSN in the piece, or if one is lacking, to use a title search. Based on a sampling of a week's issues, approximately 19% of the titles do not carry an ISSN in the publication. ISSNs for almost half our titles retrieve more than one hit on OCLC. Thus, it is not the most precise search key. However, it is far superior to a title or author/ title search. A search enhancement, scheduled for implementation with the claims component, will greatly streamline the search process.

Once the search is keyed in (title searches are always qualified by "/ser"), the results are examined. If there is more than one match, Library of Congress (DLC) copy is selected first. If an LDR has been built on that record, it (not the bibliographic record) will appear on the screen. If not, the clerk continues searching the choices until the LDR is located.

The NEXT field is compared to the piece in hand. If they match and the expected date is within ten days of today's date (or an exact match for weeklies), the piece is checked in. Any special instructions are noted. The clerk then keys in "r," update, and send, completely checking in the piece. Should the predicted date of arrival be off by more than ten days, it is manually adjusted prior to "receiving" the issue. This expected date will be important for the efficiency of the claims component. In anticipation of its imminent implementation, we attempt to keep this data as accurate as possible.

Other operator intervention may be required in certain situations. After the completion of a volume, the RTHD field is updated manually, while CRHD is adjusted to reflect the new volume and year. The system will automatically change the volume number in NEXT after the expected number of issues are received, for example, issues 1–4 of a quarterly. The following example illustrates this action.

Vol. 10, no. 4 is received and completes the volume.

NEXT	≠v 10 ≠p 4 ≠d 830815
DTRD	830515
CRHD	≠v 10 ≠p 1–3 ≠y 1983
RTHD	≠v 9 ≠y 1982

After using the "r" function and manually updating the fields, the results are:

NEXT	≠v 11 ≠p 1 ≠d 83115	**system
DTRD	830515 830815	**system
CRHD	≠v 11 ≠y 1984	**manual
RTHD	≠v 9--10 ≠y 1982–1983	**manual

The missing command, "m," is used if an issue is skipped. When the claims component is installed, this will trigger a claim notice. Until then, we make a note to claim manually.

Double issues may be checked in by using "r" twice or manually adjusting the fields to reflect the extra issue. The latter saves the cost of one update on the system, but requires more terminal time.

New Orders

Since IIT is not an Acquisitions Subsystem user, there is no online order file. LDRs are not prepared when a title is ordered, as OCLC would show us as a holding library before we actually received any issues. Instead, a payment card is typed at the time of order and filed with the order slip in the old kardex. When the first issue arrives, the clerk can check this file after failing to locate an LDR online. The clerk then fills out an LDR workform for the Serials Librarian to review. The issue will be cataloged at this time as well. The LDR is added to the system by the clerk during regular working hours, and future issues may be checked in online. Payment cards are removed from the kardex and filed in the payment drawer.

Title Changes

When title changes are noted during check–in, the clerk provides the Serials Librarian with the piece and OCLC record numbers (we have no printer in Serials) for the old and new titles (if available). The old LDR is updated to reflect the title change by including a linking note to the new title in RMKS, deleting NEXT, CRHD, and other fields pertaining to checking in a current subscription, changing subscription status to ceased, and updating the holdings for the union list. A new LDR is input for the new title, again including a reference to its predecessor. Other library records are adjusted accordingly.

Problems

This section will identify some of the major problems en-- countered since joining the OCLC Serials Control Subsystem and our solutions. These solutions are not the only possibilities. Other librarians may have very different ideas. The local situation will often indicate the types of problem experienced.

Searching

Developing a highly sophisticated search strategy is very impor--tant to the speed and success level of the check--in process. Of course, search strategies play an important role in each OCLC sub--system, but serials present particularly difficult searches. Most journals, as earlier mentioned, contain an ISSN somewhere within the piece. Only 5% of these, based on our sample, will have no match in the data base. To these, we add the 19% with no ISSN, our IEEE conference publications, and monographic series to form a small, but unwieldy body of publications to search.

Material with a simple title usually requires no more than a title search (with a serial qualifier) and some patience. The *Economist* is an example of a publication with no ISSN in the piece. Its title search is "eco, , , /ser". This retrieves over 250 matches. Happy hunting! Fortunately, OCLC will be offering a permanent solution to this type of problem. By logging in under a special type of authorization, searches performed will retrieve only those records with the institutional symbol attached. This will greatly reduce the number of hits per search key, often resulting in an exact match on the first try.

The IEEE (Institute of Electrical and Electronics Engineers) conference publications present special problems. Their title pages are graphic wonders, but puzzling to almost all library staff. We happen to have an open order plan which provides us with at least 250 such publications each year. Many of these are serial in nature, and our policy has been to treat them as such. Other libraries may prefer to treat them as monographs. Regardless, these publica--tions are perhaps the most difficult English--language material to search successfully on OCLC. Some basic hints were developed to assist the clerks in their searching. These include 1) use an ISSN if present; 2) use name of conference as author, and proceedings, record, papers, or similar wording as title; 3) avoid cutesy names (GLOBECON) as these often change from one conference to the next. These same strategies can often be used for other types of conference publications, although reliable LC Card Numbers or Cataloging in Publication data may frequently be found in these pieces.

Series present another problem. For check--in purposes, we need to retrieve the serial record for the series. A common inclina--tion is to search by the individual title on the cover. This retrieves a monographic record for that specific volume. It is therefore necessary to determine the series entry, then do a title search to retrieve the serial record. Again, if Cataloging in Publication data is present, determining the series is not too difficult. Nor is it when the series name is prominently printed on the cover or title page. Numbered series are usually easier to identify than unnum--

bered series.

Staff already familiar with OCLC searching may find it easier to pick up the techniques for tracking down problem titles. A set of examples with some general guidelines is most beneficial.

Numbering Oddities

The system is set up to automatically update records for titles which follow a standard pattern of one volume per year, regular intervals between issues, and an established frequency. Any titles which deviate from this pattern require some type of operator intervention during check--in to maintain the integrity of the LDR.

Titles published in more than one volume per year require that strict attention be paid to the numbering of each piece. The system will never adjust the volume numbering of a monthly pub--lished in two volumes of six issues per year. It will be waiting for issue 12 to arrive before incrementing the volume number. The operator will manually adjust NEXT and CRHD to reflect a new volume after issue 6 is checked in. Many volumes published per year often create a cluttered CRHD field, diminishing its clarity. RMKS should contain a note indicating the number of issues per volume and volumes per year to facilitate check--in.

Serials published somewhat irregularly can also create some confusion. Educational titles are good examples. Many are pub--lished regularly during the academic year, but not at all over the summer. The frequency code may be monthly, but only nine issues are actually published. Again, the system is expecting 12 issues to generate a change in volume numbering. A note indicating the number of issues or volumes per year can assist the check--in staff in determining if and when to intervene. OCLC has recognized this problem and will be allowing users to set the real frequency and expected number of issues for the system.

Special Issues and Indexes

Special issues are often not numbered and may appear without warning. Where are these checked in? If the issue will be part of our periodical collection, we generally check it in with the regular issues by enclosing the date of the special issue in brackets at the far right hand side of the CRHD field. The CRHD field would look something like:

CRHD   ≠v 77 ≠p 1–8 ≠y 1983 [special issue July 1983]

Some special issues may receive special treatment. This information appears in a RMKS field.

RMKS   Special issues cataloged separately. Process as VARIES.

Regular special issues (for example, directories and buyer's guides) may be checked in on a separate bibliographic record if they are cataloged separately. A cross reference in RMKS can lead check–in personnel to the correct LDR.

RMKS   Director issue checked in on its own record. See OCLC No. 8952730.

RMKS can also be used to reflect a decision not to catalog and check--in separately.

RMKS   Stamp and shelve Directory with regular issues.

Indexes to journal titles or cumulative indexes to indexing and abstracting services offer two check--in options, separate records or all on one. We check in the cumulative indexes on the bibliog--raphic record for that cumulation. Other indexes are recorded in the RTHD field of the title's LDR. It is not necessary to use separate bibliographic records for indexes. However, we found that separate records permitted more use of the automatic check--in function, but prompted the creation of more LDRs.

Check–in by Date

The library receives a number of weekly, biweekly, and semi--monthly titles which we prefer to check in by issue date. The system automatically increments NEXT and CRHD by ones, not sevens, fourteens, or fifteens. Thus, the automatic check--in function is inappropriate for these titles. Instead, we update NEXT, DTRD, and CRHD manually. The issue date is set up in MMDD form as the issue number, with year in the volume area. Updating all three fields accurately and completely may not be done consistently. Also, unless there is a prominent note reminding the clerk to check in manually, automatic check–in may be attempted, resulting in a confusing display. Once the clerk becomes accustomed to this type of title, check--in generally progresses smoothly.

Microforms

IIT subscribes to very few microforms, so this has not been a particular problem for us. However it is a controversial issue facing many libraries, especially since the advent of AACR2. AACR2 prescribes separate bibliographic records for each different format. Therefore, it follows that separate LDRs should exist for each format. Since we have so few microforms, compliance with this rule has not been difficult nor costly. Cross references are used to assist the operator from one format to another. However, other libraries have chosen to follow the microform exception rule, building one LDR per title, rather than one per format. This saves the cost of LDR creation (currently $.45) and the projected storage fees. Our recommendation is to follow the guidelines established by your network.

Examples of actual LDRs for some of the problems identified above can be found in Appendix A.

Summary

This paper presents an overview of OCLC's Serials Control Subsystem and a description of the implementation and current procedures at one institution. Basic decisions and the rationale behind them are also discussed. Proper planning before embarking on automated serials control is extremely important. The issues presented here should provide a base from which other serials librarians can make intelligent decisions regarding the implementation of the OCLC Serials Control Subsystem. Practical and flexible procedures must be developed. OCLC has plans for extensive improvements in the system. Thus, many of the procedures mentioned here will have to be adjusted. The serials control process is ever changing, as are serials themselves, and we must be flexible enough to change with it.*

*See pages following Appendix A for enhancements.

APPENDIX A. Examples of problems

```
New York Public Library.
New technical books.
ISSN: 0028-6869  CODEN: NTBOAJ  OCLC no:  1642674  Frequn:  m  Regulr: n

   Hld lib: IAHP Copy: 1     Repr:    Subsc Stat: a  Loan: PHOTO COPY AT COST.

    1 CLNO      Periodicals
    2 LOCN      Kemper
    3 FUND      81072 FAXON 2-41903-442
    4 RMKS      New York Public Library, Fifth Ave. and 42nd St., New York, NY
    5 RMKS      ROUTE--PB/ALA/JL/MB/DD/JK/SD/NB/Return for shelving
    6 RMKS      Ten issues yearly, none published Aug-Sept.
    7 DEFN      $v vol.  $p no.
    8 NEXT      $v 68 $p 8 $d 330918
    9 DTRD      830328 830531 830726 830728 830729 830818
   10 CRHD      $v 68 p 1-7 $y 1983
   11 RTHD      $v 13-66 $y 1928-1981
   12 SCHD      $d 8211 $g 0 $e 4 $v 13- $y 1928-
   13 SIHD      IAH $d 8211 $g 0 $e 4 $v 13- $y 1928-
   14 BNDG      Do not use
```

Irregular publication pattern.

```
Lecture notes in physics.
ISSN: 0075-8450 CODEN: LNPHA4  OCLC no:  1606610  Frequn:      Regulr: x

   Hld lib: IAHC Copy: 1     Repr:    Subsc Stat: a  Loan: 3 WEEKS

    1 CLNO      VARIES
    2 LOCN      Kemper
    3 FUND      S00043 Direct 2-41903-442
    4 RMKS      Springer Verlag, 175 Fifth Ave., New York, NY 10010
    5 DEFN      $v vol.
    6 NEXT      $v 185 $d 830913
    7 DTRD      830518 830613 830713 830713 830713 830823
    8 RTHD      $v 13-14,32-33,39,41,44-47,50,53-54,56,60,63,66-75,77-85,87-103,
105-136,138-184
    9 SCHD      $d 8306 $g 0 $e 4 $v 13-
   10 SIHD      IAH $d 8306 $g 0 $e 4 $v 13-
   11 BNDG      BIND
```

Series check-in screen.

Figure 2.

Telecommunications digest /
ISSN: CODEN: OCLC no: 9384538 Frequn: w Regulr: r

Hld lib: IAHP Copy: 1   Repr: Subsc Stat: a Loan: PHOTO COPY AT COST

```
 1 CLNO       Periodicals
 2 LOCN       Kemper $b Current two years only
 3 FUND       81072 FAXON 2-41903-442
 4 RMKS       Telecommunications Reports, 1293 National Press Bldg.,
Washington, DC 20045
 5 RMKS       Must check in manually. Update NEXT,DTRD,CRHD yourself. "R" will
not work properly for this title.
 6 DEFN       $v year $p MMDD
 7 NEXT       $v 1983 $p 0830 $d 330830
 8 DTRD       830719 330726 830802 830809 830816 830823
 9 CRHD       $v 1983 $p 0315-0323
10 SCHD       $d 8304 $g 0 $e 4 $f 6 $n retains current two years
11 SIHD       IAH $d 8304 $g 0 $e 4 $f 6 $n retains current two years
12 BNDG       Not in use
```

Check in by date. Note RMKS field.

Process: architecture.
ISSN: 0386-037X CODEN: OCLC no: 4049049 Frequn: u Regulr: u

Hld lib: IAHP Copy: 1   Repr: Subsc Stat: a Loan: PHOTO COPY AT COST

```
 1 CLNO       Periodicals
 2 LOCN       Kemper
 3 FUND       81080 Direct 2-41903-442
 4 RMKS       Japan Publications Trading Co. Ltd., P..O.Box 5030 Tokyo
              International, Tokyo,Japan
 5 DEFN       $v year $p no.
 6 NEXT       $v 1983 $p 40 $d 830816
 7 DTRD       830128 830208 830504 830519 830726 830817
 8 CRHD       $v 1983 $p 31-39
 9 RTHD       $v 1977-1982 $p 1-22,24-30 [supplement to no.27 rec'd]
10 SCHD       $d 8210 $g 0 $e 4 $v 1-22,24- $y 1977-
11 SIHD       IAH $d 8210 $g 0 $e 4 $v 1-22,24- $y 1977-
12 BNDG       Do not use
```

Special issue.

Figure 3.

```
Chemical engineering.
Chemical engineering(New York)
ISSN: 0009-2460  CODEN: CHEEA3  OCLC no:  1553962  Frequn:  e  Regulr: r

   Hld lib: IAHP Copy: 1     Repr:    Subsc Stat: a Loan: PHOTO COPY AT COST

    1 CLNO      Periodicals
    2 LOCN      Kemper
    3 FUND      81072 FAXON 2-41903-442
    4 RMKS      McGraw Hill, 330 W.42nd St., New York, NY
    5 RMKS      One issue per year is "Equipment Buyer's Guide". Stamp and
shelve with current issues.
    6 RMKS      Continues "Chemical and metallurgical engineering"
    7 DEFN      $v vol. $p no.
    8 NEXT      $v 90 $p 18 $d 830905
    9 DTRD      830613 830623 830711 830722 830805 830819
   10 CRHD      $v 90 $p 1-17 $y 1983
   11 RTHD      $v 53-89 $y 1946-1982
   12 SCHD      $d 8210 $g 0 $e 4 $v 53- $y 1946-
   13 SIHD      IAH $d 8210 $g 0 $e 4 $v 53- $y 1946-
   14 BNDG      Not in use
```

Special issue.

```
Journal of differential equations.
ISSN: 0022-0396  CODEN:          OCLC no:  1754537  Frequn:  m  Regulr: r

   Hld lib: IAHP Copy: 1     Repr:    Subsc Stat: a Loan: PHOTO COPY AT COST

    1 CLNO      Periodicals
    2 LOCN      Kemper
    3 FUND      20187 Direct 2-41903-442
    4 RMKS      Academic Press, 111 Fifth Ave., New York, NY  10003
    5 RMKS      Four volumes per year
    6 DEFN      $v vol. $p no.
    7 NEXT      $v 49 $p 3 $d 830921
    8 DTRD      830408 830419 830511 830701 830722 830817
    9 CRHD      $v 47 $p 1-3 $v 48 $p 1-3 $y 1983 $v 49 $p 1-2
   10 RTHD      $v 1-46 $y 1965-1982
   11 SCHD      $d 8210 $g 0 $e 4 $v 1- $y 1965-
   12 SIHD      IAH $d 8210 $g 0 $e 4 $v 1- $y 1965-
   13 BNDG      Do not use
```

Multiple volumes per year.

Figure 4.

Business periodicals index.
ISSN: 0007-6961 CODEN: OCLC no: 1537913 Frequn: a Regulr: r

Hld lib: IAHH Copy: 1   Repr: Subsc Stat: a Loan: PHOTO COPY AT COST

```
 1 CLNO      Periodicals
 2 LOCN      Stuart
 3 FUND      63272 Direct 4-50075-442
 4 RMKS      H.W. Wilson Co.,950 University Ave.,Bronx, N.Y. 10052 Account no.
5-07088-000
 5 RMKS      ANNUAL VOLUMES ONLY!!! CHECK IN MONTHLIES ON OCLC #5574615!!
 6 RMKS      Send annual to be shelflisted
 7 DEFN      $v vol.
 8 NEXT       $v 26 $d 840608
 9 DTRD      810403 820310 830309 830608
10 RTHD       $v 1-25 $y 1958-1982/83
11 SCHD       $d 8303 $g 0 $e 4 $v 1- $y 1958-
12 SIHD      IAH $d 8308 $g 0 $e 4 $v 1- $y 1958-
13 BNDG      Do not use
```

Business periodicals index.
ISSN: 0007-6961 CODEN: OCLC no: 5574615 Frequn: m Regulr: n

Hld lib: IAHH Copy: 1   Repr: Subsc Stat: a Loan: PHOTO COPY AT COST

```
 1 CLNO      Periodicals
 2 LOCN      Stuart
 3 FUND      63272 Direct 4-50075-442
 4 RMKS      H.W. Wilson Co., 950 University Ave., Bronx, NY  10052
 5 RMKS      MONTHLY ISSUES ONLY!!! CHECK IN ANNUAL ON OCLC# 1537913!!!
 6 RMKS      Superseded by annual volumes, therefore we will not maintain a
RTHD field.
 7 DEFN       $v vol. $p no.
 8 NEXT       $v 25 $p 11 $d 830808
 9 DTRD      830228 830308 830405 830516 830608 830706
10 CRHD       $v 25 p 1-10 $y 1982/83
11 SCHD       $d 8302 $g 0 $e 4 $f 6 n retained until annual cumulation is
received
12 SIHD      IAH $d 8302 $g 0 $e 4 $f 6 $n retained until annual cumulation is
received
```

Figure 5. Cumulative index

Addendum

On September 6, 1983, OCLC introduced its first enhancement since the moratorium had been announced. Release 1, as it was called, radically altered the serials check–in process. Several of the problems described in the body of this paper have been solved, other improved, and an online claims feature added. I would like to briefly describe these changes and how they have affected our procedures.

A. Search Enhancement

When logged into serials control with full, partial, or search authorization, any search done will retrieve only records with your holdings already attached. In other words, your search is limited to your own database of records. If desired, this option may be changed at any point by "selecting" another. The other options are searching the entire online union catalog or searching a particular union list group's records. To summarize, these options are:

selectoluc   to search the online union catalog

select[union list group code]   to search the holdings of a particular union list

select[OCLC code]   to search only your own records

select?   this command results in a help screen detailing the options and the proper command structure

For check–in, this has the obvious impact of reducing the number of matches to any search key. The *Economist* example mentioned earlier retrieved over 256 entries, after this search enhancement the same search key retrieves only six! This allows faster and more accurate retrieval of records to be used for check–in purposes.

It is important to remember to change the select option as necessary, especially when doing any general bibliographic searches. The system will respond "the records retrieved did not match your search option" if you attempt to search for records your institution does not already own. The OCLC record number is exempt from this restriction.

B. DEFN Update

Three new subfields have been added to the DEFN field to improve the accuracy of predicting the next issue's arrival. These are ≠e (exception to publications cycle format), ≠f (frequency value), and ≠g (enumeration level update sequence).

≠e indicates the months, weeks, or days a serial is published. Zeroes in this field indicate when a serial is not published. ≠f indicates the frequency pattern to be displayed in ≠e, and also the increment pattern for NEXT ≠d. Exceptions found in ≠e will override the values in ≠f. Examples will follow to help illustrate these functions. ≠g contains the number of issues per volume, thus allowing the system to automatically increment the volume number when appropriate.

We have had to enhance our existing LDRs for current titles to incorporate the new features of Release 1. We were used to the frequency code from the bibliographic record controlling NEXT ≠d, now it is controlled by ≠f and ≠e in DEFN. As we check in each piece, we concentrate on adding the new bits of information in DEFN as well as the fields necessary for online claiming. This has resulted in a slowing of our check--in rate during this process, but has been less disruptive on our staff's workflow than a title by title review. We have taken approximately three months to input the new information for the majority of our titles. The two claiming fields, to be described later, require more time and effort than upgrading DEFN. For libraries now considering OCLC's Serials Control Subsystem, all appropriate information may be input at once, instead of adding bits and pieces with each new release, as we have had to do. Nonetheless, we are very glad to have these enhancements from OCLC.

EXAMPLES

1) Quarterly publication

The Quarterly journal of mechanics and applied mathematics.
ISSN: 0033-5614   CODEN: QJMMAV   OCLC no: 1334524   Frequn: q   Regulr: r

```
 5 DEFN    $v vol.$p part$e 0 2 0 0 5 0 0 3 0 0 11 0$f m$g [$p 4 ]
 6 NEXT    v 37 p 2 d 840507
 7 DTRD    820816 821116 830308 830517 831031 840207
 8 CRHD    v 37 p 1 y 1984
12 PURC    A$i 068703$o 81072$s 32868$t 41285
13 CLMS    s$b 3$c 12262$d 2m$e 41285$i 41285
```

NOTE: 4 issues per volume $g, 0's for months not published
      PURC and CLMS fields are used in online claiming

2) Bimonthly publication

```
Industrial design magazine :ID.
ID. Industrial design magazine
ISSN: 0192-3021  CODEN:          OCLC no:  4689675  Frequn:  b  Regulr: x

    6 DEFN    $v vol. $p no. $e 0 2 0 4 0 6 0 8 0 10 0 12 $f m $g [ $p 6 ]
    7 NEXT    $v 31 $p 1 $d 840325
   12 PURC    P $i xxx $o 80159 $s subscription $t 41285
   13 CLMS    s $b 3 $c 41947 $d 2m $e 41285 $i 41285
```

NOTE: 6 issues per volume in $g

3) Not published in certain months

```
New York Public Library.
New technical books.
ISSN: 0028-6869  CODEN: NTBOAJ  OCLC no:  1642674  Frequn:  m  Regulr: n

    6 RMKS    Ten issues yearly, none published Aug-Sept.
    7 DEFN    $v vol. $p no. $e 1 2 3 4 5 6 7 0 0 10 11 12 $f m $g [ $p 10 ]
    8 NEXT    $v 69 $p 2 $d 840211
```

More examples will follow the body of this text.

C. Claims

The online claiming capability is now available. Claiming may be system controlled (automatic), system and user controlled (semi-automatic), or manual. Most libraries will opt for semi-automatic, as did we. The system will identify potential claims, while the user will have the final decision to claim or not.

Two new fields, CLMS and PURC, in conjunction with NEXT and DEFN, are needed. CLMS contains information regarding the maximum number of claims to be generated for a title, delay period, supplier address code from the Name Address Directory, response address code, and other claiming options. PURC contains the financial and subscription information – order number, account number, invoice number, and the like. NEXT ≠d is examined each night to determine if an issue is overdue, based on the delay period in CLMS. For instance, if Vol. 10, no. 11 is due on 11/1/83 and the delay period is one month, the system will identify that issue as a potential claim on 12/2/83 if it has not yet been checked in. Skipped issues will automatically be tagged for potential claiming, provided the proper fields are present. This is not done immediately, but overnight.

These delay periods are user defined and should be based on your own experiences. Reviewing the potential claims file requires the same type of judgment exercised in reviewing a kardex file. You should continue to use the knowledge and skill acquired from the manual claim process in the online version.

Once an actual claim is generated, forms are printed and mailed by OCLC personnel. No paper copies need be kept by the library if they so choose. An online claims file keeps track of claims generated until they are resolved. The system will automatically reclaim an item after 45 days if it has not yet been received.

D. Conclusion

There are many more aspects to OCLC's Release 1 for Serials than have been discussed here. The above was an attempt to briefly expose readers to the basic changes since September 6, 1983. The enhancements are still new enough that we have probably not realized their full potential. The impact on our departmental procedures has been great. We are now able to claim titles which we never realized had lapsed, and we no longer need to keep paper claim files. It requires more terminal time to review the potential claims file and send off the claims. However, the benefits of online claiming far outweigh this additional time requirement. The adjustment period has been filled with frustration, confusion, relearning, and impatience, but most of all with the knowledge that the system has definitely improved and that our procedures must keep pace with these improvements to better serve our users.

Acknowledgment

I would like to acknowledge the use of the following OCLC publications for the technical descriptions of their subsystem.

Serials Control: Users Manual, September 1979.
Serials Control: Training Manual, 2nd ed., 1981.
Serials Control: User Manual, 1983.

ADDITIONAL SAMPLES OF DEFN, CLMS AND PURC

```
Library journal.
Library journal(1976)
ISSN: 0363-0277  CODEN:          OCLC no:  2351916  Freqqn:  s  Regulr: n

  7 DEFN     v vol. p no. e 1,0 2,2 3,3 4,4 5,5 6,6 7,0 8,0 9,9 10,10 11,11
12,0 f s g [ p 20 ]
  8 NEXT     v 109 p 3 d 840220
  9 DTRD     831102 831118 831201 831212 840124 840206
 10 CRHD 1   v 109 p 1-2
 11 RTHD     v 101 p 9-24 y 1976 v 102-108 y 1977-1983
 12 SCHD     d 8306 g 0 e 4 v 101:9- y 1976-
 13 SIHD     IAH d 8306 g 0 e 4 v 101:9- y 1976-
 14 PURC     A i 055096 o 81072 s 32868 t 41285
 15 CLMS     s b 3 c 12262 d 2w e 41285 i 41285



Electronics.
ISSN: 0013-5070  CODEN:          OCLC no:  1567758  Freqqn:  e  Regulr: x

  5 DEFN     v vol. p no. e 1 0 3 0 5 0 7 0 9 0 11 0 13 0 15 0 17 0 19 0 21
 0 23 0 25 0 27 0 29 0 31 0 33 0 35 0 37 0 39 0 41 0 43 0 45 0 47 0 49 0 0 0 f
w g [ p 25 ]
  6 NEXT     v 57 p 4 d 840216
  7 DTRD     831020 831102 831117 831201 831221 840112 840207
  8 CRHD     v 57 p 1-3 y 1984
  9 RTHD     v 1-56 y 1930-1983 [we lack Oct-Dec 1981]
 10 SCHD     d 8210 g 0 e 4 v 1- y 1930-
 11 SIHD     IAH d 8210 g 0 e 4 v 1- y 1930-
 12 PURC     A i 042843 o 81072 s 32868 t 41285
 13 CLMS     s b 3 c 12262 d 2w e 41285 i 41285
```

274

The New leader.
ISSN: 0023-6044 CODEN: OCLC no: 1643783 Frequn: e Regulr: n

    5 DEFN   v vol. p no. e 0 2 0 4 0 6 0 8 0 10 0 12 0 14 0 16 0 18 0 20 0
22 0 24 0 0 27 0 0 0 31 0 0 34 0 36 0 38 0 40 0 42 0 44 0 46 0 48 0 50 0 52 f
w g [p 24]
    6 NEXT   v 67 p 4 d 840210
    7 DTRD   831014 831101 831116 831130 831216 831229 840116 840130
    8 CRHD   v 67 p 1 y 1984
    9 RTHD   v 48 p 3-25 y 1965 v 49-66 y 1966-1983
   10 SCHD   d 8210 g 0 e 4 v 48- y 1965-
   11 SIHD   IAH d 8210 g 0 e 4 v 48- y 1965-
   12 PURC   A i 061940 o 81072 s 32868 t 41285
   13 CLMS   s b 3 c 12262 d 2w e 41285 i 41285

PURC A=Agent, ≠i=invoice, ≠o=order, ≠s account no., ≠t ship
      to address

CLMS s=semi-automatic, ≠b=maximum number of claims,
      ≠c=Name Address code for supplier, ≠d=delay, ≠e=
      address for response, ≠i=contact for inquiry regarding
      claim

SAMPLE CHART FOR DELAY PERIOD CODES
(m=month, w=week)

FREQ code	DELAY code ≠d
d (daily)	1w
w (weekly)	2w
e (biweekly)	2w
s (semi-monthly)	2w
m (monthly)	1m
b (bimonthly)	2m
q (quarterly)	2m
t (triquarterly)	3m
f (semi-annual)	3m
a (annual)	6m
u (unknown)	6m
z (irregular)	6m

Check--in for Indexing: NLM Serial Control System

William Willmering
Head, Serial Records Section
National Library of Medicine

Background

Automation of the serial record of the National Library of Medi-- cine (NLM) has been on--going since the mid--1970's. A modular set of files, called the NLM Master Serials System, has been devel-- oped using the commercial database management system INQUIRE. Initially the system was used for bibliographic and holdings control. Later, binding and preservation modules, as well as ordering and fiscal control were added.[1] Production of four publications[2] issued by the Serial Records Section is controlled through this same system, as is serial title authority validation for citations indexed in MED-- LINE, other NLM on--line files, and in the printed products derived from these files such as INDEX MEDICUS. By 1980, NLM's Serial Records Section was using this system to build the National Bio-- medical Serials Holdings database, a file of some half--million records representing holdings for approximately 1,000 biomedical libraries throughout the United States.[3]

Also, in 1980, the Serial Records Section began developing an internal current receipt file for check--in data. Because approxi-- mately 60% of NLM's total serial receipts are processed at remote locations by subscription agents,[4] the first priority in building the check--in file was loading the tapes from the agents detailing the material they had processed for NLM. By spring 1981, in--house staff augmented the tape loaded data by adding on--line data for material sent directly to NLM. The Serial Records Section was able to build a file of records sufficient to permit retrieval of current receipt data and a crude claiming capability. Although pleased with this initial success, the staff was disappointed by the overall slow processing rate and the uneven quality of data, resulting from the delay caused by the overnight batch loading of data.

In the fall of 1982, planning began for a new check--in system which would be interactive, with multiple users adding records to the file immediately, using formatted screens. This check--in

Figure 1

```
ENTER ISSN:    ____-____
ENTER TK:      SCA/J/O/I      KEYWORD  SCANDINAVIAN_____
ENTER SEQ:     _____



*****************************  1   ************************************
SCANDINAVIAN JOURNAL OF IMMUNOLOGY. SUPPLEMENT

PL: OSLO                    PU: UNIVERSITETSFORLAGET
0301-6323  FREQ:  I     FL:  1,1973--                              OPEN
*****************************  2   ************************************
SCANDINAVIAN JOURNAL OF INFECTIOUS DISEASES. SUPPLEMENTUM

PL: STOCKHOLM               PU: ALMQUIST AND WIKSELL
0300-8878  FREQ:  I     FL: N1,1970--                              OPEN

SELECT TITLE NUMBER FOR PROCESSING


 RETURN/PROCESS F3/END SESSION F4/NEW FUNCTION F5/NEW TITLE ROLLUP
ENTER ISSN:    ____-____
ENTER TK:      SCA/J/O/I      KEYWORD  SCANDINAVIAN_____
ENTER SEQ:     _____



*****************************  3   ************************************
SCANDINAVIAN JOURNAL OF INFECTIOUS DISEASES

PL: STOCKHOLM               PU: ALMQUIST AND WIKSELL
0036-5548  FREQ:  4Y    FL:  1,1969--                              OPEN
*****************************  4   ************************************
SCANDINAVIAN JOURNAL OF IMMUNOLOGY

PL: OSLO                    PU: BLACKWELL SCIENTIFIC PUBLICATIONS
0300-9675  FREQ:  M     FL:  1,1972--                              OPEN

SELECT TITLE NUMBER FOR PROCESSING   4


 RETURN/PROCESS F3/END SESSION F4/NEW FUNCTION F5/NEW TITLE ROLLUP
```

system was designed as the initial phase of the NLM on–line index–ing system software, which will provide on–line indexing for the approximately 3,000 titles which are indexed in NLM's MEDLINE files.

The Check–in Record

Because of special indexing requirements, the NLM check–in system departs from the more conventional on–line serials check–in systems. At NLM, each receipt is a separate physical record in the file rather than one record per title or copy of a title. While this requirement makes a concise display of detailed current receipt holdings difficult, it is necessary for tracking each issue through the indexing cycle. In addition, the data entered for each item become part of the actual citation in MEDLINE and *Index Medicus.* Thus, if the data entered are: Jan 1983 volume 10 number 1, they will read into the MEDLINE file as:

$$1983 \text{ Jan}; 10 \ (1)$$

and also appear in that form in products like *Index Medicus.*

Given that each receipt is a separate physical record and also that the check–in data will go directly into the MEDLINE files as part of the indexing citation, a major consideration in designing the check–in system was to ensure consistent input of date, volume, and issue information for each issue of the same serial. That is, if each issue of a title carries a month, year, volume, number, and issue number, all of this information should be entered in every issue record for that title. The amount of information entered should not vary depending on the perseverence of the operator or his or her ability to interpret foreign language data. The answer to this problem of consistent data input was to establish a pattern code field called PROOF for each title, which provides both textual guidance and machine validation for critical data fields in each issue record for an indexed title.

The Check–in Process

The flow for the NLM check–in system follows the standard check–in process of title search, title match, order/copy match, recording receipt, and next search. The lead into the system is by one of three search arguments: 1) ISSN; 2) the title key in a 3/ 1/ 1/ 1 pattern similar to an OCLC search key, qualified by a keyword to reduce the number of hits within multiple keys; and 3) the title control number of the NLM system. Figure 1 shows

Figure 2

SCANDINAVIAN JOURNAL OF IMMUNOLOGY

```
PL: OSLO                         PU: BLACKWELL SCIENTIFIC PUBLICATIONS
0300-9675 FREQ: M          FL: 1,1972--                    OPEN
   1  *****  IM ORDER  *****  DEALER CHECKIN   *****          ********
S049306  SWETS      BEGIN:  1982  COPIES:  2   PREVD:        ORDDTE: 810929

AD:
01 S              1983    17     4                      830520 134160
02 S              1983    17     4                      830520 134161
03
D1
```


ORDER? 01   COPY? 01

                                                              ROLLUP/UP
    RETURN/PROCESS   F4/CANCEL   ROLLDN/DOWN

Figure 3

SCANDINAVIAN JOURNAL OF IMMUNOLOGY

```
FREQ: M           CALLNO: W1 SC15E                      SOURCE: SWETS
THIS IS COPY 01 OF 02 SHELVING: COLL      ROUTING: IM
REMARKS:LOOK FOR MONTH ON CONTENTS PAGE

PROOF:  MONTH YEAR VOL ISSUE
RECTYPE MONTH               YEAR     VOL     ISSUE    OTHER         INPUT
   S                        1983     17      5                      WJW
CNOTE:


REC MONTH           YEAR     VOL     ISSUE    OTHER      INPUT   DATE    ITEMNO
   S                1983     17      4                     Z     830520  134160
   S                1983     17      3                     Z     830401  124334
   S                1983     17      2                     Z     830314  117827
   S                1983     17      1                     Z     830307  115193
   S                1982     16      6                     Z     821228  93904
   S                1982     16      5                     Z     821217  90790
   S                1982     16      4                     Z     821104  78166
PROOF ==> MONTH REQUIRED
 F1/NEXT TITLE  F2/NEXT RECEIPT  F5/NEXT ORDER     F3/RECALL NOTES  ROLLUP/UP
 RETURN/PROCESS F6/RECALL RECEIPT                  F4/CANCEL        ROLLDN/DOWN
```

Figure A

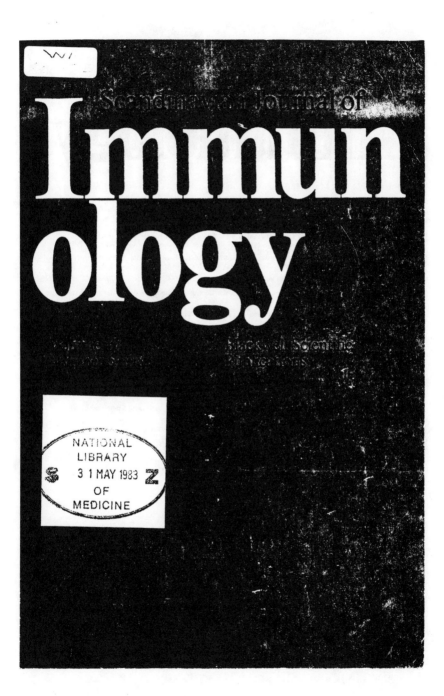

Figure B

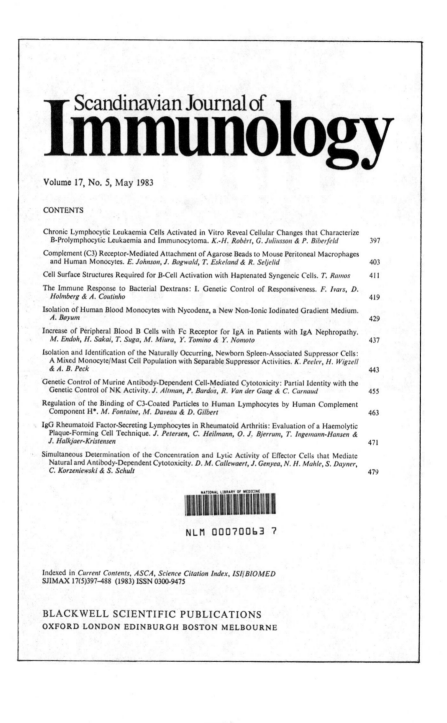

Scandinavian Journal of Immunology

Volume 17, No. 5, May 1983

CONTENTS

Indexed in *Current Contents, ASCA, Science Citation Index, ISI/BIOMED*
SJIMAX 17(5)397–488 (1983) ISSN 0300-9475

BLACKWELL SCIENTIFIC PUBLICATIONS
OXFORD LONDON EDINBURGH BOSTON MELBOURNE

a title key search for SCA/J/O/I with SCANDINAVIAN as the keyword and the resulting titles retrieved. If the title to be checked is SCANDINAVIAN JOURNAL OF IMMUNOLOGY, then the operator selects number 4 and is given a screen as shown in figure 2, a panel which shows the number of orders and the number of copies for each order. In this example, there is one order for two copies. In mid–screen appears the last receipt for each of the two copies. If the issue in hand were the one shown in figure A, the operator would select copy one and would be shown the check–in panel as in figure 3.

In the actual check--in panel, the bibliographic details such as place, publisher, ISSN, which were needed to identify the record, have been replaced by data needed for processing, such as frequency, call number, shelving, and routing instructions. The bottom third of the screen is a scrollable "window" area where previous receipts of this order/copy are listed. By scrollingg, the operator can scan all the prior receipts without leaving the fixed panel display.

Machine Validation of Check--in

In addition to specific processing information in fixed fields, there is a 150 bit field called REMARKS, which gives free text guidance to the operator. Below it is the PROOF field, which displays the data elements determined to be required to make a valid citation. In the NLM check–in system, the issue specific data reside in five fields: MONTH, YEAR, VOL, ISSUE, and OTHER. The purposes of the first four fields are obvious from the field names. The OTHER field is used to record supplements, parts, indexes, and the like.

In figure 3, the PROOF field shows that there must be four fields: MONTH, YEAR, VOL, ISSUE. Should the operator fail to enter one of the fields, as is shown in figure 3, the system will prompt the inputter in the message area near the bottom of the screen that the input is incomplete. In figure 3, the message area reads "PROOF == > MONTH REQUIRED," drawing the operator's attention to the fact that the MONTH field is blank. The free text remarks field can be used to further prompt the checker or provide guidance. As figure B shows, on this journal the full citation is only on the back contents page. The remarks field alerts the operator to look there.

In addition to identifying the absence of data, the machine validation also checks for the presence of inaccurate and inconsistent characters. For example, the YEAR field is set to accept only numeric characters and only within the range of 1900--99. The National Library of Medicine receives significant numbers of journals

Figure 4

```
SCANDINAVIAN JOURNAL OF IMMUNOLOGY


FREQ: M          CALLNO: W1 SC15E                           SOURCE: SWETS
THIS IS COPY 01 OF 02 SHELVING: COLL        ROUTING: IM
REMARKS LOOK FOR MONTH ON CONTENTS PAGE

PROOF:  MONTH YEAR VOL ISSUE
RECTYPE MONTH               YEAR    VOL     SSUE      OTHER          INPUT
  S       #                 1983    17        #       SU            WJW
CNOTE:  V.17 SUPPL - SYMPOSIUM ON CELL SURFACE STRUCTURE


REC MONTH           YEAR    VOL     ISSUE    OTHER        INPUT   DATE    ITEMNO
 S   MAY            1983    17      5                     WJW     830622  151591
 S                 1983    17      4                     Z       830520  134160
 S                 1983    17      3                     Z       830401  124334
 S                 1983    17      2                     Z       830314  117827
 S                 1983    17      1                     Z       830307  115193
 S                 1982    16      6                     Z       821228  93904
 S                 1982    16      5                     Z       821217  90790

 F1/NEXT TITLE  F2/NEXT RECEIPT  F5/NEXT ORDER    F3/RECALL NOTES  ROLLUP/UP
 RETURN/PROCESS F6/RECALL RECEIPT                 F4/CANCEL        ROLLDN/DOWN
```

not only in foreign languages but also in oriental and Cyrillic alphabets. The PROOF field is vital to ensure accuracy and consistency of data input, especially for this material, which the average checker finds difficult to record.

If the first rule of serials work is that any title can and will change, the second rule, or corollary, might be that any title which remains the same will change its frequency or its publication pattern. To accommodate fluctuations and unusual situations, the NLM check--in system provides an escape mechanism. As figure 4 shows, the use of a no. sign will cause the validation routine to be aborted and the data to be loaded even if it does not conform to the standard pattern. Here the system accepts data entered for a special symposium supplement, which has neither a MONTH nor ISSUE field.

After the data are validated against the PROOF field, they are next passed against all the prior receipts for that order/copy to check that the issue checked in is not duplicated in the file. If the data passes the duplicate check, the system accepts the new record and prompts the operator to input, via a light pen, a machine readable identifier (MRI) from a bar coded label which has been affixed to the issue. Once the MRI is read into the record, it is used for all later access to the record, thus making searching by title unnecessary for each subsequent record recall, as the issue makes its way through the indexing process. The wanding of the MRI also triggers output of printed material which is attached to the issue and is used in tracking and distribution. After these data are printed off, the system prompts the operator to enter a search for another title.

Claiming Capabilities

Like other on--line check--in systems, the NLM system permits not only receipts but also claims and claim updates to be entered in the file. Numerous special function keys permit special exits and routines. For example, in figure 4, the F2 function shown as "next receipt" at the bottom of the screen permits another record to be entered for the same order/copy. If the operator held both the June and the July issue, this function key would permit the second issue to be loaded without displaying the search and order panels. This is especially useful when a claim brings in several issues at one time. Other special function keys permit claim and not--yet--published records to be changed to receipt records when the issues are received, exits to other orders and copies, recall of text notes within the record, and of course, exit from the system entirely.

At the present time, the NLM check--in system PROOF field

does not automatically calculate the next receipt. It currently only validates the data elements, ensuring accurate data entry and a corresponding valid duplicate check. In the future, the PROOF field used in conjunction with the frequency statement could be used to calculate the next receipt. Likewise claims for missing issues, which now must be input by the operator, could be produced automatically.

While the NLM check--in system was designed specifically for an online indexing system, its use of machine validation to guide the checker and to proof the data input has potential for any system where consistent data entry on an issue--specific level is required. The use of machine validation in conjunction with free text natural language notes gives the system both the power of a machine driven file and the flexibility of a traditional manual system. Thus it uses the power of the computer to ensure consistent and non--repetitive data entry, while still permitting enough freedom to cope with the varying patterns and circumstances of serial publications.

REFERENCES

1. Martha R. Fishel and Betsy L. Humphreys, "Description of Automated Serial Control Systems, The National Library of Medicine," in *Serials Automation for Acquisition and Inventory Control,* ed. William Gray Potter and Arlene Farber Sirkin (Chicago: American Library Association, 1981), pp. 134--139.

2. *Health Science Serials* (Washington: Government Printing Office) A quarterly microfiche.
Index of NLM Serial Titles (Bethesda: National Library of Medicine) biennial.
List of Journals Indexed in Index Medicus (Bethesda: National Library of Medicine) annual.
List of Serials Indexed for Online Users (Springfield, Va: National Technical Information Service) annual.

3. "NLM's National Biomedical Holdings Data Base," *National Library of Medicine News 26,* no. 5 (May 1981): 1--3.

4. Betsy L. Humphreys, "Serial Control by Agents," in *Serials Automation for Acquisition and Inventory Control,* ed. William Gray Potter and Arlene Farber Sirkin (Chicago: American Library Association, 1981),pp. 57--76.

Union Listing On the OCLC Serials Control Subsystem

John Tieberg--Bailie
and
Elaine Rast
Northern Illinois University Library

Based upon the vast bibliographic resources of the Online Com--puter Library Center (OCLC) network, the OCLC Serials Control Subsystem offers libraries an integrated package of serial control capabilities, including serials check--in, union listing, claiming, and binding control. At the time of this writing (Fall 1983), the check--in, claiming, and union listing functions have been activated; however, binding control, the final system enhancement, is expected to be operational at a later date. Taken together, these four compo--ents of the Serials Control Subsystem will allow libraries to perform all major serials related record functions online. They also will provide for the elimination of numerous cumbersome in--house files and will allow library staff and the patron easy access to serials inventory information. For more detailed information on the OCLC Serials Control Subsystem check--in capability, readers are strongly urged to consult the accompanying article by Susan Davis.

The OCLC Serials Control Subsystem provides for the creation of local data records (LDRs) which exist in conjunction with the main OCLC bibliographic records in OCLC system memory.[1] Each local data record contains certain identifying bibliographic fields derived from the main record, as well as fixed and variable field elements describing the holding library, copy number, loan policies, call number, location, publication sequence, held issues, and other similar information. These fields also include a useful, repeatable free text field for whatever local information the entering library might deem necessary. The serials check in capability utilizes dif--ferent fields from those utilized by the union listing component, and it is not required that any library make use of both capabilities. In fact, a library wishing to make use of only the union listing component of the OCLC Serials Control Subsystem would need to enter a maximum of five data elements: holding library, copy identifier, call number, summary copy holdings, and summary institution holdings.

Given the brief data to be input, entering staff may quickly and efficiently create local data records for union listing. Once logged onto the OCLC system under an appropriate authorization, a bibliographic record representing the serial in question is first located. When such a record is found, the operator requests a Serials Control Subsystem local data record workform. This work-form contains a heading derived from the main bibliographic record which serves to identify the serial represented by the local data record to any OCLC operator, followed by a one line fixed field and the variable fields necessary for serials check–in and union listing. The entering operator then inputs all appropriate informa-tion using standard OCLC field creation and manipulation tech-niques. Once all data is entered, the local data record is updated in its entirety, and the data contained therein is immediately avail-able for use by the inputting library and other OCLC Serials Control Subsystem users. This is available either in the form of the original local data record, accessible only by the inputting library, or through a convenient union list display available to all Serials Control Sub-system users.

The OCLC Serials Control Subsystem union listing capability provides users with virtually all the advantages which could possibly be desired in the ideal union listing instrument. To begin with, OCLC represents the most widely used interconnected library system available today. Through the OCLC Serials Control Sub-system, thousands of libraries already have the ability to access immediately the holdings of dozens of union list groups throughout the country, and many more union list groups are expected to input their holdings in the subsystem in the future. Equally impor-tant, libraries which do not utilize OCLC may still join an OCLC union list group, and through offline products expected in the future these same libraries will have access to the contents of their union list in the form of regularly updated print, microfiche, and magnetic tape output. This capability provides unparalleled access to serial holdings information for all participating libraries and other interested parties. The OCLC union listing component has been designed in accordance with the *American National Standard for Serial Holdings Statements at the Summary Level* (ANSI Z39.42--1980)[2] and therefore holds the potential advantage of compatibility with other automated serial control systems, should such systems and the necessary interfaces ever be developed. The union listing component provides its users with the ability to participate in as many union list groups as desired, while requiring the maintenance of only a single database of serial holdings information. Libraries utilizing only the union listing component of the Serials Control Subsystem need only update their data as serial titles are acquired or dropped, as serials cease publication or as titles change. This

288

typically involves only a small proportion of a library's serial holdings, and as a result the OCLC union listing function boasts remarkable ease of database maintenance. The system is online, allowing instant access to all data by Serials Control Subsystem users, and most importantly, the Serials Control Subsystem is based upon the largest database of serials cataloging data currently available. Hundreds of thousands of serial bibliographic records exist in the OCLC database which have been cataloged and authenticated by the CONSER (Conversion of Serials) program, and substandard records are constantly being updated to bring them in line with current cataloging rules.[3]

In all candor, such advantages do not come without a price. The convenience allowed by the great number of CONSER–quality records is tempered by the presence of substandard and duplicate bibliographic records. With regard to serials, the OCLC database is polluted. OCLC system response time can be slow, and untold hours of terminal time may be wasted during the course of union listing as inputting staff wait for the OCLC system to respond to their commands. Finally, certain desirable Serials Control Subsystem enhancements have yet to be implemented. For example, offline output of union list serial holdings are not yet available, and there is no binding control. These considerations not withstanding, the OCLC Serials Control Subsystem nevertheless presents a remarkably elegant instrument for union listing.

OCLC Union Listing Record Creation

Union listing information is stored in Serials Control Subsystem local data records, existing in OCLC system memory in conjunction with the serial's main bibliographic record. Without a cataloging record with which to affix the local record, the local data record cannot be created. The inputting library must therefore either first locate an appropriate OCLC bibliographic record for the serial in question or create one itself before union list data entry can begin. In either case, once a cataloging record representing the serial title has been located, the inputting staff will display a Serials Control Subsystem workform containing both identifying data supplied by the system from the bibliographic record as well as the fixed and variable field elements for serial check–in and union listing (see Figure 1). The contents of the Serials Control Subsystem workform are as follows:

Figure 1:
The OCLC Serials Control Subsystem Local Data Record Workform.

```
Life.
Life(Chicago)
ISSN: 0024-3019  CODEN:          OCLC no:  4267940  Frequn:  m  Regulr: r

Hld lib: SILO Copy:      Repr:      Subsc Stat:  Loan

 1 CLNO  #b
 2 LOCN  #b
 3 FUND
 4 RMKS
 5 DEFN  #v vol. #p no. #e 1 2 3 4 5 6 7 8 9 10 11 12 #f m #g [ #p ]
 6 NEXT  #v  #p  #d
 7 DTRD
 8 CRHD  #v  #p  #y
 9 RTHD  #v  #p
10 SCHD  #d 8308 #g 0 #e 0 #f
11 SIHD  SIL #d 8308 #g 0 #e 0 #f
12 PURC  #i  #1  #m  #n  #o  #s  #t
13 CLMS  #b  #c  #d  #e  #i
14 BNDG
```

System--Supplied Data

    Main entry heading
    Title
    International Standard Serial Number (ISSN)
    CODEN
    OCLC bibliographic record number
    Frequency
    Regularity

Fixed Field

    Hld lib: Holding library
    Copy: Copy number
    Repr: Form of reproduction
    Subsc Stat: Subscription status
    Loan: Loan policy

Variable Fields

    CLNO: Call number
    LOCN: Location
    FUND: Fund
    RMKS: Remarks
    DEFN: Definition of publication sequence
    NEXT: Next expected issue
    DTRD: Date received
    CRHD: Current holdings
    RTHD: Retrospective holdings
    SCHD: Summary copy holdings
    SIHD: Summary institution holdings
    PURC: Purchasing information
    CLMS: Claiming information
    BNDG: Binding control instructions

Of these, a maximum of five fields are required for libraries utilizing
the union listing capability alone:

Fixed Field

    Hld lib: Holding library
    Copy: Copy number

Variable Fields

CLNO: Call number
SCHD: Summary copy holdings
SIHD: Summary institution holdings

The four–letter OCLC default symbol for the inputting library is supplied by the Serials Control Subsystem when a local data record workform is created. Libraries may be profiled to utilize the fourth letter of this code to indicate special locations or collections or may decide to accept the default code for all serials input. The copy field typically consists of a numeric indicator, but may in fact be any alphanumeric string up to four characters in length which the library chooses. Of course, the library may also choose not to input any copy symbol at all. As in the Cataloging Subsystem, all desired adjustments are made to each element of the fixed field, and the fixed field is then updated in its entirety.

Variable fields in the local data record are entered and updated individually. The call number field, if required or desired by the holding library, is entered in accordance with the standards for call numbers laid down in the OCLC publication, *Serials Format,*[4] or the inputting library may simply choose to enter a generic description of the materials (for example, "PERIODICALS"), an inventory number, or leave the field blank.

The Summary Copy Holdings (SCHD) and Summary Institution Holdings (SIHD) statements represent the heart of OCLC's union listing capability. It is these two fields which contain the basic data concerning which issues and volumes of a serial a library holds and which, along with the other union listing fields, are accessible by other OCLC Serials Control Subsystem users. The SCHD and SIHD fields respectively represent the holdings for the copy of the serial being represented by the particular local data record and the total holdings for the serial for the entire inputting institution. Both the SCHD and SIHD fields consist of identical elements, with the exception that the SIHD field also contains the threeletter OCLC symbol for the holding library. The fields have been established to comply with the *American National Standard for Serials Holdings Statements at the Summary Level* (ANSI Z39.42–1980)[5] and consist of coded information describing the completeness of the held title, current acquisitions status and retention policies, as well as variable length subfields for local notes, chronology, and enumeration.

When the inputting library desires to create separate union list entries for each copy of a serial title it holds, multiple local data records are created. Holdings for each copy are entered in each local data record SCHD field, while each SIHD field is identical, representing the total holdings of all copies of the serial. The system

Figure 2:
The OCLC Serials Control Subsystem Local Data Record Workform.

Life.
Life(Chicago)
ISSN: 0024-3019   CODEN: OCLC no: 4267940   Frequn: m   Regulr: r

Hld lib: SILO Copy: 1   Repr: Subsc Stat: Loan

```
 1 CLNO    AP2 #b .L54715
 2 LOCN    #b
 3 FUND
 4 RMKS
 5 DEFN    #v vol. #p no. #e 1 2 3 4 5 6 7 8 9 10 11 12 #f m #g [ #p ]
 6 NEXT    #v #p #d
 7 DTRD
 8 CRHD    #v #p #y
 9 RTHD    #v #p
10 SCHD    #d 8308 #g 0 #e 4 #f #v 1- #y 1978-
11 SIHD    SIL #d 8308 #g 0 #e 4 #f #v 1- #y 1978-
12 PURC    #i #1 #m #n #o #s #t
13 CLMS    #b #c #d #e #i
14 BNDG
```

Figure 3:
The OCLC Union List Display

SERIALS OF ILLINOIS LIBRARIES ONLINE
Time.
Time(Chicago)
ISSN: 0040-781X   CODEN: OCLC no: 1767509   Frequn: w   Regulr: n

ITEMS MARKED + HAVE FULLER HOLDINGS. REQUEST LINE NO. TO VIEW THESE.

 1 + CGP (8210,0,4) 1- 1923-
 2 + IAH (8210,0,4) 13- 1929-
 3 + IAL (8301,0,4,For microfilm see #3510888.) 11-13,17-105,107- 1928-
1929,1931-
 4 + IBA (8304,0,4) 15- 1930-
 5 + IBR (8210,0,4) 21- 1933-
 6 + IBV (8309,0,5) 1-82 1923-1963
 7 + IDJ (8301,0,4,6,Library use only. Retains current 4 issues.)
 8 + IFK (8307,0,4) 1- 1923-
 9 + IHG (8307,0,4) 77- 1961-
10 + ILO (8306,0,4,6,Retains current 12 months.)
11 + JAM (8309,0,4,6,Hard copy retained until microfilm received. For
microfilm see #1311479.)
12 + JNA (8210,0,4,For microfilm see #3510888.) 22-24,26- 1933-
13 + SPI (8304,0,4) 119- 1982-

Figure 4:
OCLC Detailed Holdings Union List Display

```
Time.
Time(Chicago)
ISSN: 0040-781X  CODEN:        OCLC no: 1767509  Frequn: w  Regulr: n
IFK (8307,0,4) 1- 1923-

 1   IFOA   (8309,0,4) 95- 1970-
 2   IFSA   (8306,0,4) 29- 1937-
 3   IGJA   (8306,0,4,6,Retains current 5 years.)
 4   IJHA   051.T  (8305,0,4) 13- 1929-
 5   IJIA   (8306,0,4) 83- 1964-
 6   IJQA   (8309,0,4) 1- 1923-
 7   IQBA   (8306,0,4) 83- 1964-
 8   IQDA   (8307,0,4) 97- 1971-
 9   IQFA   (8307,0,4) 1- 1923-
10   IQLA   (8308,0,4) 11-12,15- 1928,1930-
11   IQMA   (8306,0,4) 101- 1973-
12   IQOA   (8307,0,4) 43- 1944-
13   IQTA   (8311,0,4) 85- 1965-
14   IRCA   (8307,0,4,6,Retains current 2 years.)
15   IRNA   (8306,0,4) 49- 1947-
16   IROA   (8307,0,4) 75- 1965-
```

mandates that all local data records for a given serial title have identical SIHD fields. After one local data record is created, additional workforms for that serial have the preexisting SIHD field supplied by the system. Similarly, when multiple local data records exist for a serial, the adjustment of a single SIHD field affects the SIHD fields of all holdings records. If only one copy of the title exists at a library, both the SCHD and SIHD fields will be identical, and inputting staff need not enter both the SCHD and SIHD fields manually. They may instead enter only the SCHD field and then update the local data record. The contents of the SCHD field will then be entered automatically into the SIHD field. The time required for input is thereby reduced, and the opportunity for errors in transcription is eliminated. Because of these labor saving innovations in the Serials Control Subsystem, combined with the individual characteristics of the inputting library, as few as one or as many as five fields may need to be input on a single local data record for union listing purposes. Of course, if the inputting library is also utilizing the serials check–in capability, far more extensive data input will be required.

Once the holdings information has been input successfully, the local data record is updated as a whole and becomes part of the Serials Control Subsystem database (see Figure 2). When this occurs, the holdings symbol for the inputting library is entered in the OCLC online catalog, accessible by "display holdings" commands, and the data contained in the five union listing fields of the local data record is immediately available in a concise and convenient union list display to all Serials Control Subsystem operators. OCLC users desiring to learn which members of a union list group hold a serial title first locate the appropriate bibliographic record and then request the union list display (see Figure 3). The display indicates the name of the serial union list being searched and provides serial identifying information as in the local data record itself, followed by numbered holdings statements representing the SIHD fields of the serial holdings records. Copy specific displays indicating the contents of the SCHD fields as well as copy and call numbers are also available by searching the appropriate line numbers from the broader union list display (see Figure 4).

OCLC Bibliographic Record Selection

As any experienced OCLC user is aware, the OCLC database is immense, and often contains duplicate bibliographic records for a given title. For monographs and other formats, these duplicates may occur as works are issued in new editions or as a result of faulty cataloging by OCLC member libraries. For serials, the

Figure 5:
Multiple Returns On an OCLC Title Search (qua, jo, of, s/ser).

To see title for a COLLECTIVE ENTRY, type line#, DEPRESS DISPLAY RECD, SEND.

1 QUARTERLY JOURNAL OF SCIENCE (3)
2 QUARTERLY JOURNAL OF SCIENCE AND (4)
3 QUARTERLY JOURNAL OF SCIENCE LITERATURE AND (4)
4 Quarterly journal of science, religion, philosophy   Los Angeles,
Calif., 1930   s
5 The Quarterly journal of speech.   [Baton Rouge, La., etc.]   1915   s
6 The Quarterly journal of speech.   [Baton Rouge, La., etc.]   1915   s
7 The Quarterly journal of speech.   [Falls Church, Va., etc.,   1928   s
8 The Quarterly journal of speech.   [Baton Rouge, etc.,   1928   s
9 The Quarterly journal of speech   Annandale, Va. :   1967   s
10 QUARTERLY JOURNAL OF SPEECH EDUCATION (4)
11 Quarterly journal of St. Luke's Hospital Center, New York   New York.
1969   s   NLM
12 QUARTERLY JOURNAL OF STUDIES ON ALCOHOL (17)
13 Quarterly journal of surgical sciences.   Calcutta.   1965   s

situation is more complex. Most commonly, the presence of multiple records is a direct result of the change from latest entry serial cataloging to successive entry cataloging mandated by the advent of the *Anglo–American Cataloguing Rules,* second edition.[6] Formerly, cataloging information for a serial undergoing a title change would be filed under the most recent title, with references made from earlier titles. Under the second edition of the *Anglo–American Cataloguing Rules,* each title change a serial experiences must be cataloged separately and receive a separate bibliographic record. As a result, numerous serials are represented in the OCLC cataloging database by successive entry records for each title change, as well as any number of older latest entry records created under previous rules. In addition, multiple returns on an OCLC search will occur because of the presence of records representing different formats of a serial title, such as microfilm or microfiche, as well as the occasional inaccurate record entered by institutions unfamiliar with proper serials cataloging practices. As a result, it is common to perform a title search for a serial and have the system return a half dozen or more bibliographic records (see Figure 5).

Before a Serials Control Subsystem local data record can be created, a bibliographic record must be created to which it can be attached. A single library utilizing the Serials Control Subsystem will no doubt take as great care in selecting appropriate OCLC records as the members of an OCLC union list group. However, if the single library fails to select the record representing the highest quality cataloging, the results will be of little consequence outside of that institution. For the members of a union list, the selection of OCLC records is far more critical. If different libraries in the group select different OCLC records to which they attach their local holdings information, no single union list display will suffice to indicate all the libraries holding the serial, and the value of the online union list is therefore greatly reduced.

To eliminate this possibility, union list groups must establish guidelines for the selection of OCLC bibliographic records which ensure that all union list participants will attach their holdings information to the same bibliographic record for the same serial. Such rules should be simple enough for any entering staff to follow easily, and yet be sufficiently comprehensive to ensure the highest level of coherence in the union list database. The selection policies used by the Serials of Illinois Libraries Online project illustrate this point:[7]

1. Select only those records existing in the OCLC serials format.

2. Select only those records representing successive entry cata--

loging.

3. Select only those records representing the title's format, as held by the inputting library (for example, hard copy or micro-film).

4. Prefer records which have been authenticated by a CONSER Authentication Center.

5. Prefer cataloging records created by CONSER project members over those created by other institutions.

6. Prefer bibliographic records conforming to current *Anglo-American Cataloguing Rules* for serials.

7. All other things being equal, prefer the record with the most information.

In practice, such guidelines are easy to follow for both profes-sional and clerical staff alike. A hierarchy of preference is estab-lished by such a set of rules. If an authenticated, successive entry, serial format record cannot be located, a non--authenticated record may have to suffice. If a CONSER--cataloged title is available, it will be preferred over a record created by some other institution. If no record of reasonable cataloging quality can be located, the local data record may have to be attached to one of the substandard records which occasionally make their way into the OCLC database. Fortunately, thanks to the efforts of OCLC and the CONSER project, it is seldom necessary to affix a local data record to dubious cataloging. Of course, if no successive entry serial format record can be located at all, the inputting library will have to create a cataloging record itself before it can input local holdings data. This is rarely needed, save for local serial titles, newsletters, very old serials, and some foreign publications, all of which are still inadequately represented in the OCLC database. It should also be remembered that individual local data records will have to be created for each title change, and that these rules will have to be applied in each.

While a comprehensive knowledge of the OCLC serials format can be a valuable asset as bibliographic records are selected, it is not necessary that each individual inputting holdings data possesses such knowledge. Any serial format field may hold the key to the identification of a bibliographic record, but the number of fields commonly examined during the selection process is small. These typically include the following fixed field elements and variable

```
NO HOLDINGS IN SIL - FOR HOLDINGS ENTER dh DEPRESS    DISPLAY RECD SEND
OCLC: 1568783        Rec stat: c Entrd: 750824        Used: 830116
Type: a Bib lvl: s Govt pub:    Lang:    eng Source: d S/L ent: 0
Repr:    Enc lvl:    Conf pub: 0 Ctry: nyu Ser tp: p Alphabt: a
Indx: u Mod rec:    Phys med:    Cont:        Frequn: m Pub St: d
Desc:    Cum ind: u Titl pag: u ISDS:     .1 Regulr: x Dates: 1969-1981
 1 010    70-12659
 2 040    MUL #c MUL #d FUL #d NLM #d NSD #d OCL #d NSD #d DLC #d NSD #d DLC
#d NST #d DLC #d NST
 3 012    3 #b 3 #e s #k 1 #l 1 #m d
 4 022 0  0014-7249
 5 035    sf03267000 #b FULS
 6 042    nsdp #a lc
 7 050 0  RA773 #b .F17
 8 060    W1 FA449G
 9 082    613/.05
10 049    SILO
11 222 00 Family health
12 245 00 Family health.
13 260 00 [New York, #b Family Media, etc.]
14 265    Family Health, 149 Fifth Ave., New York, NY  10010
15 300    13 v. #b ill. (part col.), ports. #c 28 cm.
16 310    10 no. a year #b , July/Aug. 1979 -June 1981
17 321    Monthly, #b Oct. 1969-
```

Figure 6 (cont.)

```
18 350     $12.00
19 362  0  v. 1-13, no. 6; Oct. 1969-June 1981.
20 650  0  Health #x Periodicals.
21 650  2  Health #x periodicals.
22 690  0  Hygiene #x Periodicals.
23 780 05  #t Today's health #x 0040-8514 #g Apr. 1976
24 785 00  #t Health (New York, N.Y. : 1981) #w (OCoLC) 7580247 #x 0279-3547
           #g July/Aug. 1981
25 850     AAP #a AU ArU #a AzTeS #a AzU #a CCC #a CL #a CLSU #a CLU #a
   CNoS #a CSt #a CU #a CU-AM #a CU-Riv #a CU-SB #a CaAEU #a CaBVa #a CaBVaS #a
   CaMBC #a CaNBFU #a CaNSH #a CaNSHD
26 850     CaOKQH #a CaOLU #a CaOONH #a CaOSuL #a CaOTU #a CaOWA #a caOWtU #a
   CaQMG #a CaQMU #a CaSRU #a CaSSU #a CoFS #a CoU #a DGW #a DLC #a DNAL #a DeU #a
   FMU #a FU
27 850     GASU #a GAT #a GEU #a Gu #a IC #a ICJ #a ICRL #a ICarbS #a IEN-M
   #a IEdS #a INS #a IU #a IU-M #a IaAS #a IaU #a InLP #a InU #a KMK #a KPT #a
   KyLoU #a KyU #a KyU-M
28 850     LU #a MB #a MBCo #a MBU #a MMeT #a MShM #a MWwelC #a MdU #a MdU-H
   #a MiEM #a MiU #a MnU #a MoSU #a MoU #a MsSM #a MsU #a N #a NIC #a NNNAM #a
   NNStJ
29 850     NSyu #a NcCU #a NcD #a NcGU #a NcRS #a NcU #a NcU-H #a NcWsW #a
   NdU #a NhU #a NjP #a NjR #a NmU #a OCU #a OkS #a OkU #a OrU #a OrU-M
30 850     PBL #a PPT #a PPi #a PPiD #a PPiU-H #a ScCleU #a ScU #a
   TNJ-M #a TU #a TU-M Ea TxArU Ea TxDaM #a TxHMC #a TxHR #a TxLT #a TxU
31 850     ULA #a UU #a Vi #a ViBlbV #a ViRCU-H #a ViU #a VtU #a WU #a Wa #a
   WvU #a WyU
32 936     Unknown #a July/Aug. 1979
```

fields of the serial format:[8]

Fixed Field

> Bib lvl: Bibliographic level
> Ctry: Country of publication
> Dates: Beginning and ending date
> Frequn: Frequency
> Lang: Language code
> OCLC: OCLC control number
> Repr: Reproduction
> S/L ent: Successive/latest entry designator

Variable Fields

> 010: Library of Congress card number
> 022: International Standard Serial Number (ISSN)
> 040: Cataloging source
> 042: CONSER Authentication Center
> 086: Government document number
> 100: Main entry, personal name
> 110: Main entry, corporate name
> 111: Main entry, conference or meeting name
> 130: Main entry, uniform title
> 245: Title statement
> 246: Varying form of title
> 250: Edition statement
> 260: Imprint
> 362: Numeric and/or alphabetic, chronological or other designation
> 533: Photoreproduction note
> 780: Preceding entry
> 785: Succeeding entry

As long as those performing the data input have more expert super--visory staff to defer to when confusion arises over record selection, an understanding of these few fields is usually all that is needed to identify most bibliographic records (see Figure 6).

Those administering a union listing project may feel the need to select and approve all bibliographic records to which local hold--ings information is to be attached. Generally this should not be necessary, as selection rules should guide all inputting staff to the same bibliographic records for the same titles. However, if such a route is chosen, the union list group would be advised to either create a core list of preferred OCLC records for distribution or exclude certain classes of records from the need for approval. For example, if a union list group were to allow any library to input local holdings when a CONSER--authenticated, successive entry serial format record exists, the need for record approval would be eliminated in the great majority of cases. Similarly, a core list of preferred OCLC serial records distributed to union list members would not only add to the uniformity of the union list database, but also save untold hours of terminal time otherwise wasted in searching for and selecting records. Such lists may be developed locally, but are also available from the Pittsburgh Regional Library Center[9] and the Serials of Illinois Libraries Online program.[10]

The American National Standard for Serial Holdings Statements at the Summary Level

As stated previously, the OCLC Serials Control Subsystem union listing capability has been designed to comply with the *American National Standard for Serial Holdings Statements at the Summary Level* (ANSI Z39.42--1980).[11] The data mandated by this standard is contained within the Summary Copy Holdings (SCHD) and Summary Institution Holdings (SIHD) statements of the Serials Control Subsystem local data record. Data in each of these fields is formatted similarly, except that the SCHD field does not contain the OCLC symbol of the holding library. The subfield contents of the SCHD and SIHD statements may be summarized as follows:

a: OCLC symbol (system supplied)

d: Date of report (system supplied)

g: Completeness code

    0: Information not supplied or data element not applicable (system supplied default code)
    1: Complete (95%--100%)
    2: Incomplete (50%--94%)
    3: Sparse (less than 50%)

e: Acquisitions status code

    0: Information not supplied or data element not applicable (system supplied default code)
    4: Currently received
    5: Not currently received

f: Non--retention code

  Blank: Permanently retained (system supplied default code)
  6: Retained for a limited time, or only a few issues retained
  7: Received, but not retained

n: Local notes

v: Enumeration

y: Chronology

The completeness code is intended to indicate the proportion of a title held relative to holdings reported in the enumeration and chronology fields, not the proportion of the entire published run possessed by the reporting institution. Since the ANSI standard is designed for summary statements, missing issues and partially complete volumes will often not be reflected in the enumeration and chronology fields. The completeness code is intended to give the union list user a more complete idea of what is held. Unfortu-- nately, the completeness code defaults to "0" value when enumera-- tion and chronology are reported. The acquisitions status code and non--retention code are straightforward, though it is uncertain whether there will be any need in a union listing project to create local data records for serials which are "received, but not retained." Local notes are not to be used to describe bibliographic characteris-- tics of the serial title. Such information can be found in the OCLC cataloging record. Typically, local notes are used to describe loca-- tion, limits on access or use, damaged issues or volumes and retention policies for temporarily retained material, as well as to provide cross--references between local data records created for hard copy and micro--reproduction editions of a serial. The enumeration and chronology fields describe the holdings utilizing a set of care-- fully defined punctuation. Hyphens indicate a run of held materials, commas a gap in holdings, and question marks show uncertainty in chronology. Diagonals serve as "a connector between notations that form a single entity,"[12] colons are used to connect first and second level enumeration and chronology data, and semi--colons are placed wherever the sequence of the serials publication history convolutes in what the standard refers to as a "non--gap break."[13] Typically, enumeration is reported at the broadest level, with a gap reported when more than 50% of the serial at that level is ab-- sent.[14] Chronology does not have to parallel enumeration exactly, and gaps are usually reported in the chronology field only if none of the serial published during a year is held. The following SIHD fields exemplify typical holdings statements formatted according to the ANSI standard:

SIL #d 8309 #g 0 #e 4 #f #v 6- #y 1937-
SIL #d 8302 #g 0 #e 5 #f #v 9-27 #y 1960-1978
SIL #d 8212 #g 0 #e 4 #f 6 #n Retains current 6 years only.
SIL #d 8305 #g 0 #e 4 #f #n Local use only. For microfilm see
    #4266373. #v 1-26,28,32- #y 1951-1976,1978,1982-
SIL #d 8206 #g 0 #e 5 #f #v 1 #y 183?
SIL #d 8302 #g 0 #e 5 #f #v 1:12-3:23 #y 1841-1843
SIL #d 8309 #g 0 #e 4 #f #v 1/2- #y 1978/1979-
SIL #d 8211 #g 0 #e 4 #f #n In stacks. #v 1-20;1- #y 1952-

These fields are intended to provide a summary of a library's holdings, not an issue--specific description. For libraries utilizing the OCLC serials check--in capability, such detailed data would be contained within the Current Holdings (CRHD) and Retrospective Holdings (RTHD) fields. For union listing purposes, however, such detail is not necessary. Unfortunately, no capability exists in the OCLC Serials Control Subsystem to transfer holdings data from the CRHD and RTHD fields to the union listing summary fields, regretable since this would save inputting time for those libraries using both the check--in and union listing functions. Li--braries utitlizing both may expect a certain level of redundancy in their local data record input.

The ANSI standard recommends that enumeration and chronol--ogy data be entered at the broadest level of description, most com--monly volume and year, and that the second level of enumeration or chronology be utilized only to avoid ambiguity in the holdings statement. Fortunately, most libraries maintain holdings informa--tion to this level of detail. Those which do not will have to develop the necessary data before input can proceed.

In terms of the peculiarities in publication histories so commonly encountered in serials work, the descriptive powers of the ANSI Z39.42--1980 standard must be considered weak at best. While the standard provides for simple entry in most cases, where a straightforward volume/year correspondence exists, proper enumera--tion and chronology for problem situations is far from clear. The correct format is only hinted at for multiple year volumes, tem--porary retention, unexpected changes in volume enumeration, and other similarly difficult possibilities. The proper circumstances for the use of second level descriptions and the manner in which enumeration and chronology statements are to correspond are barely covered in any way. This situation is rapidly improving through interpretive statements recently issued by OCLC[15] and its Union Listing Task Force committee.[16]   Proper format for unusual publication and holdings sequences may now be determined with the aid of these documents.   Establishing enumeration and chronology in these cases will be a professional level responsibility, but one which is required only on rare occasions.

Libraries may expect to dedicate a certain amount of time to the proper ANSI–quality formatting of their holdings data, if the information they currently maintain is not up to standard. When their serials inventory is complete and up to date, only the conversion to ANSI format is necessary. Yet if a library's inventory information is outdated, much staff time will be lost in the stacks determining the completeness of volumes or the identity of those which have been lost or stolen. The problem will be particularly acute for those libraries which have maintained serials data in latest entry form.   As current cataloging practice requires, a separate local data record will need to be created to correspond to each of a serial's title changes. While these changes usually can be identified through information supplied in the OCLC database, examination of the serials themselves often will prove necessary.

Management Considerations for OCLC Union Listing

Each OCLC union list group will have to make a number of important managerial decisions before inputting can begin, both with regard to the most effective administrative arrangement for the union list organization and with respect to the demands of the OCLC system itself. OCLC requires that one institution in each union list serve as OCLC agent for the entire group. This will be the institution which will serve as liaison with OCLC for all union listing activities, and presumably will be where the union list group's activities are headquartered and coordinated. OCLC has four Serials Control Subsystem authorization modes: agent, full, partial, and search. The partial and search modes are limited use authorizations and do not provide for the creation of local data records. The full mode allows individual libraries to create and adjust their own local data records, perform serials check–in, and search all OCLC union lists. The agent mode allows the agent library to perform all these functions, both for itself and for any other library in the union list group. Therefore, a group may organize itself to permit the agent library to update all local data records for the group, if necessary. In any case, OCLC requires an agent for each group, and one must be selected and assigned.

Of greater consequence to the ongoing health of the union list are the organizational decisions which must be made. To begin with, what libraries will participate? If a closed number of libraries

306

have banded together to share their resources, the question is irrele--
vant. But if the participation of libraries must be targeted and soli-
cited, a public relations plan must be developed. Of course, any
union list group must select some individual or group to serve in
a leadership role to its membership. This might consist of a director,
an advisory board, a voting assembly representing the participating
libraries, or some combination of these, but strong central control
is essential. Who will pay for the union listing efforts? Will each
member be fiscally responsible for the creation of its own local
data records, or will some central agency or grant--giving institution
provide the necessary funds? Will libraries be reimbursed only for
OCLC fees, or will some remuneration be offered for staff as well.
The costs of database maintenance must also be determined in addition to the expense involved in the original creation of local data
records.

Staffing must be carefully considered. While the technical
difficulty involved in utilizing the Serials Control Subsystem is
unsophisticated enough to be handled by operating staff familiar
with the OCLC system, the proper ANSI quality formatting of
holdings information can be complex and will at times require
professional level analysis. It is obvious that professionals will
be administering the union list project. However, they also must
be available for consultation on problem entry and record selection.

Union list organizations must make provisions for the training
of member library staff in the use of the Serials Control Subsystem
and in the intricacies of the ANSI format, and each group must
decide whether to pursue group or individual member training.
Union list groups may feel obligated to define which materials
are to be included in the database. Any union list will include
journals and magazines, but the holdings for annuals, almanacs,
government documents, and other less common materials might
not necessarily be desired, especially if funding is limited. While
record selection should be relatively straightforward for most serials,
a union list group may nevertheless choose to centralize its record
selection procedures, either for all serials or for certain categories
of serials.

The creation of a union list obviously is designed with the
intent of augmenting the resource sharing efforts of its members,
but the increase in interlibrary loan traffic precipitated by the
creation of the union list may require the development of special
interlibrary loan protocols. In addition, systems must be organized
for the transmission of pertinent information among all members
of the union list group. This likely will consist of some form of
newsletter or perhaps a series of regularly held meetings. Whatever
the case, formal lines of communication must be maintained between

the administrative authority for the union list and its member libraries.

Perhaps the most critical decision a union listing consortium can possibly make will be whether to organize local data record creation and maintenance in a centralized or decentralized manner. Each option possesses both advantages and drawbacks, dependent upon the local situation, but whenever possible a decentralized approach is to be preferred. Centralized inputting may be mandated by the nature of the funding supporting the union list or by political considerations. Such impetus is often augmented by the argument that a centralized inputting operation allows a single staff to develop greater proficiency in the use of the Serials Control Subsystem, thereby providing for increased consistency in holdings input and OCLC record selection, as well as eliminating the necessity for train-- ing staff members at other libraries. Unfortunately, the situation is not so simple. Centralized union listing agencies cannot readily eliminate the need to train member libraries at least partially in the functions of the OCLC Serials Control Subsystem and the peculiarities of the ANSI standards, if only because of the need to ensure that they submit standard format inputting information to the central office. Of course, a centralized inputting operation requires a larger union list staff, many of whom will be dedicated exclusively to local data record creation. While such a staff will no doubt develop great expertise, it would also require its own set of expensive OCLC terminals or access to the terminals of the parent institution. Many union list groups would not be able to afford their own terminals and still fewer parent institutions would have the terminal time to spare. Finally, a decentralized operation allows the inputting libraries to check their own holdings when encountering problem input. Faced with incomplete or conflicting holdings data, an ambiguous title, or information not compatible with the ANSI format, all a centralized office may be able to do is return to the submitting library for clarification. Typically, a great mass of paperwork will result in the event a centralized operation is chosen, and in many instances achievable inputting speed will drop dramatically. In short, by decentralizing the opera-- tions of the union list group, the need for a large central staff is reduced, the need for training only marginally increased, and the burdens of data input and maintenance are distributed among all participants in a fair and equitable manner.

A number of local management considerations must also be examined before any library takes upon itself the responsibility of entering its serials holdings data onto the OCLC Serials Control Subsystem. Is the holdings information kept by the library com-- patible with the ANSI standard? How rapidly can inputting staff create local data records, and how much terminal time will be lost to other departments as the union listing project progresses? What proportion of its held titles are actually available in the OCLC database, and how many will professional staff need to catalog first? For a small collection, the answers to these questions must be estimated; but in a larger library, holding thousands of titles and where Serials Control Subsystem input may take hundreds of staff hours, intelligent management demands more accurate evaluation.

Sampling techniques may be used by a library to determine the staff time necessary to complete the union listing effort, and with such information at hand the negative impact of a union listing project on other library operations may be minimized. Unfortu- nately, sampling is generally inconvenient unless the decision to join an OCLC union list has already been firmly made, since sampling will itself require the creation of Serials Control Subsystem local data records. Yet knowing the expected duration of a project only after the project has begun is presumably preferable to not knowing until it is finished, and a sample is strongly recommended when a large collection is to be input. Such techniques are discussed in innumerable elementary statistics texts and need only be outlined briefly here.

Libraries will first need to derive a genuinely random sample of their serial holdings. The need for true randomness cannot be overemphasized. If a librarian simply selects a number of serial titles he or she believes are typical of the library's collection, the results of the sample will be suspect. When a library maintains a printed list of serial titles, it might conveniently choose to sample the titles at the top of each page, or every fifth or tenth title. While not ideally random, this method will yield acceptable data. The titles might also be numbered consecutively, and be sampled with the aid of a random number table. For libraries which keep a card file of serial holdings, a random number table may also be used to select drawer and card combinations randomly.[17] In any case, a sample of at least a few hundred titles should be taken. The larger the sample, the more accurate the results.[18]

Once the sample has been derived, staff will create the local data records as they normally would. By keeping track of the number of titles represented by OCLC records, the proportion of titles requiring additional successive entry records for title changes, the additional time needed to develop ANSI–quality infor- mation, and the time required for actual local data record input, the expected cost and staff time required may be reliably estimated, with appropriate confidence intervals, and the necessary decisions made.

Table 1:

Associated Costs, OCLC Serials Control Subsystem
Union Listing Capability

OCLC Costs

Profiling ($35.00/hour)
Agent fees ($375.00 for first 15 libraries plus $13.00 for each
    additional OCLC library and $26.00 for each additional
    non--OCLC library annually)
Local data record creation ($0.45)
Local data record update ($0.07)
Local data record online storage ($0.03 annually)
Offline products
    Title ($0.02)
    Optional fields ($0.001)
    Summary holdings statements ($0.01)
    Copy holdings statements ($0.02)
    Index entries ($0.01)
    Paper ($0.06)
    Fiche ($7.00)
    Fiche copies ($0.30)

Staff Costs

Holdings information development
Local data record creation
Local data record maintenance
Cataloging
Bibliographic record input

Table 2:

Hypothetical Parameters for Union Listing Library.

Library Characteristics

1,000 successive entry serial titles
50 new titles per year
90% of titles in OCLC database
Clerks earn $4.75 per hour
Catalogers earn $10.00 per hour
5% of new records adjusted at input
5% of records updated annually
Clerical staff creates or adjusts 12 local data records per hour
Catalogers catalog 1 serial per hour
Clerical staff inputs 2 bibliographic records per hour
50 hours of clerical staff time needed to develop ANSI compat--
   ible holdings information

Union List Group Characteristics

50 libraries
10,000 titles
Average 3 holding libraries per title
Average 5 optional fields per title
Average 1 index entry per title
2 union list updates per year
Average 10 fiche per update
Copy holdings statements not desired

Cost estimates for participation in an OCLC Serials Control Subsystem union listing project are hardly restricted to those fees levied on its members by OCLC for services rendered. Staff expenditures make up the bulk of a library's costs for union listing and must be carefully considered. OCLC charges for the initial creation of local data records ($0.45), for updating them ($0.07), and for maintaining them in its memory ($0.03 per year), as well as for profiling individual libraries for union listing. In addition, union list groups will be charged an administrative fee for members ad for offline union list products. Each union list group will be charged a minimum of $375.00 for its first 15 members plus $13.00 for each additional OCLC library and $26.00 for each additional non--OCLC library annually. Offline products will be offered in accord-ance with a simple cost schedule based upon the number of titles, optional fields, institutional and copy holdings displays and index entries, as well as for paper, fiche, and tape output.[19] Staff costs will be incurred for the development of ANSI--compatible holdings information, local data record creation and maintenance, cataloging, and bibliographic record input. These expenses are outlined in Table 1.

The extent of these expenses may be best illustrated by example. Take a hypothetical library in an imaginary union list group. Its serial collection numbers 1,000 successive entry titles, a number currently growing at a rate of 50 titles annually due to title changes and new subscriptions. Ninety percent of its current and new titles are already cataloged in the OCLC database, clerks cost $4.75 per hour, and cataloger's salaries average $10.00 per hour. Cata-logers catalog one serial per hour while clerks create or adjust 12 local data records per hour and input two bibliographic records per hour. Five percent of new local data records are adjusted at input; five percent are updated annually, and 50 hours of clerical staff time are necessary to convert holdings data into standard format. This library is a member of a fifty--library union list group, holding a total of 10,000 titles. On the average, there are three holding libraries per title, five optional fields per title, one index entry per title, and ten fiche per semi--annual update. For the convenience of calculation, it is assumed that copy--specific holdings information was not desired in the offline product. These figures, listed in Table 2, are in no way intended to represent the typical union listing institution. The values for these parameters will vary greatly from library to library, depending on staff pay, rarity of collection, achievable inputting speed, and the quality of serials holdings information currently being maintained.

As illustrated in Tables 3 and 4, the total costs of union listing are not insignificant and are heavily biased towards personnel ex--

Table 3:

Union Listing Costs for Hypothetical Library

	Initial Costs	Annual Costs (1st year)
OCOC Costs		
Profiling	$50.00	
Agent fees		$13.00
Local data record creation	$450.00	$22.50
Local data record maintenance	$3.50	$3.50
Local data record online storage		$30.00
Offline products		$34.80
TOTAL	$503.50	$103.80
Staff Costs		
Holdings information development	$237.50	
Local data record creation	$395.80	$19.79
Local data record maintenance	$19.79	$19.79
Cataloging	$1,000.00	$50.00
Bibliographic record input	$237.50	$11.88
TOTAL	$1,890.62	$101.46

Total initial costs = $2,394.12

Total annual costs (1st year) = $205.26

Table 4:

Offline Product Costs for Hypothetical Library

10,000 titles X $0.02/title	$200.00
10,000 titles X 5 optional fields /title	
X $0.001/optional field	$50.00
10,000 titles X 3 holdings statements/title	
X $0.01/holdings statement	$300.00
10,000 titles X 1 index entry/title	
X $0.01/index entry	$10.00
10 fiche X $7.00/fiche	$ 70.00
50 libraries X 10 fiche/update X $0.30/fiche	$150.00
TOTAL COST OF UNION LIST UPDATE	$870.00

Average annual cost per library (2 updates per year) = $34.80

---

penses and towards initial inputting costs. For this example, initial OCLC fees run $503.50, while an additional $103.80 is charged during the first year. Staff costs for initial input and database maintenance for the first year are $1,890.62 and $101.46 respectively. At first glance, staff fees may seem especially high. The need for cataloging is not typical of automated union listing instruments, many of which are also less dependent on the level of holdings statement format accuracy required by OCLC. Nevertheless, the extra input expenses incurred with the OCLC union listing capability are a small price to pay for the flexibility, convenience, and accuracy which the Serials Control Subsystem allows.

Any library participating in a union listing project will likely suffer increased demands upon interlibrary loan staff for reasons inherent in the process of resource sharing as well as due to the peculiarities of the OCLC union listing component. With regard to the Serials Control Subsystem, libraries considering OCLC for union listing purposes should be aware that no interface between the Serials Control Subsystem and the Interlibrary Loan Subsystem currently exists. Though such enhancements are expected in the future, their absence could cause inconvenience. In addition, the problems encountered in selecting OCLC bibliographic records for local data record creation are paralleled in the use of the union list display. To locate holdings for a serial, the OCLC operator must first select the best bibliographic record from among the many which might be present for a given title. Ideally, all holdings information for a serial title will be attached to the highest quality cataloging record, but it is naive to presume that this invariably will be the case. In practice, it occasionally will be necessary to request multiple union list displays. Complicating matters is the present inability of the Serials Control Subsystem to display the holdings of more than one union list group at a time. A search for a rare title may require the operator to request a number of union list displays. Finally, Serials Control Subsystem users may expect interlibrary loan requests for unheld issues of a title which they own. When a local data record is created, not only are the holdings available in the union list display, but the library's symbol is attached to the bibliographic record in the Cataloging Subsystem's online catalog, accessed by the display holdings commands. Borrowing libraries often will perform a display holdings search and noting that a library holds the title will request the desired material without examining the appropriate union list display. It is hoped that this situation will be addressed by future system enhancements, perhaps as the Serials Control Subsystem/Interlibrary Subsystem is developed.

These considerations not withstanding, it should be noted

that in most cases a Serials Control Subsystem user hoping to find holdings information for a particular serial title will have little trouble. Even when multiple bibliographic records exist for a title, their numbers easily may be reduced through the elimination of records representing latest entry cataloging and those of obviously substandard quality. In most cases, an obviously superior CONSER quality record will be located easily, and only a few union list groups will need to be checked.

Such flaws are minor, are probably temporary, are relevant in only a small number of cases, and should not be allowed to negatively color the opinions of potential users to the value of an outstanding union listing system. Every automated system possesses its own unique character and peculiarities, and the OCLC union listing capability is no exception. Yet OCLC has historically proven itself committed to continual revision and improvement of its automated systems, and any problems which currently exist presumably will be rectified in the future. In the meantime, OCLC's union listing component, while imperfect, remains the most com--prehensive, flexible, easy to use system available today.

FOOTNOTES

1. All technical data throughout this paper, unless otherwise noted, is derived from the publication: OCLC Inc., *Serials Control: Users Manual* (Columbus, Ohio: OCLC Inc., 1979).

2. American National Standards Institute, Inc., *American National Standard for Serial Holdings Statements At the Summary Level* (New York: American National Standards Institute, 1980).

3. Carol C. Davis, "OCLC's Role In the CONSER Project," *Serials Review* 6 (October 1980): 75–76.

4. OCLC Inc., *Serials Format* (Columbus, Ohio: OCLC Inc., 1980), 0:45–0:82.

5. American National Standards Institute, Inc., *American National Standard for Serial Holdings Statements At the Summary Level* (New York: American National Standards Institute, 1980).

6. Michael Gorman and Paul W. Winkler, eds., *Anglo--American Cataloguing Rules,* 2nd ed. (Chicago: American Library Associ--ation, 1978), 258.

7. Elaine Rast, John Tieberg--Bailie and Carol Feiza, *Serials of*

Illinois Libraries Online: Manual of Procedures (DeKalb, Illinois: Serials of Illinois Libraries Online, 1983), 20–31.

8. OCLC Inc., *Serials Format* (Columbus, Ohio: OCLC Inc., 1980).

9. *Pennsylvania Union List of Serials Core Titles.* Pittsburgh: Pittsburgh Regional Library Center, 1983.

10. Elaine Rast, John Tieberg--Bailie and Carol Feiza, *Serials of Illinois Libraries Online: Manual of Procedures* (DeKalb, Illinois: Serials of Illinois Libraries Online, 1983), 104--194.

11. American National Standards Institute, Inc., *American National Standard for Serial Holdings Statements At the Summary Level* (New York: American National Standards Institute, 1980).

12. Ibid, 11.

13. Ibid, 14.

14. Brian P. Moore, *Union List Update No. 6, revision.* (Dublin, Ohio: OCLC Inc., 1982.)

15. Ibid.

16. OCLC Union List Standards Task Force, *Serial Holdings State-- ments at the Summary Level: User Guide to the American National Standard.* (Dublin, Ohio: OCLC Inc., 1983.)

17. Dr. James L. Divilbiss of the University of Illinois Graduate School of Library and Information Science suggests that card catalogs be sampled by first assigning numbers to every catalog drawer. A drawer is selected using a random number table, and a random distance from the front of the drawer is measured similarly. For example, given a two digit number from a random number table, that number may be measured from the front of the drawer in eighths of an inch (39 = 4 7/8 inches, 84 - 10 1/2 inches). If the distance measured extends beyond the packed contents of the drawer, another drawer and distance is selected randomly. A moderately sharp object is inserted at the measured distance, and the sampler takes the title a set number of titles before or after the title obtained with the sharp object. By taking the fifth title past the selected title every time, or the third title before, or some other set number before or after the selected title, the sampler eliminates the

possibility of error associated with the greater possibility of multiple card records being selected. While admittedly cumbersome, this method yields excellently random samples for card catalogs.

18. Confidence interval for means may be calculated as follows:

Confidence Interval = Z (s/$\sqrt{N}$),

where s equals the standard deviation of the sample, N equals the size of the sample, and Z equals the value from the normal distribution corresponding to the desired level of confidence (for example: Z = 1.96 for a 95% confidence interval).

Confidence intervals for proportions may be calculated in this fashion:

Confidence Interval = Z$\sqrt{p(1-p)/N}$

where p equals the proportion derived from the sample, N equals the size of the sample, and Z equals the value for the normal distribution corresponding to the desired level of confidence.

For an explanation of the equations and the calculation of sample confidence levels, see any elementary statistics text. For example: Murray R. Spiegel, *Schaum's Outline of Theory and Problems of Statistics* (New York: McGraw Hill, 1961), 156–159.

19. Illinois State Library. *OCLC Services of the Illinois State Library: Workform Estimating FY84 OCLC Charges* (Springfield: Illinois State Library, 1983.)

BIBLIOGRAPHY

Anderson, S.E. and Melby, C.A. "Comparative Analysis of the Quality of OCLC Serials Cataloging Records, As a Function of Contributing CONSER Participant and Field As Utilized By Serials Catalogers At the University of Illinois." *Serials Librarian* 3 (Summer 1979): 363–371.

American National Standards Institute, Inc. *American National Standard for Serial Holdings Statements At the Summary Level.* New York: American National Standards Institute, 1980.

Bloss, M.E. "In Order To Form a More Perfect Union . . . List of Serials: A Report of the Workshop." *Serials Review* 8 (Spring 1982): 67–68.

Bowen, J.E. "Quality Control: Centralized and Decentralized Union Lists." *Serials Review* 8 (Fall 1982): 87–96.

Bracken, J.K. and Calhoun, J.C. "Use of the OCLC Serials Subsystem at the Knox College Library." *Illinois Libraries* 64 (January 1982): 81–83.

Bruntjen, S. and Carter, R.C. "Pennsylvania Union List of Serials." *Serials Librarian* 6 (Winter 1979): 257–258.

Buckeye, N.J.M. "OCLC Serials Subsystem: Implementations/ Implications at Central Michigan University." *Serials Librarian* 3 (Fall 1978): 31–42.

Carter, R.C. and Bruntjen, S. "Pennsylvania Union List of Serials: Continuing Development." *Serials Librarian* 6 (Winter 1981/ Spring 1982): 47–55.

Carter, R.C. and Bruntjen, S. "Pennsylvania Union List of Serials: Initial Development." *Serials Librarian* 5 (Spring 1981): 57–64.

"Committee Established to Develop Standards for Serial Holdings." *Library of Congress Information Bulletin* 38 (November 9, 1979): 468.

"Computerized Union Listing in New York State." *Wilson Library Bulletin* 56 (May 1982): 655.

Corey, J.F. "OCLC and Serials Processing: A State of Transition at the University of Illinois." *Serials Librarian* 3 (Fall 1978): 57–67.

Davis, C.C. "OCLC's Role in the CONSER Project." *Serials Review* 6 (October 1980): 75–77.

Ellsworth, D.J. "Serials Union Lists: the CONSER Project." *Serials Review* 5 (July 1979): 99–101.

Fleeman, M.G. "Availability and Acceptability of Serial Records in the OCLC Data Base." In *Management of Serials Automation:*

Current Technology and Strategies for Future Planning, 151–161. Edited by P. Gellatly. New York: Haworth Press, 1982.

"Indiana U. To Build Model OCLC–Based Serials List." *Library Journal* 104 (October 1, 1979): 2031–2032.

"Indiana Univ. Gets $$ To List Serials On Computer." *Library Journal* 103 (November 15, 1978): 2288.

"Indiana University Libraries Recently Announced That Agreement Had Been Reached With OCLC On the Final Specifications for an On–Line Union List of Serials." *Serials Librarian* 4 (Winter 1979): 250.

Kamens, H. "OCLC's Serial Control Subsystem: A Case Study." *Serials Librarian* 3 (Fall 1978): 43–55.

Kamens, H. "Serials Control and OCLC." In *OCLC: A National Library Network,* 139–154. Edited by A.M. Allison and A.G. Allan. Hillside, N.J.: Enslow, 1979.

Lastrapes, E.P. "Consideration of the Inadequacies of the OCLC Serials Control Subsystem." *Serials Review* 8 (Spring 1982): 69–73.

Micciche, P.F. "OCLC Serials Control Subsystem." In *Management Of Serials Automation: Current Technology and Strategies for Future Planning,* 219–227. Edited by P. Gellatly. New York: Haworth Press, 1982.

Nelson, N. "Union List of Serials Project Underway at OSU Library." *Oklahoma Librarian* 30 (October 1980): 9–10.

"NEOMAL Builds Serials List of the Holdings of Nine Members." *Library Journal* 107 (May 1, 1982): 845.

OCLC Inc. *Serials Control Training Manual,* 2nd ed. Dublin, Ohio: OCLC Inc., 1981.

OCLC Inc. *Serials Control: Users Manual,* 2nd ed. Dublin, Ohio: OCLC Inc., 1983.

OCLC Inc. *Serials Format.* Columbus, Ohio: OCLC Inc., 1980.

"OCLC–based Union List in N.Y. Is Step Toward OCLC/RLIN

Link." *Library Journal* 107 (May 15, 1982): 925–926.

"OCLC's Serials Control: Problems Pegged." *Library Journal* 103 (June 1, 1978): 1122.

OCLC Union List Standards Task Force. *Serial Holdings Statements at the Summary Level: User Guide to the American National Standard.* Dublin, Ohio: OCLC Inc., 1983.

Pennsylvania Union List of Serials Core Titles. Pittsburgh: Pittsburgh Regional Library Center, 1983.

Rast, E. "Serials in Illinois Libraries Online (SILO)." In *Illinois Libraries,* 64 (May 1983) 348–350.

Rast, E. and Tieberg–Bailie, J. "SILO: Serials of Illinois Libraries Online -- Union List Agency Management." *Serials Review* 9 (Summer 1983).

Rast, E., Tieberg–Bailie, J. and Feiza, C. *Serials of Illinois Libraries Online: Manual of Procedures.* DeKalb, Illinois: Serials of Illinois Libraries Online, 1983.

Rice, P.O. "ISSN as Retriever of OCLC Records." In *Management of Serials Automation: Current Technology and Strategies for Future Planning,* 179--184. Edited by P. Gellatly. New York: Haworth Prss, 1982.

Roughton, K. "Thinking of OCLC Serials Control? Read this." *Serials Librarian* 7 (Fall 1982): 23–30.

Roughton, M.D. "OCLC Serial Records: An Update." In *Management of Serials Automation: Current Technology and Strategies for Future Planning,* 163–170. Edited by P. Gellatly. New York: Haworth Press, 1982.

Roughton, M.D. "OCLC Serial Records: Errors, Omissions and Dependability." *Journal of Academic Librarianship* 5 (January 1980): 316–321.

Sperry, T.J., ed. *Pennsylvania Union List of Serials: Procedures Manual.* Pittsburgh: Pittsburgh Regional Library Center, 1982.

Walbridge, S. "CONSER and OCLC." *Serials Review* 6 (July 1980): 109–112.

Wittorf, R. "ANSI Z39.42 and OCLC: OCLC's Implementation of the American National Standards Institute's Serial Holdings Statements At the Summary Level." *Serials Review* 6 (April 1980): 84–94.

Index

323